CASE STUDIES FOR EDUCATIONAL LEADERSHIP

SOLVING ADMINISTRATIVE DILEMMAS

Stephen F. Midlock
University of St. Francis

PEARSON

Boston Columbus Indianapolis New York San Francisco Upper Saddle River
Amsterdam Cape Town Dubai London Madrid Milan Munich Paris Montreal Toronto
Delhi Mexico City São Paulo Sydney Hong Kong Seoul Singapore Taipei Tokyo

Vice President and Editor in Chief: Jeffery W. Johnston
Executive Editor and Publisher: Stephen D. Dragin
Editorial Assistant: Anne Whittaker
Vice President, Director of Marketing: Quinn Perkson
Marketing Manager: Christopher Barry
Senior Managing Editor: Pamela D. Bennett
Senior Production Editor: Mary Harlan
Project Manager: Susan Hannahs
Senior Art Director: Jayne Conte

Cover Designer: Margaret Kenselaar
Cover Art: Getty Images, Inc.
Full-Service Project Management: Sudip Sinha/ Aptara®, Inc.
Composition: Aptara®, Inc.

Text Font: Palatino

Credits and acknowledgments borrowed from other sources and reproduced, with permission, in this textbook appear on the appropriate page within the text.

Every effort has been made to provide accurate and current Internet information in this book. However, the Internet and information posted on it are constantly changing, so it is inevitable that some of the Internet addresses listed in this textbook will change.

Library of Congress Cataloging-in-Publication Data
Midlock, Stephen F.
  Case studies for educational leadership : solving administrative dilemmas / Stephen F. Midlock.
    p. cm.
  Includes bibliographical references and index.
  ISBN-13: 978-0-13-509404-4 (alk. paper)
  ISBN-10: 0-13-509404-6 (alk. paper)
  1. Educational leadership—Case studies. I. Title.
  LB2806.M434 2011
  371.2—dc22

                                                          2009032862

www.pearsonhighered.com

ISBN-13: 978-0-13-509404-4
ISBN-10:   0-13-509404-6

Dedication

I dedicate this book to my family. First, to my wife, JoAnn, who has been at my side throughout my entire career as an educator. She has provided me with valuable inspiration, encouragement, and understanding. Secondly to my children, Noelle, a speech pathologist, and Jason, a social studies teacher. Not only have they made me proud of their choice of careers in education, including master's degrees in educational leadership, but they also have offered insight and advice to my case studies. Thirdly to my grandson, Alex, who teaches me so much about life through the eyes of a two-year-old.

CONTENTS

Preface   ix

About the Author   xi

Chapter 1   Using Case Studies and ISLLC Standards to Teach Future Educational Leaders   1

An Explanation of the ISLLC Standards   1

Organization of Case Studies by ISLLC Standard   2

How to Use the Case Studies in This Book   5

Homework   5

Spontaneous Response   6

Jigsaw Activity   6

Nonlinguistic Activity   6

Chapter 2   Instructional Leadership   8

2-1. An All-Day Field Trip Impacts the Instructional Program (ISLLC Standard 2)   8

2-2. Kindergarten and the Twins: What Is Our Vision for Learning? (ISLLC Standard 1)   10

2-3. The High School Math Department: Are We Serving All Stakeholders? (ISLLC Standard 1)   12

2-4. Parents' Agreement: No Data Means "Get Rid of It!" (ISLLC Standard 3)   14

2-5. The Physical Education Dress Code and Its Fairness to All Students (ISLLC Standard 5)   17

2-6. The Social Studies Teacher and Ethical Behavior (ISLLC Standard 5)   18

2-7. State Tests and Ethics (ISLLC Standard 6)   19

2-8. The Uncompromising Math Teacher (ISLLC Standard 3)   20

2-9. The Walkout and Related Politics (ISLLC Standard 6)   22

Chapter 3   Ethics and Management   26

3-1. An Alleged Steroid User (ISLLC Standard 6)   27

3-2. Another Assistant Superintendent Falsely Accuses One of Your Staff (ISLLC Standard 5)   29

3-3. A Board Member's Son in a Fight (ISLLC Standard 3)   31

3-4. Cell Phones, a Bomb Threat, and a Building Evacuation (ISLLC Standard 3)   33

3-5. Differing Philosophies about Discipline
(ISLLC Standard 5)   34

3-6. The Electricity Goes Out During the School Day: How to Manage
This Situation (ISLLC Standard 3)   35

3-7. Ethics and the Principal's Decision (ISLLC Standard 5)   36

3-8. Misuse of the RtI Initiative (ISLLC Standard 6)   38

3-9. A Murder Occurs a Block Away from the School: Maintaining a
Safe Environment (ISLLC Standard 3)   39

3-10. Office Politics: How Does a Conscientious Administrator Deal
with Them and Still Maintain a Vision for Learning?
(ISLLC Standard 1)   41

3-11. Disposing of an Underground Storage Tank: Legalities and
Politics (ISLLC Standard 6)   43

3-12. The Principal Has Turned the Faculty Against You: An Internal
Public Relations Situation (ISLLC Standard 4)   46

3-13. The Superintendent Uses District Funds to Fix a District Car,
Then Purchases It: What Is the Ethical Course of Action?
(ISLLC Standard 5)   48

3-14. A Tornado Strikes at Night: Should I Leave My Family to Check
on the Building? (ISLLC Standard 3)   50

3-15. Trying to Implement a "Zero-Based" Budget
(ISLLC Standard 3)   51

Chapter 4   Organization and Development of Curriculum   54

4-1. Evaluating the Reading Curriculum Revision
(ISLLC Standard 1)   55

4-2. Kindergarten Curriculum Revision: Promoting an Effective
Learning Environment Amid Politics (ISLLC Standard 3)   56

4-3. The Life Skills Curriculum: Student Learning vs. Board Politics
(ISLLC Standard 3)   59

4-4. The Math Curriculum Council: Professional Advancement
vs. What's Best for Kids (ISLLC Standard 2)   61

4-5. Middle School Philosophy and Personal Beliefs Impact Student
Learning Opportunities (ISLLC Standard 3)   64

4-6. The Mosquito Unit: When Ownership Takes Precedence over
Student Learning (ISLLC Standard 2)   66

4-7. Selecting a New Reading Series: Let's Maintain a Focus!
(ISLLC Standard 1)   68

4-8. Selling a New Assessment Initiative to Your Department
(ISLLC Standard 2)   69

4-9. The Speech Teacher's Personal Agenda vs. the Instructional
Program Goals (ISLLC Standard 3)   71

Chapter 5 Supervision of Personnel 74

5-1. Assignment of Classrooms to Benefit a New Teacher
(ISLLC Standard 5) 76

5-2. The Dynamic Reading Program Equals a Recipe for Success?
(ISLLC Standard 2) 80

5-3. The First-Year Teacher and the Supervision Process
(ISLLC Standard 2) 82

5-4. Four Internal Candidates Don't Get the Administrative Job
(ISLLC Standard 6) 86

5-5. Jake's Classroom Management (ISLLC Standard 2) 87

5-6. The Outdoor Education Program That Goes Bad
(ISLLC Standard 6) 92

5-7. The Move from Associate Chair to Department Chair:
How to Evaluate My Predecessor (ISLLC Standard 3) 94

5-8. A New Assistant Superintendent Is Chosen Over an Internal
Candidate (ISLLC Standard 3) 96

5-9. The Science Teacher's Seniority vs. the Instructional Program
(ISLLC Standard 5) 100

Chapter 6 School Community Relations and Strategic Planning 102

6-1. The Band Boosters and a Trailer: A School Community
Relations Dilemma (ISLLC Standard 4) 103

6-2. The Central Office Snitch (ISLLC Standard 3) 105

6-3. Crisis Management: A Student Fatality (ISLLC Standard 5) 108

6-4. The Dumpster Incident: Internal and External Public Relations
(ISLLC Standard 6) 109

6-5. Graduating Students' Families Get Into a Fight in the School
Parking Lot (ISLLC Standard 4) 111

6-6. Let My Son Graduate Even Though He Failed Two Courses
(ISLLC Standard 5) 113

6-7. Local Florist Complains About the Date of the Prom
(ISLLC Standard 4) 114

6-8. Media Scoops and the School's Public Image
(ISLLC Standard 4) 116

6-9. A Parent's Concerns About the Technology Curriculum
(ISLLC Standard 4) 118

6-10. The Principal Bans the Local Newspaper Editor from the
School (ISLLC Standard 4) 120

6-11. Students Against Drinking and Driving: A Good Idea Goes Bad
(ISLLC Standard 3) 122

6-12. Students Drinking in Front of the School and the Political
Implications (ISLLC Standard 6) 124

6-13. A Student Visa: A Neighboring District Charges Tuition
(ISLLC Standard 4)   125

Chapter 7   Diversity Issues in Educational Leadership   128

7-1. Bilingual Issues (ISLLC Standard 4)   129

7-2. The Blind ELL Student: Who's Responsible?
(ISLLC Standard 2)   131

7-3. Communication with a Stubborn Superintendent
(ISLLC Standard 6)   133

7-4. Faculty Issues Related to Gender (ISLLC Standard 5)   135

7-5. Homosexuality Issues and a Board Meeting
(ISLLC Standard 5)   136

7-6. Placement in the Gifted Program? (ISLLC Standard 3)   137

7-7. Pride and Snobbery Between School Districts
(ISLLC Standard 5)   138

Chapter 8   Here's What Happened   141

Chapter 2 Case Studies   141

Chapter 3 Case Studies   145

Chapter 4 Case Studies   153

Chapter 5 Case Studies   159

Chapter 6 Case Studies   165

Chapter 7 Case Studies   171

PREFACE

Having taught courses in the educational leadership programs at two universities, I am convinced that case studies provide a valuable means for practical, hands-on education for tomorrow's educational leaders. There are two compelling reasons for writing this book: (1) to provide future educational leaders with as many realistic situations as we can, so as to prepare them for the myriad of leadership challenges that await them, and (2) to make sure that students are ready to assume leadership roles whenever those opportunities present themselves.

At an advisory group meeting of adjunct faculty consisting of present and former school administrators, the question was asked, "What is the most important thing we need to teach our future administrators?" The consensus among the group was that tomorrow's educational leaders need to be prepared for the unknown situations that will challenge them almost daily. These are the situations that can't always be anticipated but require good, sound judgment in addressing them. As the advisory group was probed more, the solution became obvious: Future leaders need hands-on experiences both through actual internships as well as through "what would you do if . . ." situations (case studies).

To further verify the advice of the advisory group, the students who field-tested the case studies commented on the faculty evaluation forms how much they appreciated the case studies. Not only have they grounded the students' learning in practical applications that have caused the students to project themselves into a decision-making mode, but they've also caused the students to analyze similar situations faced by their administrators. The students admitted having asked themselves what they would do if they were the administrator in their own schools. In some cases this kind of thinking has further fueled the students' desire to become administrators/leaders themselves.

Another compelling reason for writing this book of case studies is a concern that faces most professors: that of making the teaching and learning occurring in educational leadership programs meaningful enough that it will enter and stay in the students' long-term memory until they need to draw upon it. Although many students in educational leadership programs have aspirations to become educational leaders as soon as they complete their respective programs, the reality of the job market can stymie those plans.

Not all students who complete an educational leadership program will find administrative/leadership job opportunities in their own school districts, thus causing them to seek employment in other school districts. If this requires relocation, family issues might surface, such as reluctance to move one's children out of their current schools, or inability of one's spouse to find a job in another geographic region. As a result, future leaders will sometimes delay their administrative pursuits until their children grow older, or until an administrative vacancy opens in their school district of current employment.

Similarly, because of the time commitment required by administrative/leadership positions, prospective administrators sometimes wait until their families grow older, when everyone in the family is better able to handle the time considerations and they have the necessary balance in their lives. Also, some prospective administrators/leaders realize that they love their teaching career so much that they're not in any hurry to move into administration and would rather wait for just the right position to open.

Because not all students in educational leadership programs pursue or acquire administrative positions immediately after completion of the program, it is imperative that such programs provide their students with learning that will transcend the limits of time and continue to be meaningful over a long period. Brain research tells us that one way to accomplish this task is to make sure that the learners are able to project themselves into their learning in a manner that becomes personally relevant and important to them. The use of case studies is an effective way to do this. Consequently, the case study approach is likely to ensure long-term learning and recall if the learners have projected themselves into the situations and have gleaned meaning from them.

This book is intended to help our future administrators as they prepare to lead our nation's schools in an ethical, compassionate, and caring manner.

ACKNOWLEDGMENTS

Thanks to the support of other professionals in the field of education, I have been able to write this book as a practical resource for future educational leaders. I wish to express my gratitude to the following:

- The editorial staff at Pearson for their acceptance of the original proposal and their expertise in fine-tuning it: Stephen D. Dragin, Executive Editor and Publisher; Anne Whitaker, Administrative Assistant to the Executive Editor; and Mary Harlan, Production Editor.
- The following colleagues and reviewers for their helpful comments and suggestions: Dr. Sidney L. Brown, Alabama State University; Dr. Mary Harris-John, Marshall University; and Dr. Perry R. Rettig, University of Wisconsin, Oshkosh.
- The administration, faculty, and students at the University of St. Francis for their willingness to field-test the case studies in the Educational Leadership Program and to provide valuable feedback. I especially thank Dr. John Gambro, Dean, College of Education; Cindy Wrobbel, Associate Dean, College of Education; Sharon Wysoglad, Director of Advanced Programs, College of Education; and Dr. June Grivetti, Coordinator of the Educational Leadership Program, College of Education. Their various perspectives and support were extremely valuable in the development of this book. Their dedication to helping prepare tomorrow's educational leaders is admirable and greatly appreciated.

ABOUT THE AUTHOR

Stephen Midlock was born in Joliet, Illinois, and has earned all his degrees in Illinois. The most recent is an Ed.D. in Educational Leadership from Northern Illinois University. Prior to being a college faculty member, Steve served as an educational leader in four public school districts of varied demographics and size. His positions include English department chair, assistant principal, high school principal, and assistant superintendent of curriculum and instruction. Steve is proud to have had a "balanced career" consisting of 16 years as a classroom teacher and 17 years as an administrator. During his service as an administrator, Steve also taught as an adjunct  professor at Joliet Junior College in the English Department, and later as an adjunct professor at Aurora University in the College of Education. He presently is a tenure-track assistant professor in the College of Education at the University of St. Francis in Joliet, Illinois.

Steve's experience in a variety of administrative positions and in diverse school districts has given him a rich background from which the case studies of this book have grown. He originally wrote them as instructional aids in his educational leadership courses. After sharing them with his colleagues, he was encouraged to assemble them into a casebook that could be used in other universities.

CHAPTER 1

Using Case Studies and ISLLC Standards to Teach Future Educational Leaders

AN EXPLANATION OF THE ISLLC STANDARDS

Master's degree programs in educational leadership across the nation follow a set of high-level policy standards adopted by the National Policy Board for Educational Administration. The intent of the standards is not only to provide consistency among the goals and outcomes of programs in educational leadership, but also to improve preparation, certification (licensure), and professional development of future educational leaders. These standards are known as the Interstate School Leaders Licensure Consortium (ISLLC) Standards. They not only provide a sense of continuity among educational leadership programs, but they also allow flexibility in delivery systems. In other words, universities don't all have to offer the same courses in their respective programs, but they do have to address all the standards throughout the duration of the program. Different course structures and practicum experiences can be offered to students in an attempt to meet regional needs as well as to create unique delivery systems on the part of the universities.

The standards, then, have become very important in educational leadership programs, because they provide the backbone of what students are expected to learn and to demonstrate through mastery. Employers (school districts) can be assured that students who have master's degrees in educational leadership have learned a consistent set of knowledge and have demonstrated a consistent set of performances, all of which have led to the mastery of the ISLLC Standards. Needless to say, this provides a level of professionalism and credibility to educational leadership programs as well as confidence to school districts when they hire educational leaders.

There are six ISLLC Standards, and as previously stated, they comprise the backbone of educational leadership programs, helping to define the appropriate assessments and performance measures relative to educational leadership. National accreditation agencies such as the National Consortium of Accreditation of Teacher Education Programs (NCATE) and state departments of education alike recognize the significance of the ISLLC Standards by requiring universities to demonstrate how their programs align with the standards and how their students master them. The standards are the result of leadership by the Council of Chief State School Officers, which is a non-partisan, nationwide, nonprofit organization of public officials representing various state departments of education, those of the District of Columbia, and the Department of Defense Education Activity. Additional information can be found on their website, www.ccsso.org. A free download of the standards is available to the public at www.ccsso.org/content/pdfs/elps_isllc2008.pdf.

The ISLLC Standards, which were revised in 2008, are as follows:

Standard 1: An education leader promotes the success of every student by facilitating the development, articulation, implementation, and stewardship of a vision of learning that is shared and supported by all stakeholders.

Standard 2: An education leader promotes the success of every student by advocating, nurturing, and sustaining a school culture and instructional program conducive to student learning and staff professional growth.

Standard 3: An education leader promotes the success of every student by ensuring management of the organization, operation, and resources for a safe, efficient, and effective learning environment.

Standard 4: An education leader promotes the success of every student by collaborating with faculty and community members, responding to diverse community interests and needs, and mobilizing community resources.

Standard 5: An education leader promotes the success of every student by acting with integrity, fairness, and in an ethical manner.

Standard 6: An education leader promotes the success of every student by understanding, responding to, and influencing the political, social, economic, legal, and cultural context.

These standards not only provide a framework for educational leadership programs, but they also capture the key elements and functions of such leadership. Most responsibilities and activities of educational leaders are represented by these standards. An understanding of them is key to the preparation of effective educational leaders who have a sense of vision, implementation, management, public relations, ethics, politics, and legalities of school activities and programs.

While it is beneficial for purposes of analysis and understanding to break educational leadership into the areas defined by these six standards, the reality is that most activities undertaken and decisions made by educational leaders span more than one of these standards simultaneously. The case studies in this book have been indexed to the standard that is most predominant in the resolution of the challenge presented. Readers are encouraged to examine the other possible standards addressed by the case studies. Not only will this give a better understanding of the standards, but it also will give a view of the bigger picture of educational leadership and its complexities and connections.

Organization of Case Studies by ISLLC Standard

The following case studies are listed by ISLLC Standard with the chapter in parentheses.

ISLLC Standard 1: Facilitating a Vision of Learning

2-2   Kindergarten and the Twins: What Is Our Vision for Learning? (Chapter 2)

2-3   The High School Math Department: Are We Serving All Stakeholders? (Chapter 2)

3-10   Office Politics: How Does a Conscientious Administrator Deal with Them and Still Maintain a Vision for Learning? (Chapter 3)

4-1   Evaluating the Reading Curriculum Revision (Chapter 4)

4-7   Selecting a New Reading Series: Let's Maintain a Focus! (Chapter 4)

ISLLC Standard 2: School Culture and Instructional Leadership

2-1   An All-Day Field Trip Impacts the Instructional Program (Chapter 2)

4-4   The Math Curriculum Council: Professional Advancement vs. What's Best for Kids (Chapter 4)

4-6   The Mosquito Unit: When Ownership Takes Precedence over Student Learning (Chapter 4)

4-8   Selling a New Assessment Initiative to Your Department (Chapter 4)

5-2   The Dynamic Reading Program Equals a Recipe for Success? (Chapter 5)

5-3   The First-Year Teacher and the Supervision Process (Chapter 5)

5-5   Jake's Classroom Management (Chapter 5)

7-2   The Blind ELL Student: Who's Responsible? (Chapter 7)

ISLLC Standard 3: Management of Operations, Resources, and the Learning Environment

2-4   Parents' Agreement: No Data Means "Get Rid of It!" (Chapter 2)

2-8   The Uncompromising Math Teacher (Chapter 2)

3-3   A Board Member's Son in a Fight (Chapter 3)

3-4   Cell Phones, a Bomb Threat, and a Building Evacuation (Chapter 3)

3-6   The Electricity Goes Out During the School Day: How to Manage This Situation (Chapter 3)

3-9   A Murder Occurs a Block Away from the School: Maintaining a Safe Environment (Chapter 3)

3-14   A Tornado Strikes at Night: Should I Leave My Family to Check on the Building? (Chapter 3)

3-15   Trying to Implement a "Zero-Based" Budget (Chapter 3)

4-2   Kindergarten Curriculum Revision: Promoting an Effective Learning Environment Amid Politics (Chapter 4)

4-3   The Life Skills Curriculum: Student Learning vs. Board Politics (Chapter 4)

4-5   Middle School Philosophy and Personal Beliefs Impact Student Learning Opportunities (Chapter 4)

4-9   The Speech Teacher's Personal Agenda vs. the Instructional Program Goals (Chapter 4)

5-7   The Move from Associate Chair to Department Chair: How to Evaluate My Predecessor (Chapter 5)

5-8   A New Assistant Superintendent Is Chosen over an Internal Candidate (Chapter 5)

6-2   The Central Office Snitch (Chapter 6)

6-11   Students Against Drinking and Driving: A Good Idea Goes Bad (Chapter 6)

7-6   Placement in the Gifted Program? (Chapter 7)

ISLLC Standard 4: Collaboration with Families and Communities

3-12   The Principal Has Turned the Faculty Against You: An Internal Public Relations Situation (Chapter 3)

6-1   The Band Boosters and a Trailer: A School Community Relations Dilemma (Chapter 6)

6-5   Graduating Students' Families Get into a Fight in the School Parking Lot (Chapter 6)

6-7   Local Florist Complains About the Date of the Prom (Chapter 6)

6-8   Media Scoops and the School's Public Image (Chapter 6)

6-9   A Parent's Concerns About the Technology Curriculum (Chapter 6)

6-10   The Principal Bans the Local Newspaper Editor from the School (Chapter 6)

6-13   A Student Visa: A Neighboring District Charges Tuition (Chapter 6)

7-1   Bilingual Issues (Chapter 7)

ISLLC Standard 5: Acting with Integrity, Fairness, and in an Ethical Manner

2-5   The Physical Education Dress Code and Its Fairness to All Students (Chapter 2)

2-6   The Social Studies Teacher and Ethical Behavior (Chapter 2)

3-2   Another Assistant Superintendent Falsely Accuses One of Your Staff (Chapter 3)

3-5   Differing Philosophies About Discipline (Chapter 3)

3-7   Ethics and the Principal's Decision (Chapter 3)

3-13   The Superintendent Uses District Funds to Fix a District Car, Then Purchases It: What Is the Ethical Course of Action? (Chapter 3)

5-1   Assignment of Classrooms to Benefit a New Teacher (Chapter 5)

5-9   The Science Teacher's Seniority vs. the Instructional Program (Chapter 5)

6-6   Let My Son Graduate Even Though He Failed Two Courses (Chapter 6)

7-4   Faculty Issues Related to Gender (Chapter 7)

7-5   Homosexuality Issues and a Board Meeting (Chapter 7)

7-7   Pride and Snobbery Between School Districts (Chapter 7)

ISLLC Standard 6: Political, Social, Economic, Legal, and Cultural Context

2-7   State Tests and Ethics (Chapter 2)

2-9   The Walkout and Related Politics (Chapter 2)

3-1   An Alleged Steroid User (Chapter 3)

3-8   Misuse of the RtI Initiative (Chapter 3)

3-11   Disposing of an Underground Storage Tank: Legalities and Politics (Chapter 3)

5-4   Four Internal Candidates Don't Get the Administrative Job (Chapter 5)

5-6   The Outdoor Education Program That Goes Bad (Chapter 5)

6-3   Crisis Management: A Student Fatality (Chapter 6)

6-4   The Dumpster Incident: Internal and External Public Relations (Chapter 6)

6-12   Students Drinking in Front of the School and the Political Implications (Chapter 6)

7-3   Communication with a Stubborn Superintendent (Chapter 7)

HOW TO USE THE CASE STUDIES IN THIS BOOK

Much has been written recently about the value of providing practical experiences to all students, but especially those in educational leadership programs. Having served as a public school administrator for 17 years, I can honestly say that our future administrators can't be too prepared for the many challenges that await them. Case studies can help students to project themselves into situations and to consider ways of solving them. The intent of the case studies in this book is to provide students with this opportunity. As they consider how they would solve the situations, they also can reflect on the ramifications of various solutions. In the future, they may not have that luxury as such challenges present themselves.

I have asked fellow administrators for advice in preparing our future leaders. The response most often heard is, "When I first became an administrator, I was most challenged by the situations that pop up and demand immediate solutions. If we somehow can provide students with the opportunity to analyze and solve these challenges, we would be doing our future administrators a great service." When using this book, professors are asked to keep this focus.

The case studies in this book can be used in a variety of ways: as homework, for spontaneous responses, as jigsaw activities, or for nonlinguistic activities.

Homework

Students can solve these cases individually as homework, which provides them the opportunity to carefully analyze solutions as well as to seek input from colleagues as to what they would do to solve the case studies. If the students were to seek input from practicing administrators such as assistant principals and principals, they would obtain a valuable perspective based on experience. From a technological perspective, it is helpful if the students e-mail their plan of action to solve the assigned case study to their professor prior to the next class meeting. That would not only provide the students with quick feedback, because the professor could review and grade the case studies for handing back at the beginning of the next class, but also the professor would be able to ascertain if the students need some additional explanation or teaching about how to handle the situation presented in the assigned case study. A rich discussion could ensue at the beginning of the class that would provide an opportunity for additional teaching about how to manage the situation. The discussion also would serve as a review of what was taught and learned in the previous class, because the case study would reinforce the topics taught in that class.

Spontaneous Response

Another way of using the case studies is to have the students "think on their feet" and to develop solutions immediately, which is similar to what happens in the real world of administration. An interactive discussion or conversation can result as students present their solutions in class. For expedience as well as to make this realistic, students should be asked to present their solutions in a bulleted format. In my experience, I never have had to present a term paper to a board of education or a superintendent, but I have presented many bulleted plans to them. This approach closely approximates the real world of educational leadership as it relates to developing action plans intended to solve a problem. By using this approach the professor also can determine what "holes" or "gaps" need to be filled in the students' understanding of educational leadership, as the students attempt to solve the case study.

Jigsaw Activity

Breaking students into groups of three or four members and assigning a different case study to each group is another way of using the case studies. Using a jigsaw approach of having each group explain their case study and their respective solutions, the class can add their ideas to the solutions of each case study. A variation of this approach would be to have each group solve the same case study and to present their plans to the whole class. A discussion about the similarities and differences of each group's plan would demonstrate the differences that exist among future and practicing administrators. Groups can be determined in a variety of ways. A simple counting off by threes would put all the ones in a group, all the twos in another group, and all the threes in a third group. This would result in their having to solve problems with others who might not be in their respective comfort zones. This is based on the assumption that students tend to sit with other students who are in their comfort zone. Another way of grouping students would be to make sure that each group has at least one elementary teacher, one secondary teacher, one ELL teacher, and one special education teacher in it. That would provide for a variety of perspectives that have to be addressed as the group solves the problem presented by the case study. Obviously, this approach depends on the makeup of the cohort of students. Other ways of ensuring multiple perspectives would be to break up cliques of teachers who teach the same grade level or content area and to place them in different groups.

Nonlinguistic Activity

An enjoyable activity to address the right side or creative side of the brain would be to have each group present their solutions in a nonlinguistic manner on chart paper. Providing each group with colored markers and self-adhesive poster chart paper usually results in some very interesting products. By using creative/novel approaches to learning, the brain is more likely to move such learning to long-term memory. In order to retain the novelty, this approach should be used selectively and sparingly. Overuse cancels the novelty. I use this approach only once or twice in an eight-week course. Students have commented on their evaluation forms how much they enjoyed and learned from this approach.

Because the case studies in this book are based on true stories, various ethical solutions have been included. Students can benefit not only from what really happened, but also from how the administrator could have handled the situation differently. It is important to keep the case studies in perspective. New and seasoned educational leaders are required to make many decisions throughout the day. Often limited information is available to them when making decisions, but quick action plans are needed. Hindsight often yields different approaches: "If only I could turn the clock back and replay the situation." The case studies in this book are not intended to imply that today's educational leaders are not good at making decisions. Rather, the case studies simply illustrate that all educational leaders are human and sometimes make decisions that seem good at the time, but in retrospect were not the best. If we can help our future educational leaders to benefit from these decisions and to make even better decisions when such challenges confront them, I believe we are helping them to create a better learning environment. That is the primary intent of having our students solve these case studies. We want them to be as prepared as they possibly can be for the uncertainties of educational leadership.

Although expediency often is sought when facing challenges, tomorrow's leaders have to consider the various ethical implications of their decisions. Counterpoints that cause students to consider the ethical implications have been included at the end of each case study. It is important to note that while these case studies are based on true events, details have been altered not only to maintain confidentiality for those involved, but also to make the case studies more useable as instructional tools. These case studies have not been written about anyone in particular and have been altered to maintain anonymity. Their intent is not to criticize anyone's leadership style, but rather to provide future educational leaders with a myriad of leadership challenges. It is inevitable that a protagonist and an antagonist would be part of any story, including these case studies. Furthermore, the cases are presented as tools to prepare tomorrow's educational leaders to face a multitude of challenges in an ethical and effective manner.

The case studies in this book could be used in an introductory or first course in an educational administration program, or they could be used throughout the program. Students will find the case studies in this book useful in many courses. For that reason, the book has been organized into chapters addressing the major themes of typical courses in an educational administration program. Chapter 2 contains case studies addressing issues relating to instructional leadership. Chapter 3 addresses ethics and management, Chapter 4 addresses challenges stemming from the organization and development of curriculum and its alignment with instruction with assessment, and Chapter 5 presents situations faced in the supervision of personnel. Chapter 6 projects the reader into the world of school community relations and strategic planning, and Chapter 7 presents challenges related to diversity issues in educational leadership. Chapter 8 shows what actually happened in each of the case studies, whether or not the outcomes were the most appropriate courses of action.

CHAPTER 2

Instructional Leadership

Instructional leadership is an important responsibility of educational leadership. Because the educational leader is charged with many duties and responsibilities that often require immediate attention, educational leaders can easily fall into a *reactive* mode instead of a planning or *proactive* mode. While these responsibilities need attention, they don't have to be addressed by the educational leader, often the principal. Instead, other management personnel could handle the situations requiring immediate attention. The focus of the educational leader in general, and the principal in particular, should be students' learning. Because the main mission of schools focuses on teaching and learning, and because schools' effectiveness often is measured by academic achievement, it is vitally important that the educational leader focus his or her time, energy, and priorities on instructional leadership. It also is important to remember that the principal isn't the only educational leader in the building. Often districts appoint department chairs in a high school or even a junior high school setting to provide the front-line instructional leadership. Sometimes an elementary school has lead grade-level teachers who supervise the curriculum and resources for their particular grade levels. At the central-office level, assistant superintendents and curriculum directors provide instructional leadership to the schools.

This chapter provides students with scenarios presenting various challenges related to instructional leadership. These scenarios are intended to give future educational leaders a variety of situations ranging from kindergarten to high school, from school settings to the central office. Each of them has a complex set of variables, requiring critical analysis and projecting oneself into the role of an instructional leader.

2-1. AN ALL-DAY FIELD TRIP IMPACTS THE INSTRUCTIONAL PROGRAM (ISLLC STANDARD 2)

You are the principal of an average-size high school serving a blue-collar community. Your predecessor retired after 10 years of being principal of this school. You are now in your second year as principal, and an interesting challenge confronts you. For the past

10 years, one of the English teachers has been holding an all-day, in-school field trip, participation in which is required of all students in her courses. She teaches world literature, and a major unit of study is the influence of Greek mythology and culture on world literature. The unit itself is quite comprehensive, and there is no doubt of its value. The problem is that this teacher annually holds "Greek Day" in the school's multipurpose room. During the school day, the students from all her classes come together to present skits done in the spirit of Greek literature. The participants dress in appropriate costumes and also hold a Greek festival of food as part of the day's activities.

While this sounds like a great opportunity for the students, the reality is that the teacher has taken on far more than she can handle. Except for those who are actually performing, the students are running wild with little or no supervision because the teacher is busy grading the performances. Fortunately, the students know they must stay in the multipurpose room and not roam around the building. Because the students have been excused from their other courses, the teachers of those courses are concerned about how valuable it is for their students to miss their classes in order to participate in the Greek Day events. Of course, these teachers don't recognize the parental support that accompanies this event. Decorations, costumes, and food are made and donated by parents. Students look forward to being in this teacher's classes so they can participate in Greek Day, most likely for the wrong reasons.

Needless to say, the students' rumor mill quickly spreads information about how little learning goes on during this all-day field trip. As teachers from other departments hear these rumors, they become upset, not only because participation at Greek Day has been determined to be more important than attending a math class or a science class, but also because they suspect that the day is not run very well, and the students are losing time that could be spent learning in their other classes. This has the department chairs upset, too, as they hear the complaints of their teachers.

Of course, the English department chair vehemently supports his teacher and this long-standing tradition. At today's department chair meeting, you are approached by the other department chairs to do something about this alleged misuse of school time and field-trip procedures. In addition to the concerns that this really is just a play day for the students, the department chairs question how the English department can ignore the school policy that states that on field trips there has to be one adult supervisor for every 30 students. The English department chair responds, "That policy only applies to field trips held off campus." Of course, he's right. The language in the policy manual specifically refers to off-campus field trips, but that is because there are no other in-school field trips.

As principal, what do you do to address this situation? Develop a bulleted plan that aligns with ISLLC Standard 2: *An education leader promotes the success of every student by advocating, nurturing, and sustaining a school culture and instructional program conducive to student learning and staff professional growth.*

Ethical Considerations

The principal is faced with a difficult situation in that the event has been approved by his predecessor and has been going on for so many years. For the principal to put a stop to it flies in the face of a tradition that is embraced by students and their parents alike. They look forward to this event, and some of the parents have helped with the Greek costumes and decorations. Although the other teachers have a valid point both about students' missing their courses and about supervision, the event does have the potential to be a very beneficial experience for students to demonstrate what they've learned.

Shutting down the event has potential ramifications of creating disharmony with parents and students as well as depriving the students of a potentially valuable event. On the other hand, does this event send a message that one content area is more important than another? Can these presentations be done within the time frame of the normal class period? Does Greek Day have to be an all-day field trip? Can it occur as an after-school or evening event? These are good questions that shake the tradition, but they also might represent a better way of utilizing instructional time.

Another consideration is the message that the principal wants to send about academic freedom within each department. Does the principal want to micro-manage the activities in each department? Isn't that one of the responsibilities of the department chairs? On the other hand, the department chairs apparently cannot resolve this among themselves and are seeking the principal's decision. From that perspective, the principal has to step in and make an instructional decision. If those empowered to make such decisions can't handle the responsibility, then the principal has to do so. Needless to say, this might not be a popular decision (whichever way it goes) with certain faculty members and department chairs.

2-2. KINDERGARTEN AND THE TWINS: WHAT IS OUR VISION FOR LEARNING? (ISLLC STANDARD 1)

You are the principal of an elementary school in which there are three kindergarten teachers.

- Miss Sally is a traditional teacher who uses the "letter people" to teach students the alphabet. She begins with the letter A (Mr. A is represented by an Apple; Miss B is represented by a banana, etc.) and works through the alphabet. The letter Z is the last letter that the students learn.
- Miss Cindy has a background in phonemic awareness, and she teaches the alphabet not as letters, but rather as letter sounds. Students learn that the word *cat* is composed of three sounds, "Kuh," "short A," and "Tuh." She is not as concerned about the students' learning to recite the alphabet as she is that they can sound out the sounds represented by the letters.
- Miss Mary believes in teaching the alphabet as letters that represent sounds, but she knows that certain letter sounds are easier to pronounce, and others are more difficult. She begins the year with the easiest letters/sounds and works through the alphabet by level of pronunciation difficulty.

This year there are two sets of twins in kindergarten, Adam and Kerry Smith, and Allyson and Georgie Conrad. The three kindergarten teachers all agree that it is not a good idea to put twins together in the same class. Consequently, Adam Smith and Allyson Conrad are in Miss Sally's class; Kerry Smith is in Miss Cindy's class; and Georgie Conrad is in Miss Mary's class.

Both Mrs. Smith and Mrs. Conrad are good friends, and they compare stories about what goes on in their children's classes. The year started off rather smoothly for the first week, but then Mrs. Smith complained to you that her children are learning different things, and that she finds it hard to support their learning at home. She also believes that Adam is getting a better education than Kerry is. You promise her that you will check into both kindergarten classes and get back to her, once you have a better understanding of exactly what is being taught in the kindergarten classes. Shortly after Mrs. Smith's complaint, you receive a similar complaint from Mrs. Conrad. She's concerned that while both of her children are getting what she believes to be a good kindergarten education, they can't reinforce each other's learning through worksheets and games at home because they're learning different letters and sounds. Similarly, you assure her that you will look into the situation and get back to her.

After you meet with the kindergarten teachers, you begin to understand the complexity of their concerns. All three kindergarten teachers are convinced that their teaching approaches are quite sound, and each of them has literature to support her instructional practices. Not being an expert in kindergarten instructional strategies, you are at a loss as to who's right. But you know that something has to be done to address the parents' concerns.

Develop a bulleted plan of instructional leadership that will ensure consistency across the kindergarten program. As you develop the plan, focus on ISLLC Standard 1: *An education leader promotes the success of every student by facilitating the development, articulation, implementation, and stewardship of a vision of learning that is shared and supported by all stakeholders.*

Ethical Considerations

As principal you want to keep peace in the school, but you also know that the issues brought out by the parents are real issues that need to be solved. While it would be easy for you simply to placate the parents, inevitably there will be ramifications. Not being a kindergarten teacher yourself, it is difficult to know what's best for the students as well as for the school. To further complicate the decision, ignorance can be bliss, and it would be easy just to ignore the situation or to simply put both twins in one classroom. Also, once you determine the most effective approach, you will have to ensure its implementation by all three kindergarten teachers. Even though the teachers might be upset about the decision to adopt one approach over the others, it really is unethical to continue less effective practices simply to keep peace among faculty members. Students' optimal learning is at stake here. Possible solutions might include a combination of all three practices, but that will result in change for all three teachers, which would require support in terms of retraining and staff development. Needless to say, there also would have to be support in terms of classroom resources and follow-up staff development.

To further complicate matters, the lack of a district policy regarding the placement of twins either in the same class or in different classes leaves the principal with the challenge of addressing this issue as well as the lack of a common kindergarten curriculum. Is it ethical to ignore both issues? As principal, do you want to address one without the other? How fair is that to the children? What's actually best for the children? These are all ethical issues facing the principal.

2-3. THE HIGH SCHOOL MATH DEPARTMENT: ARE WE SERVING ALL STAKEHOLDERS? (ISLLC STANDARD 1)

You are a principal of an urban high school. The demographics include 60% Hispanic, 20% African American, 18% Caucasian, and 2% Asian. More than 50% of the students are on the Free–Reduced Lunch Program, and you suspect that even more are eligible but haven't applied. This is due to the fact that the junior high schools feeding into your high school have approximately 63% of the students in the low socioeconomic status category. About 50% of the students in your school are English language learners (ELLs) in a Transitional Bilingual Education Program. The bilingual program is for Hispanic students, but you also have a Transitional Program of Instruction (ESL) for 15% of the Vietnamese students in your school.

You just received a phone call from the assistant superintendent for curriculum and instruction, indicating concern about the failure rate in freshman algebra classes. During the past three years, the failure rate has been 65%! Because the freshmen fail algebra, they have to repeat it during their sophomore year. This means that they can't take geometry until their junior year, and they never will get an opportunity to take any advanced math classes in their senior year. In addition to the academic consequences, there also is a financial issue. When 65% of the freshmen fail, additional math teachers must be hired. The assistant superintendent wants to meet with you to discuss strategies to curb the failure rate and also to improve student success.

To prepare for this meeting, you call the math department chair to discuss the issue. Mr. Peterson, the math department chair, does not seem to be very concerned about the failure rate. His stance is that the teachers are teaching, but the kids aren't performing. Whose problem is that? According to Peterson, it's about time these kids learn responsibility. By failing a math class maybe they'll learn to be more cognizant of consequences.

"The math department will *not* compromise its standards just to see more students pass a course," emphasizes Peterson.

You calmly tell him that you're not suggesting that the math department standards be compromised, but you are asking what the math department is doing to ensure student success.

"We teach math; their job is to learn it and to do well on our tests," Peterson explains. "They don't show up in class; that's why they're failing."

You ask him to meet with his department members to discuss strategies that would entice kids to come to class, and you thank him for his time. You also tell him that you'd like to meet with him and the department next week, and you set a mutually agreeable day, right after school.

Your next step is to head to the central office to talk with the data processing staff. They quickly provide you with correlations between attendance in math classes and grades. You are surprised to see no correlation. In other words, the students with the highest number of missed classes also received the highest grades! Those with the least number of absences received the lowest grades. This certainly doesn't match what the department chair told you. This leaves you quite puzzled, and you're beginning to wonder if the real problem is the attitude of the teachers toward their students.

It is now next week and you're beginning the meeting with the math department. You share with them your concerns about the failure rate, and ask them for their insight as to the root causes. To a person, each math teacher blames student attendance. Armed with the stats from the data-processing staff, you show the department that there is no correlation between absence and grades. The teachers are quick to blame the students for not completing their homework. You ask how big a problem this is and how much of the grade is contingent on completed homework. All the math teachers agree that homework is very important and that the students don't complete their homework, thereby resulting in lost points. You ask the teachers to talk to their students about why they're not doing homework, but the teachers refuse, complaining that they've already got more than they can handle with their daily workload. They insist that homework is a critical element in learning high school math. You thank them for their time and ask them to continue problem-solving among themselves about how we can turn this around. You set a date to meet with them next month (by contract you are limited to one curriculum meeting per month).

You phone the assistant superintendent and share your findings with him. You ask his help in conducting focus groups with students as to why they aren't doing their homework. He gladly agrees to come over to meet with students. You and he hold a series of focus groups during study halls, before, and after school. The students are very eager to share their concerns with you. Here's a list of the reasons given by the students:

- I'm the oldest of five children. My evenings are spent fixing supper, cleaning the kitchen, and getting the younger children ready for bed. I don't have a father, and my mother works the afternoon shift. I take over for her when I get home from school. Who's got time for homework? I try to do some of it when the kids go to bed, but I'm so tired that I fall asleep while I'm doing my homework.
- Our electricity was cut off last week. We don't have money to pay our bills, and we move from apartment to apartment as the landlord kicks us out for not paying rent. It's hard to do homework when you're sitting in the dark.
- We spent the whole night on the floor, dodging bullets from drive-by shootings. My uncle is a gang member, and the rival gang is after him. I'm so happy to be in school where I'm safe.
- I'm a teenaged mother. My mom takes care of my baby during the day, and I take care of him after school. I don't have time to do homework.
- My father is a drunk, and he's always fighting with my mother and with us kids. We can't do homework when we're hiding from him.
- Because my mother's boyfriend is abusive, my brothers and sisters and I go to relatives' houses at night. We never know whose house we'll stay at. We just keep moving around trying to find someone to take us in.

The students are very candid about why they can't do their homework. When you ask for suggestions, they all indicate that their teachers in other classes give them time to do homework at the end of the class period, but the math teachers teach right up to the bell. Some of the students explain that they don't understand the homework and do try, but give up when they can't figure it out.

You go back to the data-processing staff with names of the students that you've just interviewed. A check of their demographic information verifies that they are living in poverty, they have a number of younger siblings enrolled in the district's elementary schools, there only is a mother listed as the parent, and there are multiple address changes (indicating a lot of mobility).

Develop a plan in which you focus on ISLLC Standard 1: *An education leader promotes the success of every student by facilitating the development, articulation, implementation, and stewardship of a vision of learning that is shared and supported by all stakeholders.* Include strategies for addressing both instructional issues and failure rates. Use a bulleted format.

Ethical Considerations

It is easy to blame students for their lack of progress. Because the principal can't be an expert in every content area, there tends to be a "hands-off" approach to instructional leadership. Although the teachers are the experts in their content areas, they sometimes become self-righteous when students fail. "They knew what to do, and they didn't do it. That's why they failed, and hopefully they will learn a lesson about responsibility."

There are some harsh realities:

- Failure doesn't ensure future success.
- Repeating a course that is taught the same way as it was previously most likely will not result in additional learning.
- Although teachers often place a high level of importance on homework, students and parents often don't value it.
- Teachers are responsible for ensuring the success of all students, not just those who try.
- When students fail, it's everyone's problem, and it results in a tremendous loss in terms of time, resources, and attitudes about learning.

With this in mind, the educational leader has to utilize whatever resources are available to find a solution.

Academic freedom and content area expertise are sacred values among teachers, and the educational leader has to be careful not to cloud the issue by challenging these values. As always, the focus must be on students' learning and achievement. The ideal would be to empower the teachers to collaborate on a solution. The old adage "None of us is as smart as all of us" holds very true. Teachers also have jobs to do and cannot be expected to come up with a solution during their "free time." The educational leader must give them the necessary resources, including release-time.

2-4. PARENTS' AGREEMENT: NO DATA MEANS "GET RID OF IT!" (ISLLC STANDARD 3)

You are the assistant superintendent for curriculum and instruction in a large, urban school district that serves students from pre-kindergarten to 12th grade. The district has a sizable number of students coming from low-income homes. Although many of the parents are supportive of their children's education, there are so many issues related to working extra jobs, living in the fear of gang activity, not being able to pay the bills, and so on. It becomes obvious to you that the parents are so overwhelmed by their own problems, they often don't know how to be good parents. What seems to be obvious to educators is not even considered by the parents. The parents need to be told simple things like making sure the children have a quiet place in which to do their homework.

At the regular monthly principals' meeting you announce that you'd like to form a committee to address ways to help parents better support their children's success in school. Not only do the principals agree with your idea, but within a matter of minutes, you have a full committee. The rest of the principals also pledge their support for whatever the committee might develop. This is very encouraging to you. You announce the time and place of the first meeting.

After the first committee meeting, the committee decides upon an idea to reach into the homes of all the children. They feel confident that their plan not only will help to teach the uninformed parents, but it also will affirm the actions of other parents. Specifically, the committee would like to initiate a "parent commitment" program by which both parents and teachers would sign an agreement that ultimately would help their students. The agreement would specify what the parents are expected to do and what the teachers will do in return. The signed agreements would be displayed in two places: at home on the refrigerator, and in school on the bulletin board.

The agreement would be positive in nature. The parent promises to:

- As a family, live together in love, kindness, respect, honesty, compassion, and nonviolence.
- Make sure my child is prepared for the first of day of school (registration, immunizations, schedule pickup, school supplies, etc.).
- Make sure my child attends school on a regular basis.
- Make contact with my child's teacher(s).
- Take an active part in my child's education.
- Monitor my child's progress.

The school would agree to be supportive and proactive regarding the students' success. Faculty members agree to:

- Notify parents of any change in their child's behavior, attendance, or performance.
- Make parents feel welcome and encourage good communication.
- Encourage parental participation while allowing flexibility for parents' schedules.
- Facilitate and arrange for student support services, such as mentoring and tutoring programs.
- Make sure that the students have meaningful homework that reinforces what they've learned.
- Establish a classroom atmosphere of love, kindness, respect, honesty, compassion, and collaborative problem solving.

The agreement quickly becomes accepted by parents and school personnel alike. The children are proud to have their agreements displayed on the bulletin board of their school, which has become a positive peer pressure for all students to encourage their parents to sign it. As assistant superintendent, you not only are proud of this initiative and your committee's work, but you also are eager to talk about it at the Board of Education meeting, as well as local service club meetings. Needless to say, it becomes a powerful public relations tool.

Just when you are enjoying the success of the initiative, the superintendent calls you into his office and tells you that the district is undertaking a new direction. "Everything we do must be data-driven," he explains to you. Certainly, this is nothing new to you as you think about all the data-driven emphasis that has been placed on test scores, student achievement, teacher evaluations, and principals' evaluations. You can't believe your ears when the superintendent declares that unless your "parent commitment" initiative can generate meaningful data, it will have to be canceled. He further informs you that this is a nonnegotiable issue. He has told the Board of Education that all district initiatives will be measured by data. "If we can't measure it, we won't do it."

As you walk back to your office, you can't help but think of all the positive aspects stemming from the "parent commitment" initiative. You explore in your mind how you can employ some data-collection tool that would keep the initiative alive and not detract from its effectiveness. You immediately set up a meeting with the committee to seek their input.

At the meeting, the principals are reluctant to add a data-collection tool to the initiative. After much probing, they finally admit that they are afraid that a data-collection tool would trivialize the initiative. Certainly, each school could compete with the others to see who has the greater percentage of participation, but with all of the schools already at least with a 95% participation rate, would that really be meaningful? Because of the issues faced by dysfunctional families, there always will be a small percentage who don't value the initiative and won't participate. What are the ramifications for principals if they can't get 100% participation? Would their attempts to get compliance actually turn parents away from the school?

You admit that the principals have some very valid points. Also, none of the committee members can think of any other way to collect data about the initiative other than looking at participation rates.

What would you do? Would you terminate the initiative? Explain, in a bulleted manner, your action plan. Be sure to develop your plan in alignment with ISLLC Standard 3: *An education leader promotes the success of every student by ensuring management of the organization, operation, and resources for a safe, efficient, and effective learning environment.*

Ethical Considerations

If you try to add a data-collection tool the principals' concerns about trivializing the initiative are a distinct possibility. On the other hand, if you don't add the data-collection tool, the initiative must be scrapped. You also have to be careful not to cast the superintendent in a negative light as you explain the need for a data-collection tool. But, as you explain that need, you have to be careful that you don't lose your own credibility with the constituents. This seems to be a no-win situation. Also, you know that some of the families in the district routinely move every three months to avoid being evicted. They can't afford their rent, and as a result they move frequently. Signing the "parent commitment" agreement is not a priority for them as they are in a survival mode. To expect principals to force such signatures simply to increase their school's participation rate is not going to build a positive relationship between the home and the school. Perhaps not everything in schools (or in life, for that matter) can be measured by a data-collection tool?

As an assistant superintendent, you can't help but wonder how far to fight this before jeopardizing your own job. Although that shouldn't be a consideration, if the superintendent is on a data-driven mission, you have to gauge his ability to be open-minded.

2-5. THE PHYSICAL EDUCATION DRESS CODE AND ITS FAIRNESS TO ALL STUDENTS (ISLLC STANDARD 5)

You are a high school principal whose school serves a middle-class, blue-collar community. Your assistant principal notifies you that he has been processing an inordinate number of referrals from the physical education teachers. The cause of the referrals was refusal to wear the physical education uniform. In particular, most of the referrals have been written for overweight students.

You call a meeting with the physical education staff to establish the root cause of the referrals. To a person, each teacher tells you that it's a matter of discipline and responsibility. The school has specific uniforms for physical education classes, and the students who received referrals simply have refused to wear the uniform. You probe the teachers' thinking by asking if they would be willing to change the uniform requirement to include loose-fitting sweat clothes. They adamantly refuse to accept such an idea.

Your next step is to interview the students who weren't dressing in the uniform and consequently receiving referrals. Some of the students won't tell you why they don't dress for physical education class, but it is obvious that they are hiding something. Fortunately, one student does admit to you in confidence that he is self-conscious about his appearance. He says the physical education uniforms made him look fat, and he feels that the other students were laughing at him as his "rolls of fat shook" while he ran.

You share this information with the physical education teachers to conduct some collective brainstorming and problem solving. You are shocked to learn that the teachers really don't empathize with the obese students. The teachers seem to look down on these students because of their obesity.

After contacting other principals from area schools, you find that they have moved away from physical education uniforms and have gone with a more liberal approach of requiring sweat clothes or T-shirts and shorts. The only requirement is that the physical education clothing be in the school colors. When you share this information with your physical education staff, they reject this idea as being counterproductive to instilling self-discipline in the students.

What do you do? How would you handle this situation? Using a bulleted format, explain your plan of action. Develop your plan around ISLLC Standard 5: *An education leader promotes the success of every student by acting with integrity, fairness, and in an ethical manner.*

Ethical Considerations

The obvious answer is to move to a more liberal uniform code such as the area schools have done. To do so would be more beneficial for students, and it would decrease the number of referrals received by obese students, thereby helping their self-esteem. The problem with this approach is that you would be undermining the professional beliefs of your faculty. As principal, you can't help but be concerned with your credibility with them. Do you place more value on how they view you than you do on what you believe to be best for students?

While you are thinking about what seems to be best for students who have weight control issues, you realize the physical education teachers do present an interesting counter to your approach. Would a more liberal physical education uniform code undermine the physical fitness goals of the program? While being concerned about a small percentage of the students, are you watering down expectations for the larger percentage of the students? In the long run, is it better to be concerned about the majority or each and every individual?

2-6. THE SOCIAL STUDIES TEACHER AND ETHICAL BEHAVIOR (ISLLC STANDARD 5)

You are the assistant principal in a high school having an enrollment of 1,000 students. The high school serves a predominantly white-collar community. The social studies department is comprised of energetic teachers who find ways to actively engage their students in various activities and projects that most certainly enhance learning. One of the teachers, however, Mr. Smith, has been rather outspoken about politics. He is highly visible in the community and makes his political party affiliations well known. Smith has aggressively worked on various political campaigns, and his enthusiasm definitely has spilled into the classroom. In past elections, some of his students have been campaign workers, supporting his choice of candidates. Needless to say, this is a good thing, *if* the students have freely chosen to support these candidates. But have they been unduly influenced by their teacher to support certain candidates?

Last year, the social studies department chair expressed to you her concern that Smith has been spending too much class time in discussions about politics and campaigns. Although these class discussions have been lively and entertaining, there is an obligation for the teacher to address other learning standards. The department chair wanted to inform you that she has spoken with Smith about the need to stick with the district curriculum and the state learning standards and not to turn his classroom into a podium to express his personal politics. At that time, you agreed with the department chair's approach and suggested that she also follow up with a memo to the teacher. The memo would summarize the conversation and the recommendation that Smith cut back on the political discussions and spend more time with the district curriculum and state learning standards.

This year, you asked the social studies department chair about the situation, and she assured you that all is fine. You specifically asked her about the politics in the classroom, and she smiled while responding, "There's no problem this year." You are amazed at the rapid solution to last year's problem, but you can't help but wonder how she managed to solve it with such certainty and finality. Upon further investigation, you find that the social studies department chair purposely has given Smith the lowest-level courses to teach this year. His current students have little or no interest in politics, and they certainly are not motivated to participate as campaign workers.

Although this has solved the problem, you begin to question the ethics of such a strategy. Is this really fair to the students who would learn from campaign worker experiences and political discussions? Is this fair to the "low-level students" to give them a teacher who might or might not be skilled in teaching the fundamentals of social studies? Is this fair to the teacher, who has great talent for motivating students to learn more about the political system?

How would you approach this situation? Develop your plan around ISLLC Standard 5: *An education leader promotes the success of every student by acting with integrity, fairness, and in an ethical manner.*

Ethical Considerations

As a supervisor, you will encounter teachers who don't always comply with your or their department chair's requests, but is reassigning them the correct way to handle the situation? In this particular situation, the enthusiasm and passion of the reassigned teacher has to be questioned. Is the teacher able to sustain the same levels of enthusiasm and passion if she or he perceives that the new assignment is a punishment? Did the teacher fully understand the department chair's directions? Was the teacher given ample time and support to make the necessary changes? All these questions are left unanswered as the principal attempts to investigate.

The scary part is the likelihood that the department chair might not have given adequate explanation and support. Instead, the department chair most likely reassigned the teacher as a quick and expeditious way to solve a problem. But is this really best for the students? What the teacher was doing in the classroom was creating a good learning environment. The teacher went too far over the proverbial line, but the students were actively engaged in their social studies projects. How can this be continued without crossing the line? Isn't it the job of the supervisor to promote quality teaching while also ensuring ethical behavior on the part of the teacher? One has to ask if the reassignment was ethical behavior on the part of the supervisor. Does one kind of unethical behavior warrant another instance of unethical behavior to solve the problem? What really has been learned by the teacher and the students?

2-7. STATE TESTS AND ETHICS (ISLLC STANDARD 6)

You are the new principal of an elementary school that has struggled with its students' State Achievement Test scores. As a principal, you have been concerned that your school might not make AYP (adequate yearly progress) this year, despite the best efforts of your faculty. You are very proud of the faculty's work in preparing the students for the State Achievement Test and their attitude toward the test. Because you have a large population of ELLs who will be taking the English version of the State Achievement Test as per the new requirements, you are worried that the composite scores for your school are going to be lower than they were last year. You have shared your worry with the faculty, and they have done much brainstorming about how to prepare the students.

It now is testing time, and everything seems to be going smoothly until you discover something very shocking. Your typical routine is to walk around the building and talk with the night custodians before you leave for the evening. They appreciate your interest in their work, and it gives you an opportunity to know them better. As you walk into a classroom where one of the custodians is cleaning, you notice a copy of the State Achievement Test on the teacher's desk. Needless to say, all testing materials should have been secured for the night, but what is especially alarming is that the test booklet is open. From all appearances, the teacher must have been reading the test!

You know that teachers are not allowed to read the State Achievement Tests, and that this is a violation of the testing process. You don't know if the teacher was reading the test for her own benefit, or if she was helping her students with the test.

What should you do? Using a bulleted format, explain your plan of action. Develop your plan to align with ISLLC Standard 6: *An education leader promotes the success of every student by understanding, responding to, and influencing the political, social, economic, legal, and cultural context.*

Ethical Considerations

If you confront the teacher, you might not want to hear the truth. You rely on her students' scores to pull up the school average. If she admits any misuse of the test, you will have to report it to the central office. They will have to report this to the state, and that class' scores will not count toward your school average. You also will have to discipline the teacher.

If you don't confront her, you could avoid the situation. Maybe you should ignore your finding and not even ask about it. But is it ethical to ignore the situation? Can you sleep at night, perhaps allowing unethical behavior by your faculty?

If you confront the teacher, what would be the ramifications for the whole school? Would you be jeopardizing the future of the school? In other words, would this lead to reconstitution of the school, due to poor scores? If you keep your mouth shut, you can avoid this possibility. There is an old adage that still holds true today, "Good communication solves problems." Perhaps that is the best advice. Communicate with the teacher, both in terms of understanding her actions and in terms of conveying your expectations.

2-8. THE UNCOMPROMISING MATH TEACHER (ISLLC STANDARD 3)

You are a principal in a suburban high school. One of the initiatives of which you are proud is the special education teachers' work in transitioning students with learning disabilities into regular education classrooms and providing ongoing support to students and teachers. You can't help but wonder why one of the special education teachers makes an appointment to meet with you about a critical situation involving a special education student's placement in an algebra class.

When the special education teacher comes to your office for her appointment, you are surprised to learn that one of your best math teachers is refusing to make some simple accommodations for a student with processing deficits. The special education teacher explains how much progress the student has made even to be eligible for a transitioned placement in the algebra class. She is very concerned that the math teacher's refusal to make some simple accommodations will result in a tragic setback for the student.

You ask just what the accommodations are, and the special education teacher responds, "Because Michael has a processing deficit, his IEP (Individualized Education Plan) specifies that he be given extra time to solve algebra problems. We fully expect him to correctly solve the problems, but he just needs a little extra time to do so."

You realize that not only is this a very reasonable request on the part of the special education teacher, but because it is written as an IEP goal, it is a requirement that the math teacher comply. Furthermore, you are very surprised by the math teacher's resistance, because she usually is very cooperative and open to new ideas and change.

You assure the special education teacher that you will meet with the math teacher to address this issue, and you assure the special education teacher that you agree it is vitally important that the student be given this simple accommodation.

When you meet with the math teacher about this, she flatly refuses to "water down her curriculum." She states firmly, "I have certain standards and I am not going to compromise them." Knowing that the state learning standards don't prevent teachers from making such an accommodation, you ask, "What standards are you referring to? Certainly not the state learning standards."

"My own personal standards for teaching algebra!" she quickly responds.

You patiently explain the ethical obligation that she has to help the student with learning disabilities to succeed. Also, you remind her that she is obligated to follow the conditions of the student's IEP. Her response is shocking.

"I'm not a special education teacher, and I don't appreciate having to teach that student. He's the responsibility of the special education teacher, not mine."

You are beginning to lose your patience, but you calmly but firmly explain that this student is her responsibility because he has been placed in her class. Just as she is responsible for all her students, she is responsible for him as well. Furthermore, if one of her other students had a broken hand, she would make an accommodation; if a student suddenly became ill, she would accommodate that student by allowing him or her to leave the room and go to the washroom. In other words, she would make accommodations for other students, why not this one?

She firmly states that she is not a special education teacher. Deciding to take another approach, you ask, "What is the real problem here?" She tells you that she has gotten the students excited about doing timed speed drills, and she doesn't want to lose their enthusiasm by allowing the special student to take a little longer to solve the problems. You remind her that the goal of the program is to teach students how to solve algebraic problems, but not necessarily to solve them within a few minutes. Even the state learning standards don't require timed speed drills. Although these might be an interesting and challenging strategy for some students, not all will react positively to this approach.

You then give her a little pep talk about the value of differentiating instruction and adjusting her teaching to the students' different learning styles. She continues to argue back that her timed speed drills are very important.

What would you do? Using a bulleted approach, develop an action plan that aligns with ISLLC Standard 3: *An education leader promotes the success of every student by ensuring management of the organization, operation, and resources for a safe, efficient, and effective learning environment.*

Ethical Considerations

Being a principal can be a lonely role. You certainly want your faculty to like you and to respect your leadership. On the other hand, you also have to promote and enforce certain ethics, one of which is to ensure a quality education for all students. If you cut the math teacher some slack, you run the risk of jeopardizing the success of the student with learning disabilities. Also, you run the risk of losing the special education teacher's respect and support.

On the other hand, if you force the math teacher to comply, you not only lose her support, but you also don't really have any assurance that she will fully comply once the classroom door is shut. Unless you sit in her classroom every day, which could be misconstrued as harassment and could result in a union grievance, how will you know that she really is accommodating the student with learning disabilities? Of course, there is a chance that the math teacher could reflect on this and admit that she needs to be more accommodating. But that is a long shot.

2-9. THE WALKOUT AND RELATED POLITICS (ISLLC STANDARD 6)

You are the principal of a small-town high school of 500 students. This is your second year as principal and your fourth year in the school. You were assistant principal for two years, and then you were appointed principal when your predecessor retired. Your superintendent has been in the district just over a year, having come from a large, affluent high school. He had been the principal of that high school and was hired by your board of education as the superintendent with no prior central office experience nor any small school experience.

You are concerned about this because Dr. Meister, the superintendent, often interferes in your areas of responsibility. It seems to you that he hasn't really made the transition from principalship to a superintendency. You wonder if his lack of central office experience is the cause of this. Nevertheless, it is becoming increasingly more difficult for you to do your job well when the superintendent is acting as if he is the principal, making promises to staff when he should have referred them to you.

To complicate matters, Dr. Meister doesn't seem to understand the community very well. As principal, you are very active in community events and serve on a number of village committees. Because your high school is a single building in its own district, you have included parents from the "feeder" elementary districts in various high school committees. They and the junior high principal are on your curriculum planning committee, your principal's advisory council, and the mission planning committee. You also serve on the village economic development committee, a position that was held by the former superintendent, but handed off to you by Dr. Meister. He explained to you that he doesn't like committees and that he's delegating the responsibility of representing the high school to you.

Because your high school is in a small town, there has been an expectation on the part of the community that a family-like approach would be used in making decisions regarding what courses to offer, class sizes, and so on. Just prior to the former superintendent's resignation, the board of education supported your recommendation to offer "zero hour" classes so that students would be able to take more electives during the day. By offering boys and girls physical education as well as a fine arts course before the regular school day, you were able to eliminate some scheduling conflicts. Because yours is such a small high school, you were able to offer the specialized electives only once in a day, sometimes preventing students from taking Advanced Biology or AP History, and the like. The board unanimously approved the "zero hour" concept and agreed to pay the additional costs for teaching overloads because it afforded students more opportunities.

Back to the present. . . . Dr. Meister just called you into his office to inform you that for next year's schedule, there will be no "zero hour" courses because he's trying to trim costs. You respectfully fill him in on the background of the program as well as the board's support of it. He tells you that he has a mission to bring this small-town high school "up to the level of a large suburban school, such as the one from which he just came." You calmly counter by telling him that the "zero hour" concept is one that you originally saw at a large high school, and that when you were the principal-elect, you had assembled a team of teachers to visit that high school to check out the feasibility of the "zero hour" concept. To cancel the program now would not only take away opportunities from students, but it also would send a message to the staff that their committee work was meaningless. Dr. Meister then proceeds to tell you that the "zero hour" program will not be funded for next year. There is no discussion about it. Furthermore, he informs you that he is setting a minimum number for each class. If fewer than 15 students enroll in a class, it will not be offered.

Knowing that your current enrollment in a French III–IV class is only 12 students, but that you allowed that small enrollment in order to provide those students with an opportunity to take more than two years of a foreign language, you explain to Dr. Meister that there are some courses that have to run at small enrollments, but to offset their impact on staffing, you've run some other classes with 25 students. Staff members understand this and are willing to accept some large classes as long as they are offset by some small classes. To that comment, Dr. Meister replies, "If there are 15 students enrolled in a class, run it; but if there are 14 students enrolled, don't run it. What don't you understand about that? It's just good business to set these limits." Realizing that this will not only negatively impact students, but that it could reduce some teachers' jobs from full-time to part-time, you decide that you have to take one more shot at trying to convince the superintendent that this is not a good idea.

You explain to Dr. Meister that during your curriculum meetings, which you hold regularly with parents, members have been very pleased with the willingness of the high school to offer small classes. One of the parents explained at a recent meeting that her daughter was going to major in French in college, but if she had only had two years of that course, she probably wouldn't have made that choice. Ultimately the girl hopes to go into international law, and a background in French gives her a real advantage. Dr. Meister responds coldly, "Why can't you get it into your thick head that students actually make choices when they enroll in courses? If only 13 students sign up for a course, they are telling us that the course isn't important to them. It's a market-driven world out there." To which you respond, "It is very important to those 13." Dr. Meister then gives you very specific orders: "Meet with your department chairs and tell them that we'll have no 'zero hour' courses next year, and that we're imposing a minimum class size of 15. If they complain, tell them that we're in financial trouble and that we have to trim costs. Do not send them to me. I'm not taking the heat for this decision. As principal, you have your orders; carry them out, but do not make me the bad guy. Do you understand?"

At the next department chair meeting, you explain the new restrictions on scheduling and that these must be imposed to address budget concerns. Because you're relatively new to the role of principal and some of the department chairs have been in their positions for many years, you can tell that they are not going to support these changes, but you're not sure what they're going to do about them. Within a few days, you know what the department chairs have done.

Through the rumor mill, you hear that some of the teachers have told their students that because not enough students signed up for certain courses, some of the teachers are being fired. In reaction to this, the students are planning a walkout on Friday. The department chairs have created a fear-based scenario among their teachers, possibly with the intent of trying to leverage change through student reactions. Obviously, this is putting teachers and students in a bad position. In addition, the fear could spread to the parents as students complain at home.

That evening, one of the teachers who is loyal to you phones you at home to say that he overheard some students talking during track team practice. Apparently, they are planning a walkout in protest of the canceling of courses not having sufficient enrollment. The teacher has a sense that talk of the walkout has become a rallying force among the students. You recall that just a few weeks ago, students in a neighboring school district staged a walkout in protest of their principal's banning a long-standing tradition of having a Christmas tree in the school lobby. That walkout generated a lot of media coverage for the students. You fear that your students might be enticed by the possibility of such media coverage. Thanking the teacher for letting you know about the possible walkout, you then phone your assistant principal to find out if he has heard anything about this.

The assistant principal also received a tip from another teacher. He further informs you that one of the coaches has been stirring up the students, most likely in an attempt to win their support for him, thereby ensuring his reappointment as coach next year. He has been overspending his budget and has been worried about possibly not being reappointed. Apparently, he sees this as an opportunity to solder himself into the position via student support. It is becoming more and more obvious that this is a "perfect storm" brewing, and there are many factors at work.

Your phone rings again. It is a concerned parent who somehow has gotten your home phone number (maybe from the staff directory via one of the teachers?). The parent threatens to call the news media unless you can make sure that her daughter's French class will be offered to third-year students next year. You feel sick to your stomach as you realize that the magnitude of this problem is increasing rapidly.

If you were the principal, what would you do? Explain, in bulleted format, a process for dealing with this instructional leadership challenge. Develop your plan to align with ISLLC Standard 6: *An education leader promotes the success of every student by understanding, responding to, and influencing the political, social, economic, legal, and cultural context.*

Ethical Considerations

There are many ethical aspects to this scenario. The most obvious is what some might call an implicit contract with the students. If freshman students complete one or two years of a foreign language, doesn't the school have an obligation to provide them with years three and four? Had the students known in advance that years three and four wouldn't be offered, would they have chosen a different foreign language? If the course were going to be canceled, shouldn't it be phased in beginning with incoming freshmen?

On the other hand, can a school be expected to continue to offer courses that don't have sufficient enrollment? Doesn't the school have the responsibility to properly manage the taxpayers' money? Does fiscal responsibility have more priority than a moral responsibility to students?

The superintendent certainly wants what's best for the school, but when does the superintendent have a right to micro-manage the principal? Shouldn't a clear mission and set of expectations be understood between both the superintendent and principal?

What obligation does the superintendent have to make sure that the principal and the rest of the administrative team understand the mission and expectations set forth by the superintendent?

If the principal senses that the superintendent is sabotaging him, perhaps for an excuse to get rid of the principal, should the principal try to protect his or her own job, or should the students come first in the decision making?

The actions of some of the teachers, and the track coach in particular, are disheartening, but how much can be attributed to fear about job security? If you were the teacher of one of the courses that are "on the bubble," what would you do? Are the teachers justified in taking drastic measures to ensure their job security, especially when they feel that they have no control over their future? Certainly, using students to benefit one's job security is unethical, but isn't the whole situation based on unethical practices?

CHAPTER 3

Ethics and Management

This chapter addresses the management side of educational leadership. In addition to the instructional portion of an educational leader's duties, there are numerous managerial duties. They might include monitoring the overall physical condition of the building (often the head custodian reports to the principal), or the use of the building by outside groups, or the management of the building budget. To complicate matters, these managerial duties often can seem to take priority over the real "business" of the school, teaching and learning. Some principals get so good at managing that they prefer those duties to the instructional leadership side of educational leadership. This is especially true when the principal has to face and solve crisis situations. Principals will refer to themselves as "crisis junkies" because they thrive so much on the challenge of crisis situations.

Some state departments of education have mandated that principals spend at least 51% of their time on instructional leadership instead of on managerial duties. This mandate doesn't eliminate the managerial duties, though. How an educational leader balances both the instructional and managerial sides of the position has been the topic of various research studies. There are two distinct schools of thought about how to balance these two sides of leadership. One school says that the educational leader should not engage in managerial tasks, but should delegate them to an administrative assistant who is capable and empowered to handle them. The result could be the hiring of a school manager. The other school says that the educational leader needs to learn how to set priorities and to set a reasonable balance between instructional duties and managerial duties. This might include delegating, if appropriate to the particular situation.

Regardless of the approach, the fact remains that both the instructional and the managerial duties are under the overall responsibility of the educational leader or principal. The purpose of this chapter is to provide future educational leaders with various scenarios that provoke good, clear thinking and planning and that cause the future leader to think and plan in terms of ethics. The quick fix that short-circuits ethics might be appealing, but future educational leaders are urged always to seek the high road of moral and ethical leadership.

3-1. AN ALLEGED STERIOD USER (ISLLC STANDARD 6)

You are a second-year assistant principal in a small, suburban high school of approximately 600 students from middle- and upper-class families. Your responsibilities as the assistant principal include: disciplinarian/dean of students, director of special education, director of guidance and counseling, and director of student activities. During your first year, you were instrumental in acquiring a part-time police liaison and reactivating the Students Against Drunk Driving Club. You also forged an agreement with a local hospital to provide free drug assessments for students suspected of using drugs or alcohol. Depending on the outcome of the assessment, a program could be individually designed for the student. Such programs could be on an inpatient or outpatient basis. The program costs would be referred to the family's medical insurance, and the hospital has agreed to waive costs not covered by insurance, depending on the family's ability to pay.

You worked with the athletic director to initiate an "Athletes Take the Pledge" program in which all athletes and their parents not only attend an orientation program, but they also sign a pledge agreeing not to partake of drugs or alcohol. The program emphasizes making good choices and having fun without drugs or alcohol. Parents of the athletes also agree not to allow underage drinking in their home. Student athletes can be removed from the team if they are caught drinking or using other drugs during the season. Needless to say, you have been quite instrumental in promoting appropriate drug- and alcohol-free behaviors.

One day, you receive a tip that a student, Eric Jones, has been using steroids. Although he is not a student athlete in your school, he is a power-lifter in an area gym. You have noticed that he has "bulked up" recently, but you've attributed that to his weight-lifting. The student in question also has an Individual Education Plan (IEP) for learning disabilities specifically related to computational skills and application in math settings. Being director of special education, you know that his disability is not related to processing of information related to decision making. Acting on the tip about steroids, you ask the special education teachers if they've noticed any difference in his behaviors, or if they've heard him or the other students talk about his alleged use of steroids. You are acting in the best interests of this student by not jumping to conclusions and taking the time to investigate. Obviously, you are not looking to get him in trouble, but if he is using drugs, you would refer him and his parents to the local hospital for an assessment.

You are shocked when one of the special education teachers accuses you of trying to "put feathers in your cap" by creating situations to make you look like a savior. As you calmly explain that the best interests of the students are first and foremost in your intentions, you can't help but feel that you are on the defensive.

"Let's focus on the situation at hand," you say to the accusing teacher. "Have you noticed any change in Eric's behavior?" Each of the three special education teachers denies having seen any change in the student's behavior. You ask them why a student would give you such a tip.

"Have there been any situations that would cause other students to make up such an allegation?" you ask them.

Again, they stonewall you by saying that they have no idea why such an allegation would be made.

Knowing that the tip came from a reliable source, you recall that there have been some reports from the regular education teachers of the classes in which this student is being mainstreamed. They have indicated some aggressive behavior that just recently emerged. While walking back to your office, you decide to check the student's locker.

In situations like this, you know that it's best to have another adult witness your examination of the locker. Just as you round the corner, you see the police liaison walking toward you. As you ask her to witness your examination of the locker, she reminds you that as a police officer, she needs probable cause to conduct the search, but as a school employee, she can be a witness if you conduct the search.

You reply, "That's fine with me. I'll conduct the search, and you be my witness."

As you open the locker and begin the search, you find steroids. The police liaison verifies the label and contents as steroids. You photograph them and call the student into your office. His answer to your interview with him is that someone else put them there. As per the handbook, you contact a parent in the presence of the student and request an immediate conference.

At the conference, you explain that the parent either can take the student to the hospital for a drug assessment, or the student faces immediate out-of-school suspension pending possible expulsion for possession of drugs. The student also could face civil charges with the police. The parent agrees to the hospital assessment in lieu of suspension and possible expulsion.

You make a phone call to the hospital to inform them that the parent and student will be arriving shortly. The agreement is for the hospital to confirm that the assessment has been done.

The next day, the hospital phones to say that the parent and the student never showed up. When you phone the parent to find out what happened, you are told that one of your special education teachers has advised the parents not to have the drug assessment done. You have no choice but to proceed with an expulsion hearing, first with a designated state hearing officer, who will submit his or her findings to the board of education.

Although the due process steps will be followed, you ponder what to do about the special education teacher. How would you handle this situation? Explain, in a bulleted fashion, your plan. Be sure to align it with ISLLC Standard 6: *An education leader promotes the success of every student by understanding, responding to, and influencing the political, social, economic, legal, and cultural context.*

Ethical Considerations

It could be argued that the parents have a right to seek counsel from the special education teacher, whom they trust; however, it also could be argued that the teacher was acting as an "agent" of the school. As such, the teacher must be careful to act within the scope of his or her responsibility. The teacher is not a substance abuse counselor and would be misrepresenting the school if she or he offered advice from that perspective.

Another consideration would be the political ramifications of reprimanding the teacher. If you don't, a message is sent to the staff that it's okay to act out of their scope of responsibility and to undermine the administration. If you do reprimand the teacher, it could be viewed as retaliation for the teacher's recently having spoken out against you.

When looking at what's best for the student, obviously the assessment could yield the much-needed help that might prevent the student from making even worse mistakes related to drug use in the future. From that perspective, any attempt to prevent the student from undergoing an assessment would be detrimental to the student's well-being.

3-2. ANOTHER ASSISTANT SUPERINTENDENT FALSELY ACCUSES ONE OF YOUR STAFF (ISLLC STANDARD 5)

You are a new assistant superintendent in an affluent suburban school district that serves 8,000 students, pre-kindergarten through eighth grade. There are 15 schools, 12 elementary schools and 3 junior high schools in the district. You have prior experience as an assistant superintendent for curriculum and instruction in a large urban school district. Although you were happy in your previous district, you decided to leave due to the intense central office politics. Your new district has a refreshing air about it, in that there is a lot of attention paid to mission and vision. You appreciate this approach, and you are especially pleased with the requirement that all administrators, teachers, and students have to develop annual goals for themselves.

There is a strong emphasis on self-evaluation as administrators, teachers, and students have to maintain a portfolio that includes artifacts supporting their accomplishment of goals. All in all, this seems like a very nice school district in which to work. There is a weekly meeting of the four assistant superintendents and the superintendent scheduled for one o'clock Thursday afternoon. You are eagerly awaiting this meeting to see just how the superintendent's cabinet works.

The informal agenda of the meeting turns out to be a complete surprise to you. The other assistant superintendents engage in backstabbing and gossip about the principals, and the superintendent seems to enjoy it. You are especially surprised when the assistant superintendent for business boldly states, "There is a problem between the instructional technology services and the instruction department. They don't seem to be able to communicate with each other."

You ask for specifics, but the superintendent advises you to look into the matter and moves on with the agenda. As per his directive, you go to your technology person in the instruction department and ask what this could be about. He doesn't have the foggiest idea of what the assistant superintendent for business is talking about. You then go to the director of instructional technology services, ask the same question, and get the same response.

Your next step is to pull both of them into a meeting together, and they still say they don't know what this is about. You talk to them about how important it is for the two departments to work together, and they not only agree, but they also share with you some of the cooperative projects on which they've been working. You are pleased to hear this, but you still are bewildered by the comments made by the assistant superintendent for business. You ask if the two directors would be willing to meet with her to share with her the cooperative projects and to let her know that what she said in the cabinet meeting wasn't accurate. They agree, and you have your secretary set up a meeting at a mutually agreeable time.

During the meeting, the assistant superintendent for business seems upset that you've even called this meeting. You and the two directors are very cordial and collegial and keep the focus of the meeting on your desire to have good communication with her and to put her concerns about the two departments allegedly not working together to rest. She finally states that she heard the complaint from the principal of River Valley School. As soon as that principal's name is mentioned, both of the directors quickly say, "Oh, that one! She's always got a complaint about something and so does her learning resource director. Between the two of them, they are never pleased with anything we do for them."

You ask for specifics, and they explain how unreasonable the learning resource director recently was when the Internet-based library catalog system wasn't working correctly. It wasn't an internal problem, but rather a problem with the provider's main system. The glitch has been fixed by the provider, and all is well. The assistant superintendent of business doesn't seem too happy to hear this logical explanation, but you are relieved that the truth is out in the open and that there is no real problem.

The next day, the superintendent calls you into his office and asks for an explanation of why you called a meeting with the two directors and the assistant superintendent for business services. You give him the complete details, thinking that you've done the right thing by bringing people together to resolve an issue. You expect him to commend you for confronting a problem in a positive manner and bringing it to a good conclusion. Surprisingly, he says to you, "We don't do things like that around here."

The look on your face is one of surprise and confusion, to which he responds, "What we talk about in the cabinet stays in the cabinet."

You explain that you were merely trying to address an issue that the assistant superintendent for business brought up, and that she clearly had bad information. You felt it was necessary to clear up the matter, and your style is to reconcile differences quickly before they fester into worse problems. Again, he says, "We don't do things like that in this district. That might be the way you did things in your former district, but not here."

You don't know how to take this comment, but it is clear to you that he is protecting the assistant superintendent for business. As far as you're concerned, she had no business making such gossipy comments that can be injurious to others. That's not good for any organization. But you can't figure out why the superintendent is acting this way. Does he thrive on the gossip? Does he rely on such comments to monitor the district? Because you're so new to the district, you haven't yet learned the interpersonal workings or the administrative culture. But with the superintendent's focus on mission and goals, you're very surprised by his comments.

What do you do? You certainly want to make a good impression on him. You're still very new in your position in this district. But you don't want to become part of dirty politics and backstabbing. You wonder if he expects you to dig up gossip and report it at the cabinet meetings. It's obvious that the assistant superintendent for business has run behind your back to the superintendent to complain about you. How do you handle this interpersonal relationship situation with the superintendent and with the assistant superintendent of business?

Develop a bulleted plan of action aligned with ISLLC Standard 5: *An education leader promotes the success of every student by acting with integrity, fairness, and in an ethical manner.*

Ethical Considerations

As indicated in the case study, there are many different ways this can impact your future. What seemed to be the best course of action, to address the allegation head-on, actually was used against you. This certainly helps you to understand the motivation and possible insecurity of the assistant superintendent for business. When a person makes allegations, she or he should have had the integrity to check on the accuracy of the allegations before making them public. Sometimes when people use such allegations to make themselves look good, they are insecure in their own positions and try to divert attention from their own performance to that of others.

A puzzling issue is the motivation of the superintendent as to why he chose to support the assistant superintendent for business in her false allegations. Perhaps he was showing support because he felt an obligation to do so. That would be somewhat comforting to you, to know that the superintendent will back his assistant superintendents, even if they're wrong. But you're also one of his assistant superintendents, and he isn't backing you right now. Of course, you're still new, and that might be why he's supporting someone who has been there longer than you.

Another possibility is that the superintendent himself feels somewhat disconnected from the schools, and he relies on such reporting to keep him apprized of what's going on in the district. That's dangerous, because he could be forming opinions based on false information, and he could be the victim of reporters' using this vehicle to better their own personal causes. Knowing that this is a possibility, you probably wouldn't want to challenge the superintendent and try harder to get him to accept your plan of action. While your plan usually is the preferred venue to address problems, if the superintendent feels that your plan would jeopardize his reporting system, he will try to squelch your actions immediately.

If you were to consider this experience as a learning tool and file it away for the future, the superintendent most likely would be relieved to see that you're not pursuing it any further. But the assistant superintendent's behavior would have been rewarded and she would see that you have been reprimanded. That could complicate your working relationship with her in the future. Of course, there is the chance that she might think twice about making such allegations in the future, knowing that you are willing to confront such behavior head-on.

What probably is most important to you right now is to note that the superintendent has "corrected" you, but he hasn't written you up. You need to gauge the dynamics of the assistant superintendents and the superintendent in future meetings. If you see this kind of behavior repeating itself, you either can continue to defend your staff and run the risk of being "corrected" again, or you can seek a school district that has a healthier way of conducting business in the cabinet meetings.

As an educator, you most likely believe in the potential of everyone to learn and to grow. You probably hope you can enlighten your colleagues and try to teach them new and more appropriate behaviors. But, if they are receiving praise and encouragement for their reporting, then you might not be able to change them. Hopefully you won't change by falling into the same trap that has ensnared them.

3-3. A BOARD MEMBER'S SON IN A FIGHT (ISLLC STANDARD 3)

You are a new assistant principal of a small high school of 550 students. Because the high school is relatively small, there is no dean of students. As assistant principal, you are responsible for student discipline. The student-parent handbook specifies that students involved in fighting must receive from 3 to 10 days of out-of-school suspension, depending on the severity of the fight. For "teddy bear" fights (some pushing and shoving), the usual consequence is three days of out-of-school suspension. Because this is specified in the handbook, you don't have any leeway regarding the consequences.

After school, one of the teachers brings you two boys who were allegedly pushing and shoving each other. The teacher broke up the "teddy bear" fight before it could escalate. As you bring both of the boys into your office, it is obvious that the tension between them has run its course, and for all practical purposes the "fight" is done. They are not going to carry the fight elsewhere. As you begin your investigation, they both admit that they were fighting over a girl. From their responses, you recognize that they were "posturing" to show their manliness, and they really had no intentions of doing any more than shoving each other. They both admit that they were and are friends, and that it was a bad decision to let their emotions lead them into a "teddy bear" fight. When you tell them that they both will have to serve a three-day out-of-school suspension, they are relieved. At first they were worried that their suspension would be longer. Everything is going well as you have each of the students phone their parents to explain what happened. Then you speak with each boy's parent regarding the out-of-school suspension and the required parent conference prior to re-entry to school on the fourth day.

One of the parents, Rick Rufus, was calm and very understanding. The other parent, Don Anderson, is a member of the board of education. He also understands the handbook and its consequences because some revisions were recently approved by board action. You give each of the students a lecture about making good decisions, and they admit that they have learned a valuable lesson. The two students shake hands and agree not to let a girl jeopardize their friendship in the future.

As you are shutting down your computer for the day and putting tomorrow's work on your desk, the phone rings. Your secretary tells you that it is Don Anderson. You take the call, wondering why he is calling you back after you just finished speaking with him on the phone about 20 minutes ago. Don proceeds to tell you that after talking things over with his wife, he wants to exert his authority as a board member. He does not think it is appropriate for a board member's son to be suspended. After all the time and hard work that he has given to his job as board member, Don believes that he is entitled to special consideration. You tactfully explain to him that you are obligated to follow the requirements of the handbook, which the board of education approved. Also, it is important for the overall integrity of discipline policies that there not be a double standard. He admits that he understands this, but his wife is very upset. "When momma ain't happy, ain't nobody happy in my house," he explains to you.

Before you can respond to this comment, he reminds you that your annual contract is up for renewal next month. He says, "One hand washes the other. You help me out with this situation, and I'll make sure you not only get a contract renewal, but also that you receive a good pay raise."

You are astounded by this comment.

"Think about it and call me tonight with your decision," Don says as he hangs up the phone.

You know that you should phone the superintendent about this, but you also realize that Don is highly influential with other board members. Despite the superintendent's recommendation to renew your contract, it has to be approved by the board of education.

What do you do? Explain, in a bulleted format, your plan aligned with ISLLC Standard 3: *An education leader promotes the success of every student by ensuring management of the organization, operation, and resources for a safe, efficient, and effective learning environment.*

Ethical Considerations

On the one hand, your first impulse to notify the superintendent is the most ethical way to handle this situation. The superintendent should communicate with board members about their duties and their ethics.

You do need to recognize that Don Anderson could be offended by your "reporting" him to the superintendent. As such, he could use his influence on other board members. Your administrative future in this district is dependent on how well the superintendent can persuade the board to accept his recommendation to renew your contract.

On the other hand, do you want to serve in a district in which board members micro-manage assistant principals? This is only the beginning. What comes next? Will Don Anderson second-guess every decision you make? What will this do to your authority?

3-4. CELL PHONES, A BOMB THREAT, AND A BUILDING EVACUATION (ISLLC STANDARD 3)

You are the principal of a suburban high school having an enrollment of 3,000 students. The district office has created a crisis management plan for all 25 schools in the district and for just about any crisis that could ever happen. Although the central office personnel are very proud of this accomplishment, you and the other principals are skeptical about implementing some of the plans. Fortunately, you have not had to utilize any of the crisis plans, because the school year has been rather calm.

It is a sunny October day and the students are all in their classes. Your common practice is to walk through the school during the first period and to "pop" into some of the classes for informal visits, not for evaluation purposes, but rather to be visible to the students and to show your interest in what they are learning. As you are making your rounds, you can't help but think how fortunate you are to be the principal of this school. The teachers and students all are actively engaged on this beautiful fall morning.

Your thoughts are quickly interrupted by your cell phone. You notice it is your secretary calling you. She informs you that the receptionist just received a bomb threat. The caller sounded very serious. As per the district office plan, you have the secretary begin evacuation notification while you phone the police. The students and teachers quickly and orderly file out of the building to the football stadium. They proceed to their designated areas, and all seems to be going according to plan.

The police arrive within a few minutes, and they begin to sweep the building in search of any suspicious-looking item that could be a bomb. Your assistant principals are in the football stadium, and you are in the building with the police and your chief building engineer. You receive a phone call from one of the assistant principals indicating that you are needed in the football stadium. As you walk to the stadium you are shocked to see a long parade of cars parked alongside the football stadium. Knowing that parking is not allowed in the road, you wonder why those cars are there. As you look toward the street, you notice more cars pulling in. You then notice that all the cars are occupied by drivers, and the students no longer are seated in their designated areas, but rather are lining up to exit the stadium.

Your phone rings again, and your assistant principal informs you that the students have been using their cell phones to call for rides home. They are asking to leave. Some of the parents have gotten out of their cars and are approaching you. They begin to express concern for the safety of their students, and they want to remove them from this dangerous situation. You explain that you are following the district procedures for bomb threats and that everyone needs to remain calm until the building is checked. Then school will resume.

The parents continue to demand that their students be released to their custody.

In bulleted format, explain how you would handle this situation. Be sure to align your plan with ISLLC Standard 3: *An education leader promotes the success of every student by ensuring management of the organization, operation, and resources for a safe, efficient, and effective learning environment.*

Ethical Considerations

Although parents have the right to remove their children from school, you also have to employ some way of keeping track of who is leaving and who is requesting that they be dismissed. It's not as simple as dismissing them. Also, your average daily attendance will be negatively impacted, which has a bearing on state funding in some states. To allow the students to leave is not a simple matter.

If you don't allow the students to leave, you run the risk of mob action. Even when the school is safe, the students most likely won't be cooperative in their classes. They feel their rights are being violated.

Another consideration is the practicality of the central office's plan for your school. Didn't they anticipate this? Also, by holding all the students in the football stadium, aren't you putting them in danger of any drive-by shooters? What about any flying debris should there be a bomb and it were to explode in the school? Is the stadium really far enough away from the building to provide a safe refuge for the students? How are the teachers supposed to maintain order in the stadium? Doesn't sitting in a stadium cause "stadium-like" behavior?

What is your first responsibility? To the students or to the central office directive?

3-5. DIFFERING PHILOSOPHIES ABOUT DISCIPLINE (ISLLC STANDARD 5)

You are the principal of a middle school that has a faculty of two distinct age groups: half of the teachers are in their 50s and half are in their 20s. Needless to say, their philosophies about student discipline are different. Generally speaking, one group of teachers believes that discipline should be rigid and stern, resulting in punishment. The other group of teachers believes that discipline is a learning experience resulting in the students' reflection about how the situation could have been prevented.

As their principal, you always are criticized either for being too harsh or too soft on the students when dealing with discipline matters. You recognize that what is missing among your faculty is a common belief or value about the purpose of discipline. Because you have been emphasizing the importance of good parent and teacher communication, you now are concerned that some of your faculty might be criticizing your discipline of students. Just recently, you received a phone call from a parent who complained that the discipline in your school is too rigid, and kids can't be kids. Later that day, you received a phone call from another parent who complained that the discipline in your school is too lax and that she's afraid to send her child to school, because the "kids get away with everything."

You remember from your history and philosophy classes that this is not a new issue. For centuries, educators have struggled with the purpose and implementation of appropriate student discipline. Obviously your faculty are rooted in different philosophies, which were prevalent in different historical periods. Whose philosophy is right? Regardless of right or wrong, you recognize that your faculty are at odds over this issue, and it's spilling into the parental community. It must be addressed before morale and eventually student learning suffer from the tension among the faculty.

How would you lead your faculty to develop a contemporary philosophy of discipline that is reflective of the values of the community your school serves?

Develop a plan in a bulleted format. Include how you would get both groups of the faculty to come together on a mutually acceptable philosophy of discipline. Please align your plan with ISLLC Standard 5: *An education leader promotes the success of every student by acting with integrity, fairness, and in an ethical manner.*

Ethical Considerations

It is a difficult situation for the principal when the faculty are divided about the purpose of discipline: punishment or a learning experience. For the principal to side with one group or the other would further promote the division in the faculty. Although the principal most likely has his or her own philosophy about discipline, she or he has to be careful not to be an autocrat by simply dictating what the faculty's philosophy should be. However, this would be an expeditious way to resolve the conflict.

The veteran faculty are an important group in the school. They represent the tradition and foundation of the school. On the other hand, the newer faculty represent creativity and enthusiasm. Both groups are key proponents of the school, and they provide a rich experience for the students. If the veteran faculty want their legacy to continue, they have to earn the respect of the young faculty, and if the young faculty want the expertise and advice of the veteran faculty, they have to be open to different opinions. The principal clearly has to work on team-building based on acceptance of diversity of thinking.

There is no quick and effective way to bridge these two groups. It will take time and shared experiences to bring them together. Perhaps most important would be the recognition that both groups have the same motivation: to help their students to be successful. What's missing is that realization. One might successfully argue that both groups are correct in the effectiveness of their approach to discipline, but when either group's approach is utilized is situational.

3-6. THE ELECTRICITY GOES OUT DURING THE SCHOOL DAY: HOW TO MANAGE THIS SITUATION (ISLLC STANDARD 3)

You are a junior high school principal in an urban setting. Your school has 600 students, and your faculty members are represented by various age groups. In other words, you have a nice mixture of ages in your faculty. The school is a 90-year-old building consisting of 3 floors. All of the classrooms have plenty of natural light, but the washrooms don't have any windows.

It is one o'clock in the afternoon when the electrical power goes out. This means that not only have the lights ceased to function, but also the intercom system, the phone system, and the fire alarm protection system. And, while you still have water, the washrooms are dark. The class period will be over in 15 minutes, but because the intercom system now is nonfunctional, the bell won't ring to announce the end of the period. You have your secretary place a call to the power company, and you learn that they are aware of the power outage, but their estimate for resumption of service is up to 2 hours.

Although the classrooms have plenty of natural light, and the teachers can continue with teaching, discussion, and, hopefully, learning, the technology applications obviously aren't working in specialized classrooms such as science, art, and computers. Your teachers are resourceful, and you don't see a problem with continuing the last two periods of the day, but the washrooms and fire alarms are a problem. Perhaps you should dismiss early.

You phone the bus company, but the dispatcher informs you that she cannot round up the bus drivers with such short notice. Even if she could, by the time they got to the school, it would be very close to normal dismissal time. You consider dismissing anyone who either walks or can get a ride and holding the other students until they can get a ride or until the buses come, but two hours could be a long time to simply place students in a holding area.

What would you do? Consider your biggest concerns: fire alarms and washrooms. Develop a bulleted action plan that is aligned with ISLLC Standard 3: *An education leader promotes the success of every student by ensuring management of the organization, operation, and resources for a safe, efficient and effective learning environment.*

Ethical Considerations

The ethics of simply dismissing students without prior parental notice most likely would prohibit your doing that. How can you just release junior high students from your supervision to an unsupervised situation without even giving the parents an opportunity to make arrangements? Not only would that be unethical regarding safety and responsibility, but it also could easily become a public relations nightmare.

On the other hand, how can you ethically keep the students in school without ample washroom facilities? You have water, but the washrooms are dark. Another consideration is what to do with the students for the next two hours. Do you move them into the next period and run the school as normally as you can, or do you hold them in their current period and classes for the next two hours? Will your teachers have enough planned to keep them meaningfully engaged for two more hours? Or should you move into the next period because you know that the teachers do have enough planned for each period?

There are certain parties with whom you have to communicate throughout this process. They include your custodians and maintenance staff, your teachers, the secretaries, the fire department, and eventually the media.

3-7. ETHICS AND THE PRINCIPAL'S DECISION (ISLLC STANDARD 5)

You are the new principal of a high school in a rural town. One obvious area of need is a policy regarding student use of alcohol and other drugs. You and a committee of teachers, parents, and students research such policies from other high schools and develop one, which includes prohibiting students from attending school functions if they appear to be under the influence of alcohol or drugs. The process would be to notify the parents and to have them come to the school function to pick up their son or daughter, rather than to have the suspected student drive home while under the influence. Also included in the policy is a provision for parents to take their son or daughter to a nearby hospital for assessment at no charge to them. In lieu of suspension, the student could enroll in either an inpatient or outpatient rehab program, depending on the assessment results.

When presented to the faculty and to the students, the new policy was met with widespread acceptance. The board of education unanimously approved it to become an official policy of the school. The press presented positive coverage of the new policy, and you were attributed with success as the leader of the committee. As a result of the community's acceptance, you also begin an Operation Snowball chapter in which students learn teamwork and how to have fun without the use of alcohol or drugs. Many students join the chapter and participate in its activities, and again, the press gives you very positive coverage.

On the night of the prom, two students who clearly have been drinking attempt entry to the event. Your faculty, who are monitoring student entry, notify you. In accordance with the policy, you call the parents, explain the situation, and ask them to pick up their sons because you will not allow them to drive home. One of the parents becomes very belligerent and does not want to drive there to pick up his son. You explain that you cannot allow him to drive home, and if the parent won't pick him up, your only choice is to have the police bring him home. This further upsets the parent, and he begrudgingly agrees to pick up his son.

When the parent arrives at the prom, he is accompanied by a member of the board of education who also has the other student's father with him. The two fathers and the board member become loud and obnoxious to you as they clearly express their displeasure with your decision not to allow the boys into the prom. You calmly appeal to their sense of reason and explain the policy, its intent, and the dangers of condoning the boys' behavior. The parents counter by stating that their sons are seniors, and this is their last prom. Because of you, their senior year now is ruined. The board member then loudly declares that unless you allow these two boys into the prom, your job is in jeopardy.

As you quickly think of your options, you also realize that the superintendent is new and somewhat weak when it comes to any disagreement with the board of education. Obviously, the superintendent looks at the board members as his "bosses." Will he support you? You're unsure.

- Do you refuse to allow the boys to enter the prom and jeopardize your career?
- Do you allow them into the prom and violate the policy that you worked so hard to develop?

If you allow them into the prom, what impact will that decision have on your reputation with the community (parents, students, faculty)?

Using a bulleted format, explain what you would do and why. Be sure to align your plan with ISLLC Standard 5: *An education leader promotes the success of every student by acting with integrity, fairness, and in an ethical manner.*

Ethical Considerations

This is a difficult situation with entangling repercussions regardless of the path taken to solve it. Administrative positions are hard to get, and to lose one's job can be detrimental to the individual as well as to the family. Also, when principals are dismissed from their jobs for political reasons, there can be a negative impact on the faculty as well. Morale within the building can hit a low spot that takes years to overcome. Does the principal want to risk losing a job, causing stress on the family, and negatively impacting the faculty?

On the other hand, to let the boys into the prom would represent a serious compromise regarding the policy. It would send a powerful message to the students and parents that policies can be changed for certain individuals. It also would convey that you can be "bought."

Situations like this typically cannot be quickly solved with a rational approach because of the emotions involved. One also has to recognize that this has no easy solution, and either one's credibility or one's job most likely will be lost depending on the decision made to resolve it. The proverbial "bottom line" is that the situation is far greater than your control. It's analogous to trying to steer a tornado. Your ethics and your ability to live with your decision will guide you.

3-8. MISUSE OF THE RtI INITIATIVE (ISLLC STANDARD 6)

You are employed by a district that has a designated special education coordinator at each building. This is a low-level administrative position in that the building special education coordinator meets regularly with the special education faculty and provides direction and support to them. The special education faculty includes special education classroom teachers in the learning disabilities program, the behavior disorders program, and the emotional disorders program; resource teachers; the school psychologist; the speech pathologist; the occupational therapist; the physical therapist; and the social worker. You are the building special education coordinator, and you report both to the principal in your building as well as to the district special education director.

Recently, the district office told all principals that they will have one full-time resource person to facilitate their schools' Response through Intervention (RtI) initiative. Although the initiative is intended to provide interventions to students who might not qualify for special education services, in some respects it competes with the special education program. In your role as building special education director, you have the responsibility to make sure that the caseloads and assignments of the special education faculty are in compliance with state laws.

Recently, some new families have moved into the district and into your school's attendance area in particular. Each of these families has a child with an IEP, thereby increasing your school's number of students needing special services. As you review the existing IEPs, you notice that three of the children need speech services. When you notify your building's speech pathologist, she willingly accepts the additional students on her caseload, but she informs you that these students will put her over the maximum legal number of speech students she can serve.

A quick check of the records verifies that the speech pathologist does indeed have a larger caseload than she should have. Knowing that the building has an allocation for one more resource person, you approach the principal asking for a half-time speech pathologist to bring the caseloads back into legal compliance. You are shocked when the principal tells you that he will not use the resource allocation for speech services. He is determined to use the allocation for an intervention specialist. You caution him that his school is out of compliance.

His response is completely unethical in your eyes. The principal tells you to remove three students from the speech program, thereby bringing the numbers back into compliance. You explain to him that the children are receiving speech services because they have deficits that negatively impact their learning. They need speech services in order to improve their communication skills and ultimately improve their academic performance in their content areas. You also explain that none of the children currently receiving speech services is ready to be removed from the program. To do so would hinder their learning as well as their self-esteem. These children are self-conscious about their speech, and consequently they don't communicate with others for fear of being embarrassed.

The principal accuses you of being a "bleeding heart" and tells you to remove three students from the speech program.

What would you do? Explain, in a bulleted format, your plan of action aligned with ISLLC Standard 6: *An education leader promotes the success of every student by understanding, responding to, and influencing the political, social, economic, legal, and cultural context.*

Ethical Considerations

Knowing that you report to the district special education director, but you were selected by the principal from a pool of other possible candidates, you are reluctant to immediately run to the district special education director. If you report your principal, you could lose your position and be placed back into the ranks of special education teachers. You worked hard to get this directorship, and you don't want to lose it.

On the other hand, you have credibility to maintain among your special education faculty. What would they think of you if you were to prematurely remove students from the program? Furthermore, can you live with this decision when you know it will negatively impact children's lives? Although you could rationalize that the children will adjust and compensate just fine without speech services, such rationalization goes against your own professional beliefs. If such were the case, why do we even have special services?

This is a tough situation, and you don't want to snitch on the principal, but there are some real ethical considerations at play here.

3-9. A MURDER OCCURS A BLOCK AWAY FROM THE SCHOOL: MAINTAINING A SAFE ENVIRONMENT (ISLLC STANDARD 3)

You are the principal of an elementary school in an urban setting. Your particular school is located in an area that has a high concentration of Section 8, federally subsidized housing sometimes called "the projects." These housing units are inhabited by gang members who are in the process of establishing their turf. As a result, the area surrounding your school often is the site of shootings in the evening hours. Fortunately, the school grounds, which occupy one square block, have not been disturbed by gang graf-fiti. Also, during the school day there is no visible evidence of gang presence. The gang activity only occurs at night.

A reality with which you must deal is that many of your students live in the same housing complex with gang members. A second-grade teacher once asked her class how many of the students had ever seen a gun or heard it fired. Every student in the class raised his or her hand to acknowledge having seen a gun and having heard it fired. Sometimes the children don't do their homework because they spend the night on the floor, away from windows out of fear of drive-by shootings.

Fortunately, the children and their parents see the school as a safe zone. Often just before winter break, spring break, summer vacation, or even school holidays the stu-dents will tell their teachers that they wish they could stay in the school rather than having to be at home during the break. They seem to appreciate the security of the school and the support of the teachers and other adults in the school. A big concern is getting the children to read at home during breaks. They simply don't have books at home. You have built up your school library, and you have encouraged the students to take books home.

Today has been a good day in that the students and teachers all seem very much engaged in classroom activities. Everyone appears to be in a good, cheerful mood. It is almost dismissal time, and you are in the hallway just leaving a classroom when you get an emergency phone call from the central office. Your secretary meets you in the hall and tells you that the superintendent is on the phone and must speak with you immedi-ately about a critical situation. You take a deep breath and hurry to your office to take the phone call.

The superintendent explains that he has received a call from the police depart-ment that a murder (most likely gang-related) has occurred a block away from your school. Because most of the children will walk past the murder scene, and there is a like-lihood that many of them would know the victim, the police are asking that the school not dismiss the children until the police feel it is safe to do so. In addition, there is a con-cern that more shooting could occur in the area surrounding the murder scene as well as in the housing complexes. Needless to say, the children would be walking right into those areas on their way home from school.

You have 15 minutes to pull together a plan of action. How will you notify faculty and staff in this short period of time? Will you make an announcement via the intercom system? Or would such an announcement cause fear among the children as they won-der if one of their relatives has been the victim? Where will you hold the children—in classrooms? In a large area, such as the gym, cafeteria, or library? Should you request assistance from the central office?

Using a bulleted format, develop a plan of action aligned with ISLLC Standard 3: *An education leader promotes the success of every student by ensuring management of the or-ganization, operation, and resources for a safe, efficient, and effective learning environment.*

Ethical Considerations

In addition to the questions already asked about whether to tell the children what has really happened, you also have the ethical question of asking staff and faculty to stay with their students for what might be a long period of time. They most likely would not disagree with the responsibility to stay with the students, but they might have family responsibilities of their own, such as picking up their own children from day care. Can you require all faculty to stay as long as it takes, regardless of their own family responsibilities? Would you really want to put any of your faculty in this position? On the other hand, is it fair to expect only the single, nonparent teachers to stay? Most likely it would be best simply to ask for volunteers and hope that you will get a good response. Certainly, you have a right to expect the faculty to stay for at least 30 minutes after dismissal as per their teaching contract.

Another question is that of the faculty and staff members' safety should they have to leave 30 minutes after the usual dismissal time. Despite their family responsibilities, would you be allowing them to put themselves into jeopardy as they drive past the housing complex on their way home? Should you remind them of this, or would you be causing them to panic? These are difficult decisions that can't be answered generally or unilaterally. The answer to these questions lies with the individuals and your relationship with them. But you certainly have to take all this into consideration.

3-10. OFFICE POLITICS: HOW DOES A CONSCIENTIOUS ADMINISTRATOR DEAL WITH THEM AND STILL MAINTAIN A VISION FOR LEARNING? (ISLLC STANDARD 1)

Bob Smith has the management style of a dictator. The words "You're fired!" roll easily off his tongue. During his 10 years in the district, there have been a number of well-respected, hard-working people who were terminated by Dr. Smith. An assistant principal was fired, supposedly because of enrollment shifts, but most people suspect the superintendent really was creating a position for the school board president, who openly admits that she is seeking an administrative position in the district. Of course, she quickly adds, "That is because I would love to work for a superintendent like Dr. Smith. He is my role model and mentor." Most of the district employees suspect that Smith really has "bought" her votes by offering her promises that he'll never be able to keep. Nevertheless, the board president has a record not only of voting to support every one of Smith's recommendations, but also of publicly questioning those board members who vote "no." Shortly after terminating the assistant principal, due to enrollment shifts and for financial reasons, Smith created a new administrative position at the central office. Because many staff members have questioned his motives and have accused him of creating a vacancy for the board president, he did not fill the position even though he had the board's approval.

Taking personal credit for all building renovations, Dr. Smith has led the movement to rebuild all 15 schools during the past 10 years, even though the schools were far more elegant than most in the state. Each of those schools now has a bronze plaque adorning the entryway. That plaque not only contains the names of the board members, but also has Smith's name prominently displayed. Under Smith's leadership, the board has opted not to seek voter permission to finance the rebuilding of the schools and instead has taken Smith's recommendation to "spend down" the district's reserves. As Smith explained to them in a private work session, "If the public were to see how much money we have in reserves, they would question us. By spending down our reserves, we not only don't have to seek their permission, but we also can show them some tangible use of their tax dollars."

To make sure the business manager wouldn't question such a recommendation, Smith offered to promote her from manager to assistant superintendent. Of course, a large increase in pay would accompany the promotion. He told the board that a woman of her expertise and work ethic is hard to find. Using scare tactics, Smith convinced the board that a neighboring school district was trying to woo the business manager to join their ranks. According to Smith, the only way to keep her in the district would be to promote her and to give her a raise in pay. The board, at the president's urging, agreed to Smith's recommendation. His financial strategies would be defended by her and financial reports to the board would support whatever he recommended to the board. In short, he bought the business manager's allegiance and now owned her.

The other assistant superintendents wondered about the sudden promotion of someone with no administrative experience to their rank. To gain the support of the assistant superintendent of human resources, he publicly stated to the board that she was his most trusted employee. Because of the nature of her work, confidentiality is of utmost importance. That compliment was enough to satisfy her ego, and in her mind she now was in a position of greater closeness to Smith than any of the other assistant superintendents. She actually believed that the new assistant superintendent for business had threatened to leave the district for another position and that Dr. Smith had been quite wise to entice her to stay. The assistant superintendent for human resources further believed that Smith placed her above the new assistant superintendent because of her loyalty to the superintendent.

As one might expect, the other two assistant superintendents felt as if they were on the bottom of the pecking order. To shore up her value in the superintendent's eyes, the assistant superintendent for special education immediately began to compete for the superintendent's attention. At meetings, she would proclaim, "Dr. Smith, you are a god! You're so intelligent." His ego having been stroked, he would blush and smile at her—much to the jealousy of the assistant superintendent for human resources.

You are the assistant superintendent for curriculum and instruction and you refuse to compete for the superintendent's attention, resulting in a plan on the part of the superintendent to get rid of this supposed non–team player. At cabinet meetings, the superintendent would criticize the instructional program, and the other assistant superintendents would chime in with their fabricated stories of teachers who supposedly had complained about the quality of instructional materials. The assistant superintendent for business (who never has taught a day in her life) frequently has "ideas" about how to improve the instructional program. Interestingly, more than 85% of the students annually met or exceeded standards on the state test. The assistant superintendent for business boldly announces that she has found a program that will raise all students' scores, and she has found an account in your budget that will cover it. You see this as an intrusion into your area of responsibility, and you know that no single program can result in the raising of all students' scores.

Your focus is on fostering the vision of learning throughout the district that affirms the learning potential of each individual. What would you do in this environment? In accordance with ISLLC Standard 1: *An education leader promotes the success of every student by facilitating the development, articulation, implementation, and stewardship of a vision of learning that is shared and supported by all stakeholders*, create a series of steps or strategies that define how you would continue to promote quality instructional programs despite the "office politics."

Ethical Considerations

It's human nature to want to protect one's job, and it would be easy to simply agree to a canned program, but knowing that student success is far more complicated than any single program could ever address, you also know that this would not only be a waste of district money, but also an insult to the teachers and students alike. On the other hand, you are definitely on the outside of the superintendent's close-knit circle of confidants. How much will the superintendent listen to you, and how much will be perceived as your trying to block one of his favored staff?

The president of the board of education clearly is in the superintendent's pocket and has political influence over the rest of the board. How much support you would have from them is doubtful. As much as your job security is important, you have to remind yourself that you are giving the best hours of each day and the best years of your life to this job. Are you making the best use of your talents? Maybe it's time to move on to another district? Or would that be like abandoning the ship?

3-11. DISPOSING OF AN UNDERGROUND STORAGE TANK: LEGALITIES AND POLITICS (ISLLC STANDARD 6)

You are the principal of a small rural high school consisting of some building sections that are 100 years old. Although the facility is in good structural shape and has been maintained to a very pleasant level of appearance, the infrastructure was beginning to show its age. The original heating system main boiler failed one day and had to be re-tubed because the lines were corroded and clogged. The backup boiler was put into service and functioned fine, but unlike the main system, which was fueled by natural gas, the backup system was fueled by heating oil. When the underground storage tank was topped off with fresh heating oil, the building engineer checked the log and found that this system hadn't been utilized for at least five years. Similarly, the underground storage tank hadn't been refilled for at least five years.

Because the main boiler was so old, parts have to be ordered, and some have to be fabricated as repair technicians rebuild the boiler. The anticipated completion date keeps getting moved back. This means that the backup system will be the main system for a longer period of time than anticipated. The building engineer is concerned about this not only because of the age of the backup boiler, but also because of the unknown status of the heating oil and its underground storage tank. He explains to you that there is a likelihood that the heating oil might be contaminated with moisture, which could have corroded the underground storage tank.

He asks you to approve a request for an underground storage tank inspection company to evaluate the condition of the tank. Not only are there environmental issues if the tank were to spring a leak, but there also are legal ramifications should any leakage leach into the wells of surrounding homes, thereby contaminating their drinking water. Needless to say, there are ethical issues also. Such leakage could have serious health effects on your neighbors and your students. Of course, you approve the request for the inspection. You are somewhat afraid of the inspection, though.

You ask your building engineer some questions. "What if the tank is found to be leaking? How do we solve that problem? What would it cost?"

The building engineer admits that he also has been worried about that scenario. He tells you that if the tank is leaking, it has to be removed as per state law. You ask if the tank simply can be drained and left empty. The building engineer explains that not only is such a course of action not permissible by the state, but it also could have disastrous ramifications on the high school building's foundation should the tank begin to "float" from a buildup of underground water in a heavy rain. You then ask if the tank could be filled with sand to prevent its floating. The building engineer smiles and says, "I wish it were that simple. There most likely is an accumulation of sludge on the bottom of the tank, which would have to be pumped out. Then a hole would have to be cut in the top of the tank, and a technician would have to be lowered into the tank to scrub it clean. If the tank is found to be leaking, the surrounding soil has to be removed and replaced. Because the soil would be contaminated, it would have to be disposed of by a licensed hazardous waste management company."

Needless to say, all of this would be very expensive. You ask how much it would cost to remove the tank and the surrounding soil. Because the building has sections added onto it over the years, the building now surrounds the tank, which is buried in a maintenance courtyard. Access to the courtyard is via a garage door on the south side of the building. The small maintenance vehicles fit through the garage door, but any large vehicles needed to remove the tank never would fit. This means that the tank would have to be drained, scrubbed, and cut apart in pieces. This is a very, very expensive endeavor.

The building engineer also tells you that he strongly suspects that the results of the underground storage tank inspection will show leakage under the tank. This is due to the age of the tank. You are upset that your predecessors never gave consideration to this possibility when they added onto the building. Why didn't they remove the tank back then? The building engineer explains that environmental concerns were not in anyone's thinking when the building additions were built. You ask the building engineer, "What do you think this would cost? I know you're not an expert in this, but what do you think would be a very rough estimate?" The building engineer offers to contact the building engineers in neighboring school districts to get an idea of cost. He is certain that one of the neighboring districts faced a similar problem last year.

A few days later, the building engineer gives you a rough cost estimate, and he informs you that the inspection is scheduled for tomorrow morning. The inspection company will send a camera down into the tank and determine its condition. The rough estimate should the tank need to be replaced is an amount equal to what you were going to spend to renovate two science labs! After the building engineer leaves your office, you quickly phone the superintendent to keep him in the communication loop. You also share with him all the possibilities, even the worst-case scenario of having to remove the underground storage tank.

You are surprised by his response. "You have your capital improvement budget. Use it for removal of the tank." Even though you remind him that the capital improvement budget has been earmarked for science lab renovation, which is sorely needed, especially since you've begun to offer an advancement placement science course that could result in college credit for the students, he quickly replies that you have a choice to either spend the money on the science labs or spend it on removal of the underground storage tank. But you can't do both.

You know that you really don't have a choice. If the tank is found to be leaking, you can't in good conscience ignore it. But the superintendent seems to be implying that you could just ignore the situation. You probe a little deeper. "I'm not sure I understand. Are you suggesting that I could just leave the storage tank alone?"

"It's been there longer than you or I have been alive. Sometimes it's best to let sleeping dogs lie," the superintendent replies. "It's your choice as the building principal, and I'll support your decision . . . whatever it is. Give yourself some time to think about it. We are in a small rural district that is strapped for cash. Our constituents don't have the resources to bail us out of this problem. They expect us to act with fiscal responsibility. Would they want us to spend their money by digging up a tank that hasn't bothered anyone? How do we know what else might be leaching into the wells? Are we responsible for the fertilizer that is spread on farmland and washed into the wells by rainfall? Is this really an issue for the school district? Or is this a fabrication by environmental alarmists? Again, it's your decision. The board pays you to manage that building. Make a judgment call, and I'll support it."

Wow! What do you do? Should you ignore the situation and hope that underground leaching of oil won't impact anyone's drinking water? Should you take the precautionary route and use the science lab money to remove the tank and surrounding soil? The students, parents, and the local newspaper all have been begging the school to update its science labs. Is the superintendent right about this issue being fabricated by environmental alarmists?

Develop a bulleted action plan taking into consideration two possible scenarios: One would be that the inspection report shows no leakage, but removal is advisable; and the other would be that the inspection report shows there is leakage and removal is strongly recommended. Kindly align your plan with ISLLC Standard 6: *An education leader promotes the success of every student by understanding, responding to, and influencing the political, social, economic, legal, and cultural context.*

Ethical Considerations

Fiscal responsibility and test scores seem to be the two primary drivers in today's school districts. Some leaders are willing to compromise or even ignore ethics in order to show a balanced budget. Of course, the taxpayers always complain about having to pay taxes. The news media thrives on budget issues of public-supported entities such as school districts. It's no surprise that the superintendent would suggest that leaving "sleeping dogs lie" might be the best decision. It's akin to the old adage, "What we don't know won't hurt us." Needless to say, we've all faced situations in which that old adage isn't true.

As a principal, you have a lot of responsibility. It is true that the board of education has hired you to manage the building, to exercise fiscal responsibility, as well as to be the instructional leader. But hopefully they also hired you to make ethical and moral decisions. If even one person were to get sick from contaminated drinking water, would you be able to sleep at night with that on your conscience? Also, if it were determined that you knew about this and could have prevented it, what would happen to your credibility? To your career? Although the approach of ignoring the problem might be enticing to you and even fiscally responsible, it most likely will end up costing the school district lots of legal fees and possibly fines in the future. Whether you and the superintendent can move on to another district before any of that is determined is a risky and unethical way of weighing the options.

Many people are skeptical of reports about asbestos, radon, carcinogens, ground-water contamination, and so on. Their skepticism doesn't remove the hazard and possible injury to others. You can understand the superintendent's jaded response, but you also know that when people's safety and health are the issue, you shouldn't dismiss it as being a fabricated alarm. Although renovation of the science labs would be a popular use of the money and would generate positive press for you, knowledge of the potential danger lying underground would supersede the benefits of using the money this way.

It's unfortunate that this is a small district that has neither the financial resources nor the people resources to solve the problem. A larger district might have a grant writer who could look for state or federal environmental grants that might apply to the removal of underground storage tanks. Sometimes cash-strapped school districts don't look beyond the obvious to solve their problems. Perhaps letting the public know about the problem might generate interest from sources you haven't even thought about. Would anyone be willing to donate science equipment such as new microscopes that could be used in the existing labs? Knowing that the school is acting honorably and ethically might be the incentive for the public to be willing to provide assistance. To hide the truth from the very people that you serve is insulting to them. Ethics and moral values should win on this one.

3-12. THE PRINICPAL HAS TURNED THE FACULTY AGAINST YOU: AN INTERNAL PUBLIC RELATIONS SITUATION (ISLLC STANDARD 4)

You are the brand-new assistant principal in a small suburban high school of 750 students. The principal is retiring in two years, and you have been hired as the school's first assistant principal. There are many responsibilities in your job duties, including dean of students, special education director, student services director, guidance office director, as well as the normal assistant principal duties of overseeing the scheduling of extracurricular uses of the building, making sure the building is in compliance with various county and state codes, acting as the school liaison with the village economic development council, being the administrative representative to the parent-teacher organization, and supervising all home athletic contests. Having been a department chair in a large high school in a district about 20 miles away, you have some administrative experience with budget planning and managing line items, evaluating staff, revising curriculum, adopting textbooks, and providing staff development.

The assistant principalship is considered to be an entry-level administrative position, and you are very grateful for it. You were the successful candidate from a pool of 40 applicants. In addition to the excitement of getting your first administrative position, you are even more excited about the possibility that awaits you in two years. The superintendent has confided in you that the principal is retiring in two years, and that the board of education has authorized him to find an assistant principal who would be able to quickly learn the principalship and step into that position when the retirement occurs. Of course, that person is you. If you work out well during the upcoming two years, you will have a good shot at becoming the next principal.

For this reason, the superintendent has advised you to get to know the principal and to learn as much as you can about his job. According to the superintendent, the principal has been told by him to teach you as much as he can about the principalship so as to prepare you for that position. Again, you are excited about this opportunity. During your interview with the principal before you were hired as assistant principal, you found it hard to read the principal, but he seemed to be supportive of your candidacy. You don't know how much input he had in the decision to hire you, but the principal definitely was part of the selection and interviewing process.

It now is September, and you've been in your new position since July first. During the past two months, you've tried very hard to get to know the principal and his job, but you have found the principal to be very unapproachable. Now that the school year has begun, you can't help but notice that the principal also is unapproachable to the faculty. He frequently closes his office door and will not accept any interruptions, even from you. This forces you to make administrative decisions without his input and without much knowledge of the culture of the school. You do your best, and the faculty seem to like you, but their interactions with you are superficial. Knowing that it is imperative to win their respect and trust, you try to get to know each faculty member on a personal level, but you sense resistance on their part. How can you be an effective leader if those whom you are leading aren't willing to interact with you?

Not knowing what to do and not wanting it to seem as if you can't handle the situation, you are reluctant to run to the superintendent. You know you probably should, but you are afraid you might seem too inexperienced in his eyes. In your role as assistant principal, you are the guidance department director, so you approach one of the guidance counselors in confidence and explain your concern. The counselor tells you that the principal has managed the faculty by fear over the past few years. He routinely calls one faculty member into his office each week and scolds him or her for something. It doesn't matter what the issue is. All that matters is that the faculty member gets a scolding and leaves the office fearing the principal.

In addition, the principal has sent out an informal message to the faculty that they are supposed to avoid any interaction with you. Supposedly, his intention is to give you a chance to get to know your job, but you suspect he is "poisoning the well" against you to prevent your becoming his successor. What would you do? Explain, in a bulleted manner, your plan of action, aligned with ISLLC Standard 4: *An education leader promotes the success of every student by collaborating with faculty and community members, responding to diverse community interests and needs, and mobilizing community resources.*

Ethical Considerations

You certainly have a legitimate concern about your future, about how effective you can be as a future principal, and how you can be an effective leader if you can't get to know your faculty. Although you'd like to run to the superintendent with this newfound revelation from the guidance counselor, you also don't want to implicate the guidance counselor, who has been kind and trustful to share such information. You also don't want to create even more of a rift between you and the principal. You would like to earn the principal's respect and get to learn as much as you can from him. Can you do all this in the next two years?

On the other hand, you also know that the superintendent is the principal's direct supervisor. The superintendent evaluates the principal and is the only one who really can initiate change in the principal's behavior. The way that he treats the faculty is demoralizing to the faculty and has left them without any genuine leadership. Can you allow this to continue for two more years? How many faculty members will become calloused and ineffective in their teaching as a result of the way they are treated by the principal? Can you run the risk of jeopardizing the teaching and learning that should be occurring in the classrooms for the next two years? Should you contact the superintendent about this situation, would the superintendent see you as a snitch, or as a responsible and concerned administrator who would like to solve the problem?

3-13. THE SUPERINTENDENT USES DISTRICT FUNDS TO FIX A DISTRICT CAR, THEN PURCHASES IT: WHAT IS THE ETHICAL COURSE OF ACTION? (ISLLC STANDARD 5)

You are the principal in a small rural high school of 500 students. Yours is the only school in the district, and there are three administrators in the district: the superintendent, the principal, and an assistant principal. All of the district and school administrative duties fall on the three of you. There also is a bookkeeper who takes care of payroll, purchase orders, and state financial reporting. Because the superintendent is expected to attend various community functions including village board meetings, he has a district-owned car for his use. The superintendent does not live in the district, but rather lives about 30 miles away. Because he uses the district-owned car for commuting as well as for use at home, he pays the district $50 per month for personal use of the car. As a condition of his contract with the board of education, the superintendent's district-owned car is replaced every five years.

Because there are only three administrators in the district, you and your assistant principal do as much if not more driving for school district–related business as the superintendent does, but you and your assistant principal receive mileage reimbursement. Prior to all board of education meetings, the three administrators are expected to review the list of expenditures (purchase orders) that will be presented for board approval. If any board members were to question a particular expenditure, one of the three administrators would provide the explanation. In large school districts, the business manager typically provides this information, but again, there are only three administrators in your district.

As you are reviewing the list of expenditures, you notice that the superintendent's district-owned car recently had some preventive maintenance work done, including a new battery and tires. You find this unusual, because you know that the board of education has been soliciting bids for a replacement car for the superintendent. Because the work on the car already has been done, the board of education has no choice but to approve the superintendent's recommendation for payment of this bill. They really can't send the tires and battery back if they don't agree with the purchase.

In your previous district, the superintendent authorized maintenance work on a district-owned vehicle for his use, and a month later the board of education traded the vehicle for a new one for the superintendent. The dealer who accepted the trade (and did the maintenance work) then sold the same vehicle to the superintendent for his wife's use. The board president of that district caught wind of the deal at the next board meeting when bills were presented for payment and sought to have the superintendent removed from his position for misuse of school district funds. Specifically, she accused the superintendent of using school district money to spruce up a car that he intended to purchase for his wife. She questioned how the superintendent could justify purchasing new tires, a battery, and a tune-up for a car that he knew would be traded in for a new vehicle in just a month after the maintenance work had been done. He couldn't give an appropriate answer, and the board of education took action to remove him from the superintendency.

It's possible that your current superintendent wouldn't have heard about this occurrence in another district a few years ago, but nevertheless, the situation appears very similar. You realize that you have to reserve judgment and that there might be a legitimate reason for the superintendent to authorize the maintenance work. Also, the new car hasn't been purchased yet, as the bids are just being sought. You opt to "park this in the back of your mind."

A few months later, the superintendent's new district-owned vehicle is purchased, and you don't know what happened to the old car because the only cost showing up on the bills presented to the board of education is the total cost of the car, which is the amount of the successful bid. There is nothing indicating a trade-in value. You know that the district can't just sell a vehicle without accepting bids for it. You wonder what happened to the old car, but it really isn't your concern as principal. That's an issue for which the superintendent and the board of education are responsible. Nevertheless, you can't stem your curiosity about this. Of course, if you were to go to a member of the board of education with the question, it would appear that you either don't trust the superintendent, or that you are doing an "end run" beyond the chain of command, possibly to make yourself look good. That could backfire on you, and you really don't want to get entangled in those politics.

It is now the summer, and students are out of school. There are a few student workers present who have been hired to do some painting and landscaping around the school grounds. The board of education recently approved their seasonal employment, as the board does each summer. Interestingly, one of the student workers is the superintendent's son. One morning, as you drive into the parking lot, you notice the old car that once was the superintendent's district-owned vehicle. It is parked in the employees' section. Now your curiosity really is piqued. You are certain that it is the superintendent's former district-owned car because of a certain scratch on the rear bumper of the car. The car also has temporary license plates, which indicate that it has been purchased within the past two months and the official tags haven't yet been received from the Department of Motor Vehicles. Rather than make a big deal about it by questioning people, you decide to make yourself visible in the parking lot at the time when the student workers and full-time maintenance workers end their day.

You are surprised to see the superintendent's son get into the car and drive away. He waves at you as he drives past, and there is no doubt in your mind as to his identity and the identity of the car. You are shocked by this, knowing that the superintendent has purchased the very car that he had fixed at the district's expense. You also know that while this might not be illegal per se, it certainly smacks of unethical behavior.

What do you do? Should you confront the superintendent? Should you contact a member of the board of education? Develop a bulleted plan of action explaining your rationale. Please align your plan with ISLLC Standard 5: *An education leader promotes the success of every student by acting with integrity, fairness, and in an ethical manner.*

Ethical Considerations

If you confront the superintendent, in his mind you actually are accusing him of doing something unethical. Even though this does appear to be unethical, he is your direct supervisor. Will he cover his tracks by giving you an unsatisfactory evaluation? Unfortunately, a superintendent can subjectively declare that an administrator under his supervision no longer is performing up to standard. Most boards of education would accept the superintendent's assessment of the principal, because they recognize that he is the direct supervisor of his administrative staff. Also, administrators typically have one-year contracts, which are subject to renewal pending successful evaluation of performance. In other words, your contract might not be renewed, and the reason given could be fabricated.

On the other hand, if the superintendent is acting unethically, how can you sleep at night knowing that you didn't at least question it? Don't you take pride in your ethics? If you noticed the car, wouldn't other school district employees also notice it? Would they consider you to be "in on the deal" if you don't at least question it? Would your credibility be at stake also?

It would be easy just to close your eyes and to blank this from your mind, but can you really do that? What if the board of education "cut a deal" with the superintendent? This also would be unethical, but if you questioned it, they might want you terminated. Can you single-handedly incriminate the board members and the superintendent? Or would your actions be dismissed as those of a disgruntled employee?

3-14. A TORNADO STRIKES AT NIGHT: SHOULD I LEAVE MY FAMILY TO CHECK ON THE BUILDING? (ISLLC STANDARD 3)

You are a junior high school principal in an old city, which has most of its electrical power delivered via overhead power lines. The geographic area is the Midwest, and the season is spring. Although this is an encouraging time of the year as the trees begin to bud and the grass turns green, it also is a dangerous time of year because it is tornado season. The state department of education requires all schools to hold tornado drills prior to the beginning of spring, and your school has complied.

It is the evening of what was a beautiful day, and you are sitting outside on the patio when suddenly the sky north of you turns dark and the air becomes very still. Having lived all your life in this area, which is about 15 miles from your school, you know what this means. Your wife has been watching the television, and as you come into the house she tells you that a tornado has just struck the town in which your school is located.

Your first reaction is, "I've got to drive there to check on my school." Your wife reminds you that severe weather is in the area for the next hour and that you possibly will encounter some downed trees and power lines as you try to drive to the nearby town. She also tells you that your own town is under a tornado warning. Although you don't want to leave her in any danger, you also know that if things get bad, she will go into the basement. But for the time being, things seem to be calm here.

You are concerned about the away–sports events from which your students will be returning in the next hour. Shouldn't you be there to make sure they all get home safely? On the other hand, isn't that the job of the coaches? You also have a night crew of four custodians that is scheduled to work until midnight cleaning the school. Are they okay? Did the tornado strike the school? When you call 911 to try to get some information, you get your own area's service. The personnel politely tell you that they don't have jurisdiction in your school's area and that you should contact the nonemergency number. You try to phone the police department in the town, but their nonemergency number is nonfunctional. Of course, no one answers the phone at your school.

Do you attempt to drive to the school? In the chain of command, the district director of buildings and grounds should be the one to check on the building, but as principal you feel a responsibility to go there. Should you jeopardize your safety while driving into an area that has been struck by a tornado? Would you be hampering rescue efforts by adding to the traffic problems that result from the curious who are out driving around? Should you stay home in case a tornado were to develop near your own home? You have a cell phone. Will you have service, or have the cell towers been impacted by the tornado?

Develop a bulleted action plan of what you would do, using ISLLC Standard 3: *An education leader promotes the success of every student by ensuring the management of the organization, operation, and resources for a safe, efficient and effective learning environment.*

Ethical Considerations

Although one could rationalize that he should stay home and stay off the streets, that's not an easy thing for a responsible principal to do. On the other hand, upon arriving at the school, what exactly can the principal do? If the building has been destroyed by the tornado, he won't be able to get into it, but if the building hasn't been hit by the tornado, could it be used as a safe area for any students coming home from the away–sports events? Also, would the school be used as a community safe area by the American Red Cross? There is an agreement with the local emergency services association to use it for that purpose. Of course, that's really a central office agreement signed by the district director of buildings and grounds.

Another issue is the safety of the staff at the school. Even if they're okay, wouldn't they appreciate seeing the principal and knowing that he cares? But if there's no electricity, will the principal be able to find his way through the building in the dark? The emergency lights only have a 90-minute battery life. To go to the building might be considered above and beyond the call of duty by some, but in the world of principals, it would be an expectation.

3-15. TRYING TO IMPLEMENT A "ZERO-BASED" BUDGET (ISLLC STANDARD 3)

You are a new high school principal in an urban setting. For years, each department chair has managed his or her own department accounts, and each year each department would receive a small percentage increase over the previous year's budget. It is the spring, and you are engaging your department chairs in budget discussions.

The science department chair announces that he needs a sizable increase in his budget to purchase new microscopes. The other department chairs all chime in with their requests.

You suspect they are trying to get as much out of the new guy as they can, but you hear their requests with interest. After each has made a request for an increase in the budget, you share with them the total amount that has been budgeted for department accounts. As you add up their requests, the chairs all can see how unreasonable they are in relation to the budget. They begin to grumble, but you offer them a possible solution.

You explain the concept of "zero-based" budgeting in which each department would determine its real needs. There would be no guaranteed increase over last year's accounts, but rather each department would have to justify its needs for next year. You further explain that you would like them to be honest about their true needs because by pooling the money the departments with great needs could have them met, and the other departments could wait their turn until their needs justify the larger pool of money. You ground the explanation by showing how they all could contribute to the need for microscopes for next year, but the following year another department could acquire something that it needs. Each department would receive enough to meet its basic operational needs, but any "fluff" items would not be purchased, and that money would be used to help the science department to purchase microscopes. All of the division chairs express hope and delight with this new concept. You ask them to bring their budget requests to next week's meeting.

At that meeting, you are surprised to see that all the department requests are identical to those originally submitted. Needless to say, the microscopes cannot be purchased if all the department budgets remain the same. As you probe with questions, one of the department chairs finally says, "With all due respect, your idea for zero-based budgeting is fine. But here's the problem. If we agree to accept smaller amounts of department money, and you decide to take a better position elsewhere, where does that leave us? What if your successor doesn't believe in this process and gives us the same amount of money that we had this year? Those of us who have decreased our budgets to help the science department would lose."

The other department chairs express agreement with this one. Now what do you do? How do you get the zero-based budgeting approach to work? Or do you give up and let the science department purchase one or two microscopes at a time?

Develop a bulleted action plan aligned with ISLLC Standard 3: *An education leader promotes the success of every student by ensuring management of the organization, operation, and resources for a safe, efficient, and effective learning environment.*

Ethical Considerations

The department chairs have a valid concern, but they also have an excuse not to try anything new. Isn't it important for a leader to take risks that could lead to a greater end? If we all choose to keep things status quo, how will the organization grow? Although that might be a comfortable and safe approach from some perspectives, is that really beneficial to the students? How many department chairs really spend all of their allocated accounts? How many wildly order things at the end of the school year just to spend down their accounts so they won't be cut next year? Can the principal allow this to continue? What is the principal's fiscal responsibility to the organization, to the taxpayers, to the students?

On the other hand, can the principal just step in and arbitrarily reallocate funds without losing credibility with the department chairs? Wouldn't that be micro-management? Don't we have department chairs so the principal can focus on his job, and they can focus on theirs? What message would be conveyed about empowerment? Can the principal take more time and educate them about the value of calculated risk-taking? Can he convince them that not every administrator is upwardly mobile? And most importantly, how can the principal focus them on what's best for students instead of what's best for their departmental structures?

CHAPTER 4

Organization and Development of Curriculum

Schools today are faced with the challenge of providing the public with evidence of student learning through standardized test scores. Although there is much disagreement about the use of standardized tests in this manner, the reality is that federal legislation requires such use of standardized test scores through the No Child Left Behind (NCLB) Act. Some proponents have suggested that assessment drives everything we do in the schools. This seems to be true as the media reports about "successful schools" and "failing schools" in terms of standardized test scores, but most educators agree that a balanced approach of curriculum, instruction, and assessment is the key to good, long-term learning.

The importance of organizing and developing curriculum in alignment with sound, effective instruction and multiple assessments is very important to the educational leader. Although test scores are tangible measures that seem to be desired by the publics we serve, ultimately parents want their children to be good, long-term learners. For 40 years, Phi Delta Pi has been conducting a survey about what parents and the public expect of their public schools. Each of those 40 years' worth of surveys indicates the same common goal of wanting schools to prepare students to be more than good test-takers. The role of the educational leader most definitely requires a thorough knowledge of good curriculum, good instruction, and good assessment practices.

Complicating the educational leader's job in the area of developing, organizing, and aligning curriculum is the ownership of individual teachers regarding their own lessons and activities. Students don't always come to school ready and eager to learn, and the teacher often has to provide motivation and incentive to get students to a point of wanting to learn. In addition, most human beings learn more if the experience is enjoyable. For these reasons, teachers often develop very creative activities and lessons, which their students absolutely love. The problem facing the educational leader is that of getting the teachers to understand that their lessons have to align with the curriculum, and their approach has to include differentiation so as to include all students and their preferred learning styles. Obviously, the creative activity also has to result in measurable learning (test scores).

This chapter provides scenarios intended to challenge future educational leaders' ability to solve problems related to curriculum development; curriculum planning; textbook adoption; alignment of curriculum, instruction, and assessment; teachers' personal, creative lessons that might or might not align with the curriculum; evaluation of curriculum; adopting a new textbook series; and other situations that jeopardize alignment of curriculum, instruction, and assessment. These situations not only provide our future educational leaders with opportunities to engage in critical thinking and problem solving, but they also represent the guiding principles of the heart and soul of what goes on in the schools on a daily basis: teaching and learning. Because curriculum is managed and controlled at the central office level as well as at the building level, the scenarios presented in this chapter project future educational leaders into a variety of administrative positions. This is important not only for them to understand the various elements impacting curriculum decisions, but also for them to be prepared should they seek any of these leadership positions themselves.

4-1. EVALUATING THE READING CURRICULUM REVISION (ISLLC STANDARD 1)

You are the principal of an elementary school in a small district consisting of an elementary school and a middle school. Two years ago, you chaired the committee that revised the reading curriculum and chose a new reading textbook series along with resource materials for students above or below grade level. You and the committee are very pleased both with the process and with the way that the faculty has implemented the new curriculum and materials. It is now the spring of the first year of implementation. As you visited the classrooms, you were very impressed with the engagement on the part of the students. From your perspective, everything is working well in the world of reading instruction. Because the reading series included many new resources, you have cautioned the teachers not to become overwhelmed by them. Rather, they should concentrate on the district's reading curriculum and experiment with the new materials as appropriate. No one expects them to utilize every resource, and in fact, the resources are intended to support individual reading needs.

In December, you reported this to the superintendent and to the board of education, and they seemed pleased to hear your report. However, you cautioned the superintendent and the board that it takes time for teachers to really learn all of the resources and materials. The first year of implementation is a learning process for the teachers as they experiment with the various resources and determine which ones work better, how much time to allocate for the various materials, and how to teach the new curriculum. The superintendent and the board members nodded their heads to show understanding as you explained this.

It now is April, and the superintendent has asked you to meet with her about how you plan to present to the board an evaluation of the new curriculum and textbook series. You are shocked by this, because you thought that both the superintendent and the board understood that it takes time to implement a new program and that you weren't planning on showing any evaluation results until next year. When you meet with the superintendent, you explain this, but she wants data now!

You tell her that you had planned to involve the faculty in a debriefing session at the end of the school year, during which you and they would determine what worked well, what didn't, and what changes would be made for next year. You ask the superintendent if you could present these findings at the July board meeting, but the superintendent wants more than that. She is willing to postpone the reading evaluation presentation to the board until the fall, but she wants hard data, like test scores.

What would you do to maintain a focus on the district's vision of learning? Using a bulleted format, show the process of how you would handle this situation. Be sure to align your plan with ISLLC Standard 1: *An education leader promotes the success of every student by facilitating the development, articulation, implementation, and stewardship of a vision of learning that is shared and supported by all stakeholders.*

Ethical Considerations

This situation is more common that one might think. When a board of education allocates a large sum of money for new textbooks and other related curriculum materials, they typically want to see immediate results for their expenditure. Who can blame them? They are responsible to their constituents for good fiscal responsibility. On the other hand, there is a learning curve that must be taken into consideration whenever new texts and materials are implemented into the classroom. The teachers need time to explore the various nuances of the texts and materials, and they need time to gauge their students' reactions to them.

Of course, the superintendent wants to be attentive to the needs and questions of the board members. Because superintendents often are so immersed in the "big picture" aspects of the district's financial state as well as in the political climate that impacts the district from city or village boards to township assessors, they can be out of touch with the instructional issues that confront their schools. Needless to say, that's one reason why we have principals! As a principal, you have an obligation to keep the superintendent apprised of the progress of such issues as textbook adoption and implementation, but how attentive the superintendent might be to those issues depends on what critical issues she is facing at that moment. As much as you want to set the superintendent straight about the realities of the learning curve, your attempts could very easily fall on deaf ears. Instead, the superintendent might think that you haven't been diligent in your supervision of the implementation of the new texts.

On the other hand, your teachers are going to feel that they've been given an unfair ultimatum if you ask them to provide the data that's being requested. They and you know that there is a likelihood that student achievement test scores will dip slightly during the first year of implementation of a new textbook as both teachers and students familiarize themselves with the new materials. The goal is for the scores to rise during the subsequent years of the textbook adoption.

You'd like to explain all this to the superintendent and to the board members, but again, you run the risk of sounding as if you're making excuses. How embarrassing would it be if you did present achievement test score data and the results were lower than for previous years?

4-2. KINDERGARTEN CURRICULUM REVISION: PROMOTING AN EFFECTIVE LEARNING ENVIRONMENT AMID POLITICS (ISLLC STANDARD 3)

You are an elementary school principal in a suburban school district in which there are 11 elementary schools. The district has just completed a two-year process of revising the reading program/curriculum and adopting new reading texts that meet the varied needs of learners who are below, at, and above grade level. The faculty across the district and in your building are very pleased with the revisions and the new texts, but the kindergarten teachers are apprehensive about their role as the "first reading teachers" that the kids encounter upon entering the district.

The kindergarten teachers in your building would like to develop a districtwide kindergarten curriculum that would support the reading curriculum in an interdisciplinary approach. They would like to identify specific activities that would teach and reinforce reading acquisition in various content areas. Your kindergarten teachers have been talking with kindergarten teachers in another district elementary school, and they are convinced that this could be a districtwide initiative.

You phone the assistant superintendent for curriculum and instruction and share this idea with him. He is very supportive and agrees that the project should be districtwide and supported by his office. He believes that a group of kindergarten teachers should be compensated to work on this project. You are very happy about his support, and you carry that message back to your kindergarten teachers. When you tell them that the assistant superintendent is willing to compensate a representative group of kindergarten teachers for their work after school and on weekends, the teachers immediately counter that instead of compensation, they would like to use the district inservice and institute days to do this work. Their rationale is that they need *all* district kindergarten teachers to work on this project to ensure ownership and implementation. You agree to talk with the assistant superintendent about this.

During your conversation with the assistant superintendent, you find out that the superintendent has a plan that encompasses all the inservice and institute days for the next two years. He wants the district to engage in an award-winning, data-driven model that will result in each school's completing an application and undergoing a review process by an external team. The superintendent's ultimate goal is for every school to receive an award for excellence in data-driven decision making. He plans to use the inservice and institute days for each faculty to meet with the award organization representatives and to develop their comprehensive applications for this award. Needless to say, this will necessitate that all teachers from all grade levels participate in the districtwide inservices and institutes during the next two years. Although the goal seems to be a noble one, some of the teachers, especially the kindergarten teachers, see it as window-dressing to get an award. The superintendent's plan is to acquire representatives from schools who already have received this award to act as coaches who will help with the writing of each school's application. These coaches will be paid for their time and service. It will require much committee work involving faculty, principals, and parents from each school in the district.

You and the assistant superintendent both recognize the value of having a uniform and consistent kindergarten curriculum, and you personally have placed it higher on the priority list than the plan to have each school acquire an award. As you and the assistant superintendent engage in some brainstorming about how to get the superintendent to accept the kindergarten teachers' proposal, you both realize that the support of other elementary school principals is necessary to convince the superintendent. The assistant superintendent cautions you not to appear to be against the data-driven award plan, because in some cabinet meetings, the superintendent chastised the assistant superintendent for even questioning how the award plan would improve teaching and learning. The superintendent wants the awards, and he has rationalized that the application process will result in improved test scores. He equates improved test scores with good teaching and learning. Of course, the premise upon which this thinking is based is a belief that test scores show what students really are learning.

Although the assistant superintendent agrees with you and will support both your recommendation and the implementation of the kindergarten curriculum revision process, he believes that it will be better received by the superintendent if it comes from the principals. He agrees to put this on the agenda of the next monthly district elementary principals' meeting. You agree to present the idea to the group.

- How will you introduce this to the principals?
- How can you be assured of their support?

Knowing the superintendent's plan for inservice and institute days for the next two years, how will you present the idea in a way that will convince him to release the kindergarten teachers from the district meetings so that they may use the time to work on the district kindergarten curriculum?

Develop a bulleted plan in alignment with ISLLC Standard 3: *An education leader promotes the success of every student by ensuring management of the organization, operation, and resources of a safe, efficient, and effective learning environment.*

Ethical Considerations

This is a difficult situation because you and the teachers don't see the same value of the award acquisition process that the superintendent does. Furthermore, from an instructional perspective, the need for a consistent districtwide kindergarten curriculum is of critical importance. Needless to say, the ownership that comes both from the kindergarten teachers' initiation of the idea and from their willingness to work on it to successful completion is very valuable. The superintendent might recognize some of the value of this, but he obviously places a higher value on the award acquisition process. For you to take a position against the superintendent might be detrimental to your career, or it might result in increased respect from the superintendent because of your passion for good teaching and learning that ultimately will result from the kindergarten curriculum.

Do you take the risk of challenging the superintendent? Can you live with yourself if you don't? What will happen to your credibility in the eyes of the kindergarten teachers if you don't carry their initiative forward? On the other hand, if you do carry it forward and the superintendent rejects it, how can you not make him out to be the "bad guy"? But, if you try to sugar-coat the rejection, will the teachers see you as not being honest with them? Of course, if you blame the superintendent for rejecting the proposal, he most likely will think less of your leadership ability because you've blamed him.

The assistant superintendent is willing to help, and that is your key to success. If two members of the superintendent's administrative team were to present a proposal to him, he might be more likely to consider its merits, even if the proposal runs counter to his plans for inservice time. Furthermore, if you can enlist the support of the other elementary school principals, the viability of the proposal becomes even greater. Of course, if one of them were to report to the superintendent that you are trying to present an initiative that would compete with his plans for inservice time, you would be at a disadvantage. The ideal would be for you to get to the superintendent before any of your colleagues can do so.

There is another perspective, that of the superintendent. He firmly believes in the value of the awards acquisition process. Although you and the assistant superintendent don't see it as being more valuable than the kindergarten curriculum initiative, you might want to put yourself in his shoes. What is so appealing about the awards acquisition process? Why would he want it so badly? Trying to understand his position before presenting yours is valuable to both you and him.

4-3. THE LIFE SKILLS CURRICULUM: STUDENT LEARNING VS. BOARD POLITICS (ISLLC STANDARD 3)

You are a newly appointed assistant superintendent for curriculum and instruction in a unit district consisting of 11 elementary schools, 3 junior high schools, and 1 high school. The superintendent has decided to initiate a junior high school study process in which he wants participants to examine middle school philosophy as contrasted to the current junior high school philosophy. He has asked each of the three junior high principals, two board members, and you to serve on the newly formed Junior High Study Committee. After sending formal letters to each one, inviting/commanding them to serve on the committee, he now is seeking someone to chair it. Even though you are very new to the district, you have a strong secondary education background, having previously served as a high school principal in another district. You volunteer to serve as the chair, and the superintendent gladly accepts your offer. He asks that you carve out two hours to meet with him to talk about his unwritten goals for this committee.

During the meeting with the superintendent, you receive a list of what he calls "non-negotiables," which are items that he expects you to put into place under the auspices of the committee. He tells you that you should present them to the committee members as the "superintendent's non-negotiables," and they will understand what to do. You wonder to yourself why he formed a committee, if he's already created a list of changes, but you are intrigued by what seems to be an open-ended challenge. The superintendent would like the current home economics program to be revised to be more reflective of life skills that extend beyond the traditional sewing, cooking, and child-care units. Having already met with the three home economics teachers (one from each junior high school) as part of your plan to acclimate yourself to the district curriculum issues, you know that one of them would like to move to a computer-based modular approach in which students would work cooperatively to learn various modules and then to create a project that demonstrates what they've learned. Although this approach is appealing to your philosophy about teaching and learning, you notice that the other two home economics teachers are not as enthusiastic about this concept. One of them is so preoccupied with purchasing 25 new sewing machines (one for each student in her classroom) that she can't fathom how a teacher could have students working on different modules simultaneously. Her approach is a lockstep, everyone-does-the-same-project approach. One of the board members on the Junior High Study Committee is a retired home economics teacher who shares the same philosophy as this teacher. The other board member holds a futuristic outlook that supports computer-based modules. Because the superintendent hasn't identified a specific outcome (non negotiable) for this aspect of the committee's work, you are excited about the prospect of engaging your committee in true problem solving. You have asked the home economics teachers to join the study committee for this aspect.

A few years ago, the former vocational education program for junior high school students consisted of woods, metals, and electricity basics. For various reasons, that program evolved into a computer-based modular approach that has two students working on various modules such as wind tunnel/aerodynamics, plastic-injection molding, screen-painting of T-shirts, interior design, stress engineering on structures made of balsa wood, and so on. The program has been very successful in terms of student interest and performance outcomes. The same company that markets the voc-ed computer modules also has a home economics program of modules. You have found out that a neighboring school district uses these modules, and you suggest to the committee that you and they visit this school both to see the modules and to view how they are operationalized during a normal school day.

You and the school board member who is a retired home economics teacher visit the neighboring school to see the modular curriculum in action. After an impressive overview by the teacher, you and the board member are invited to walk around the class and to look at the various modules. When the bell rings and the students enter the room, the teacher tells them to welcome the visitors and to explain their respective modules as well as their feelings about the program. As you and the board member visit with the kids, you get very positive feedback from them. All of the kids are on task, and they seem to be self-directed to complete their respective modules. Some of the students are working on interior design, others on soil and spot removal from fabrics, others on making fudge in a microwave, others on baking a cake in a convection oven, others on cooking the main entrée on an electric cooktop, others on sewing from a pattern, and so on. You notice that the board member seems quite pleased to see the range of options for the students. Just as you begin to think that the board member will support this curriculum, she whispers, "Let's see what these two boys are doing." As you approach their module, you see two boys dunking a baby doll feet first into a tub of water. You quickly ask them to explain their module, and through their laughter, they tell you that their module is about how to give a baby a bath. Needless to say, the board member is appalled and reprimands the boys for not taking this seriously. The teacher, who is at the other end of the room helping some other students, is oblivious to these boys' actions.

All the way back to your district, the board member is ranting and raving about how this new modular curriculum is "an accident waiting to happen." You try to tell her that classroom management plays an important role and that the teacher should never have paired these two boys together, but the board member won't hear of it. She now is bound and determined that the only way to provide a good life skills curriculum is to have every student doing the same thing at once. You try to explain to her that it would be cost-prohibitive to buy 25 new sewing machines and cabinets and to retrofit new kitchens to accommodate 30 students simultaneously, but she insists that it worked when she was teaching, and it still works today, regardless of the cost.

When you and the other subcommittee members debrief about the visit, the board member isn't shy about expressing her opinions. The other board member quickly argues with her, stating that not every student even wants to learn how to sew or cook. He gives an example of his wife, who sends any sewing out to be done by someone else. He states that their microwave is used far more often than the range, and that when guests are invited to his house for a meal, his wife orders catering from the local delicatessen. Now the two board members begin arguing about what children should learn.

You and the life skills teachers know that you have to bring things back to focus, and try to get the board members to agree on a common curriculum plan that you can recommend to the superintendent.

What would you do in this situation? Create a series of steps or strategies that define how you would continue to promote a state-of-the-art life skills curriculum for the middle schools. Be sure to align your plan with ISLLC Standard 3: *An education leader promotes the success of every student by ensuring management of the organization, operation, and resources for a safe, efficient, and effective learning environment.*

Ethical Considerations

It's always difficult when a member of the board of education tries to micro-manage the decision-making process. It's even more difficult when that board member has been a teacher, but her experience is far removed from the experience of today's teachers. To disagree with her could be taken the wrong way. You don't want her to think that you're being disrespectful to her, to her position, or to her experience. On the other hand, when she is oblivious to the dynamics of today's classroom, someone has to politely help her to get in touch with reality. After all, she is making decisions that have an impact on students and teachers.

Although it would be easy from a "protect my career" perspective to let the opinionated board members drive all the decisions, would you really want that for the teachers and students? Will the board member respect you more if you are willing to agreeably disagree with her? Hopefully, you can get her to the point of agreeing to disagree with each other. Often that kind of relationship leads to a deeper understanding of perspectives and ultimately results in better decision making.

The dynamic existing between the two opposing board members might initially appear to be embarrassing, because no one wants to see that kind of disagreement in public. But it is indicative of a healthy relationship when board members can take opposing viewpoints and still be respectful of each other. It is said that unlike in Western cultures where we seek to resolve opposing viewpoints through compromise, in Eastern cultures an attempt is made by both parties to get as close as they can to each other's viewpoint. The resulting viewpoint usually is richer than any compromise of the two could ever be. What a great learning experience for all, if the assistant superintendent could work with the two opposing board members to seek that third choice instead of a compromise!

4-4. THE MATH CURRICULUM COUNCIL: PROFESSIONAL ADVANCEMENT VS. WHAT'S BEST FOR KIDS (ISLLC STANDARD 2)

You are an assistant superintendent in a large, urban unit district. One of your personal goals is to ensure a smooth transition of curriculum from one grade level to the next. To that end, you have carefully nurtured curriculum councils for each content area. These curriculum councils are comprised of teacher representatives from the primary, intermediate, junior high, senior high, special education, and bilingual education areas. Although most of the curriculum councils are functioning quite well and have developed a K–12 curriculum based on the Illinois Learning Standards, the math council is struggling. You meet monthly with the council chairs, each of whom gives the group an update and shares curriculum documents. During the past few meetings, you have noticed that the math council isn't producing the same quality of work as the other councils. Having a list of the meetings for each of the councils, you decide to attend the math council meetings. Here's what you notice:

- The primary, intermediate, junior high, and special ed. teachers are working well together.
- The high school representative is very argumentative. He also has assumed an air of superiority and treats the members as if they don't know as much as he does about math.
- The bilingual teacher also has a similar attitude and treats her elementary-level colleagues with the same air of superiority.
- As you observe the dynamics, you realize that the egos of these two are poisoning the group and preventing progress.
- The appointments to the council are annual appointments, and the members receive a small stipend of $250 per semester for their work, which includes monthly meetings; at least the equivalent of three full days' worth of curriculum work on weekends, evenings, or days off; and three days' worth of work at the end of the school year.
- The bilingual representative already has informed you that she won't be able to fulfill her end-of-the-year responsibilities because they conflict with her duties as a bilingual teacher.
- The bilingual director, who reports to you, but who has a direct pipeline to the superintendent's office, is very adamant about getting more bilingual teachers involved in district committees, regardless of their qualifications. You've been trying to get her to understand that although they need better representation from the bilingual staff, they have to be careful to choose the best representative. Many of the bilingual teachers are on provisional teaching certificates (pending completion of required teaching courses) and aren't highly qualified by NCLB standards. You certainly agree with her in concept, but you want to be sure that you have the best person on the committees.
- The high school representative also is not liked, nor is he respected by the other members of the high school math department. His teaching methods are questionable, and he recently aligned himself with a particular math textbook series, which has resulted in his acting as a salesperson for that publisher. This really has irritated the other math department members, who prefer to look at the newest and best from all publishers. Interestingly, he has a doctorate and for that reason was appointed department chair a few years ago, by another principal.
- The high school representative, whom none of the other council members likes, has befriended the superintendent because he teaches the superintendent's son. Interestingly, the superintendent's son has worked the system in such a way that his teachers have allowed him to "skate by" without having to do much work. This is because the teachers fear the superintendent and don't want any confrontation with him. Although the superintendent's son has barely squeaked by with a low C, he's now earning Bs in the high school math class! The superintendent attributes this new success to the teacher, and he has told you that he's very impressed by the quality of this teacher's work.

- So the superintendent doesn't appear foolish, you try to caution him about the teacher's reputation, but the superintendent won't hear you.

You know that you need not reappoint the high school representative and the bilingual representative, but you also know that this will cause major headaches for you with both the superintendent and the bilingual director.

In a bulleted format, explain how you would handle this situation if you were the assistant superintendent. Be sure to align your plan with ISLLC Standard 2: *An education leader promotes the success of every student by advocating, nurturing, and sustaining a school culture and instructional program conducive to student learning and staff professional growth.*

Ethical Considerations

It's always difficult when an administrator has to step in and act in a directive manner. Ideally, the council would be able to operate in a collegial and collaborative manner, but that always isn't the case. If the members cannot solve their interpersonal issues, then the assistant superintendent has to do something to address the problem. What complicates this situation is that the teachers are seeking assistance and want someone to step in and assume leadership. To take sides inevitably will result in someone's being angry with you and someone's being pleased with your action. In either case, you are a winner or a loser depending on whose perspective you are considering. Of course, popularity shouldn't be the driving force in your decision making.

Before taking sides, it is imperative that all the facts be gathered in order to provide sufficient information from which a good decision can be made. Although the high school teacher seems like the proverbial bad guy, there most likely is some reason as to why he is so passionate about a particular textbook series. Before you dismiss that motivation as being for personal gain, you need to thoroughly examine that premise. A quick judgment based on emotions might not be the best approach. There is a chance that the high school teacher firmly believes in the textbook, and his affiliation with the publishing company is of little concern to him. This doesn't remove the conflict of interest, but knowing his motivation certainly helps you with your decision. If the teacher's motivation is not for personal gain, you might be able to reason with him as you and the committee brainstorm other approaches to teaching math.

Similarly, the bilingual teacher's inability to lead the group might make her seem like the antagonist in this scenario, and her resistance certainly is counterproductive to the work of the committee. Again, you have to thoroughly investigate this situation. Can something be negotiated with the director of bilingual education so that the bilingual teacher could perform the responsibilities of both duties: that of math curriculum council chair and that of bilingual teacher? If this conflict cannot be resolved, then a choice has to be made by the teacher as to which role is going to receive the majority of her time. Again, investigating the facts is imperative prior to making any judgment or drawing any conclusions.

The popular opinion in this case would be to dismiss both the high school teacher and the bilingual teacher from their roles on the council, but the assistant superintendent's credibility would be enhanced if she or he were to carefully investigate prior to making a decision. If the decision is to remove both of them, it would be important for the other members to know that it was not made arbitrarily or hastily.

4-5. MIDDLE SCHOOL PHILOSOPHY AND PERSONAL BELIEFS IMPACT STUDENT LEARNING OPPORTUNITIES (ISLLC STANDARD 3)

You are the principal of a junior high school in a wealthy suburban district in which there are 6,500 students in 10 elementary schools and 3 junior high schools. The board of education has had its own mission of renovating a school each year. The last elementary school is being completed this year, and the superintendent has asked the three junior high principals to consider who would like to be the first junior high to be renovating in the district. There are certain advantages to this, but you also realize that to be the first one is to be the proverbial "guinea pig," especially because the board members are so involved in the renovations. You have heard horror stories from the elementary school principals about how their buildings were thrown way off schedule because of change orders made by the board. Those change orders have been for rather trivial things, like adding a window in one hallway but removing a window from an office; not allowing the wooden cabinetry that the staff chose, because a board member prefers metal to wood, and so on. Fortunately, the district has a vacant school due to declining enrollments about 10 years ago. That vacant school has been the place to which each of the respective elementaries have moved during their renovations. Even though plans are for renovations to take no more than one year, because of the board's change orders for design, color, and cabinetry, some schools have been in the vacant building for more than a year!

You are very proud of your junior high school staff because of their innovation and willingness to embrace change. Your school was the first to have a modular technology lab in which students can explore various careers through computer programs. Two students are assigned to a module that takes about 10 classes to complete. The modules include designing and testing bridges, aerodynamics, rocketry, plastic-injection molding, and so on. Your vocational technology teacher spearheaded the program a few years ago and has since assisted his colleagues in the other two junior high schools as they have adopted this program. Knowing this, as well as the fact that any renovations done to the junior high schools will have to be done in the summers only, because the vacant elementary school isn't big enough to house any of the junior high enrollments, you feel somewhat calm as you enter the junior high school principals' meeting with the superintendent. You know that the agenda is to discuss junior high renovations.

You are very surprised when the superintendent announces that the three junior high schools are not only going to receive renovations during the next few summers, but that they all will be undergoing various renovations simultaneously during the summers. In the past, the board has undertaken one school at a time; this certainly will be interesting to see how the board will micro-manage three projects! The real shock comes when the superintendent states that the junior high schools are going to become middle schools. At first you wonder just what he means by this—is it simply a change in the nameplates on the doors of the schools? Is it a redistribution of grade levels? The superintendent goes on to explain that he wants all three junior high schools to move away from the traditional "high school preparation" philosophy to a middle school philosophy. He also explains that he expects the junior high principals to do this in "repayment" for his getting them the building renovations. In other words, he sees this as a "quid pro quo" or "one hand washes the other" situation.

You and your colleagues have had discussions about both philosophies, and all three of you feel that you have adopted the best of both into your programs, schedules, advisories, and teaming. In light of the fact that many districts feed into the high school district, you and the other junior high principals want students to be well prepared to compete and be successful in large high schools of 3,000 students. One of your colleagues speaks up, sharing that information with the superintendent. You are surprised when the superintendent announces that his idea of a middle school philosophy is that the traditional language arts curriculum be replaced by two separate programs, reading and writing! Although you are shocked at the superintendent's limited understanding of middle school philosophy, you are baffled about how middle school philosophy equates with a move backward to separating language arts into reading and writing, instead of integrating them.

When the superintendent further explains that he's looking for one "middle school" to start this approach during the first year and for the other two to follow later, he stares directly at you. Neither of your colleagues volunteers, and the superintendent directly asks you to "carry the torch." He further directs you to visit a neighboring school district that has moved from the junior high school philosophy to a middle school philosophy. One of the board members expresses an interest in going with you.

On a visit to one of the schools using the middle school approach, you very cordially ask the board member to ride with you to the school. In the car, you see another side to her—that of a caring and concerned person. She tells you that she's worried that the superintendent might not have the well-being of the students first in his plans, and that she sees her role as one of stopping him from bulldozing his way through meetings. She further explains that she has voted "no" on many items recently, because she wants to prevent him from ramrodding his views and ideas through the board, but that her colleagues are pushovers. She's asking you help to derail the move to the middle school approach.

Here's your challenge:

- You believe in the middle school philosophy and would like your school to adopt it.
- You know that it takes time and that the staff must have ownership.
- You were planning to slow down the process and to empower your junior high staff.
- How do you work both with a superintendent who wants this done tomorrow and a board member who wants to derail it?
- How can you get the other junior high principals to take a more proactive role?

Using a bulleted format, explain what steps you would take. Be sure to align your plan with ISLLC Standard 3: *An education leader promotes the success of every student by ensuring management of the organization, operation, and resources for a safe, efficient, and effective learning environment.*

Ethical Considerations

Politics are inevitable in any organization, and usually acquisition of power is at the root of motivation. Superintendents are hired by boards of education, but things change and the superintendent's power base sometimes changes over time. Sometimes differences of opinion cause the change. Other times, the more board members and superintendents work together, the more they realize how diametrically opposed their opinions and philosophies are. Another reason for a shift in the power base occurs as the result of an election when the board members who originally hired the superintendent no longer are on the board. For these reasons, superintendents are in a very tenuous position regarding job security and length of service.

Principals and other administrators have to be aware of the political climate as they accept challenges and as they make recommendations. Rarely are things as simple as determining what's best for the students. Usually, there are many opinions as to what's best for students. The belief on the part of the people who are asked or expected to implement new programs usually determines the success of those new programs. If the superintendent wants to implement a middle school philosophy that is highly supported by current literature, but the principals and the teachers don't believe in it, the likelihood of success is slim to none. Even worse, if the superintendent picks out certain aspects of the middle school approach, but ignores other critical elements, the program won't work.

To make such a change, a lot of "behind-the-scenes" work has to be done with the principals and teachers. They need time to investigate what other schools do. They also need to understand why a change is important. If they believe that all is well under the current structure, they will be reluctant to change for the sake of change. Data should be used to show why a change is needed. Also, human nature being what it is, principals and teachers will most likely reject any attempts to force something on them. Although the superintendent might have the best of intentions, and he might be educationally correct in his choice, the way by which this is presented to the principals and teachers is critical.

For the board member to recognize this dynamic is a benefit to the district, but for the board member to subvert the normal chain of communication by bringing this to the principal definitely is not beneficial to the district. Not only has the board member put the principal in a very difficult position, but whatever the principal does with the information can have a negative impact on her future in the district. If she tells the superintendent, the board member most likely will be embarrassed and angered. If the principal doesn't tell the superintendent, and he later finds out about it, the principal will no longer be trusted by the superintendent. In either case, there is a high risk of jeopardizing one's future career.

In addition to the principal's future in the district being at risk, the junior high school faculty and students also will suffer when a program is forced on them. For the principal not to discuss these possible ramifications with the superintendent would lead the faculty and students to believe that the principal either doesn't care about them, or doesn't know any better. Obviously, her credibility among faculty and students (and parents) would suffer. On the other hand, if the superintendent is very adamant about changing the junior high schools, he might not see the principal's questions as resistance to change.

4-6. THE MOSQUITO UNIT: WHEN OWNERSHIP TAKES PRECEDENCE OVER STUDENT LEARNING (ISLLC STANDARD 2)

You are a junior high school principal of a school of 750 students. During the past five years, your school has had four principals. Your predecessors left to take jobs in other districts, but you know that had they been happy, they wouldn't have looked in other districts. Your staff is split, insofar as half are veteran teachers and half are relatively new teachers. Because of the turnover of principals, the veterans have amassed a certain power base that has caused your predecessors some problems. The veterans believe that they should get preferential treatment and that they should be involved in all decision making. The young teachers would like a say in decision making, but it seems that when a young teacher comes up with an idea, the veterans all reject it. As a result, your faculty meetings have been challenging as you try to educate your staff in a collaboration model.

You have taken the approach of "winning them over one at a time." And that has been working as you continue to get to know each teacher individually. Today, however, you have been hit with a new dilemma. Two of your young teachers are in a terrible spat that involves curriculum. As you begin the fact-finding steps of a process to resolve this situation, here's what you have found:

- During the first semester, the seventh-grade teacher, in an attempt to integrate science and art learning standards, created a mosquito unit. The students not only conduct research about the habitat and living conditions of mosquitoes, but they also construct models of mosquitoes using pretzels, gumdrops, pipe cleaners, and marshmallows. The unit seems to have been successful, as measured by the students' involvement, collaboration, and acquisition of knowledge about mosquitoes. In some respects, it has resulted in a mini–science fair.
- The sixth-grade teacher was asked to judge the mosquito projects, and she really liked this unit. She liked it so much that she incorporated it into her second-semester lessons.
- The seventh-grade teacher found out that the sixth-grade teacher did this and became furious to think that her colleague would steal this unit. Furthermore, now that the sixth-grade teacher has incorporated it into her second-semester plans, when those students get into seventh grade, the unit will be "old hat" to them.
- In addition to the difficulties surrounding two teachers who once worked together and now are barely speaking, there are some curriculum questions. When should this unit be taught? Does one teacher have ownership rights to a unit? Does another teacher have the right to take a seventh-grade unit and use it in sixth grade?

In a bulleted format, explain how you would handle this situation if you were the principal. Kindly align your plan with ISLLC Standard 2: *An education leader promotes the success of every student by advocating, nurturing, and sustaining a school culture and instructional program conducive to student learning and staff professional growth.*

Ethical Considerations

Determining who has the right to use the mosquito unit isn't an easy determination. One might want to declare that whoever wrote it, owns it. But, in this era of educational learning standards, ownership of a unit isn't as important as how well the unit supports the appropriate grade-level standards. This is a difficult concept for some educators to accept, because for years they've been developing interesting and creative units that not only engage students in their learning, but also make it entertaining and fun. For students and teachers alike, an engaging, entertaining, and enjoyable learning activity is a valuable commodity. Not only do classroom management problems diminish, but the whole lesson moves more smoothly than if the students are not engaged. Most teachers try to develop engaging, entertaining, and enjoyable lessons every day, but they don't always go as planned.

A winner like the mosquito unit is a real gem. One can understand why the originator of the unit would feel victimized if a teacher in a previous grade level were to use it first. Even though one could argue that the unit could be redone in the next grade level because the students would be able to dig deeper into the concepts, the novelty of the unit would be gone. Also, not all students develop intellectually at the same rate. Whereas some would dig deeper into the unit, others would not be able to do so and would see it merely as a repeat. So using the same unit in two grade levels might seem like a good resolution to the problem, but it most likely won't be effective.

Ideally, the two teachers should be able to work this out as adults and as professionals, but when an individual believes his or her personal rights have been violated, such a resolution can be difficult. For this reason, the educational leader has to be involved. That person has to provide focus and keep things from becoming too emotional. The principal should be able to focus the discussion on the grade-level learning standards and lead the teachers to a decision as to which grade level would be the appropriate place in which to teach the unit in question. Although the originator might not like the outcome of this discussion, at least she will know that her input has been sought and valued.

What if the seventh-grade teacher created the unit, but it is determined that the unit is more appropriate in the sixth grade? Although an objective, rational explanation might be obvious, it doesn't remove the emotional feelings that also have to be addressed. Not only will the seventh-grade teacher feel a loss in terms of her lesson planning, but she also will feel that one of her colleagues has taken something from her without permission. This is another issue to address with both teachers. Ideally, we all should willingly share our creative ideas and units with each other, ultimately to benefit the students. Isn't that what we learned in kindergarten? A big part of the kindergarten curriculum is for students to learn how to share.

Of course, sharing and taking without permission are different. The seventh-grade teacher has a valid complaint that the sixth-grade teacher used the unit without permission. The principal has to work on vertical articulation and team-building among the grade levels. To make a decision as to where the unit belongs without addressing this interpersonal dynamic would be a mistake.

4-7. SELECTING A NEW READING SERIES: LET'S MAINTAIN A FOCUS! (ISLLC STANDARD 1)

The current reading series has been in use for 10 years. It no longer is appropriate for the changing needs of today's students. The series does not have a Spanish component, nor does it have any supplemental materials for students who are below grade level in their reading ability. Similarly, it does not have enrichment materials for those students who are significantly above grade level in their reading ability. With more and more kindergarteners coming into the district not knowing their letters, letter-sounds, or nonsense words, the primary teachers are asking for the resources to help these students to get up to grade level before they fall any farther behind. It is obvious that the new reading series is needed, but there is apprehension among the teachers in the district.

Prior to your coming to the district, your predecessor involved teachers in the selection process of the reading series, but after the teachers decided upon one series, the former assistant superintendent for curriculum chose a different series. Needless to say, this not only offended the teachers, but it also "poisoned the well" for future teacher involvement on committees. You want to engage the teachers in a new reading selection process, but you also realize that not all the teachers value the need for a Spanish component. Also, even though 10 years have passed, some teachers still are skeptical about putting forth effort on this committee because they were "burned" during the last process.

- How would you initiate a text selection process?
- How would you address the teachers' concerns?
- How would you ensure acquiring a series that meets the needs of all students?

Develop a plan for selecting a new reading series that supports both the district's vision for learning and addresses the teachers' concerns. Please align your plan with ISLLC Standard 1: *An education leader promotes the success of every student by facilitating the development, articulation, implementation, and stewardship of a vision of learning that is shared and supported by all stakeholders.*

Ethical Considerations

Often central office personnel make the decision of what texts to pilot or even which texts will be adopted. They simply ask the teachers' input after the decision has been made. I would consider this expeditious but borderline unethical. How can we expect teachers to support the new texts if they haven't been part of the choice? Furthermore, what does this say about how we view the teachers' expertise? If our teachers are the content experts, they certainly need to be respected and engaged for their expertise.

One important ethical consideration is that of influence by textbook representatives. Many publishers will want to shower the teachers with dinners and gifts in an attempt to woo them toward their respective textbooks. Personally, I believe that if the textbook representative has an expense account for such incentives, she or he should use that account for teacher resources. In other words, "save your expense account for now, and let your product speak for itself. If it's chosen as the text to be adopted, then you can use your expense account to provide the teachers with resources and staff development." I consider this to be the ethical way of utilizing expense accounts and not using them to influence the choice of the textbook.

4-8. SELLING A NEW ASSESSMENT INITIATIVE TO YOUR DEPARTMENT (ISLLC STANDARD 2)

You are the English department chair at a suburban high school, which serves mostly a middle-class, blue-collar community. Although the students do well on state exams and college entrance tests, the board of education has expressed concern that there are no other accountability measures by which they can judge the performance of the school. The assistant superintendent for curriculum and instruction recently called a meeting of all the department chairs to announce a new initiative that will address the board's need for more assessment scores.

Knowing the "turf" issues associated with content areas at the high school level, as well as the reluctance to adopt standardized tests as department accountability measures, she introduced a proposal by which departments would write their own quarterly tests, which would be scored in-house, and the data would be used for program improvement as well as for individualization of instruction. The idea sounds great to you, but you notice that your colleagues are not accepting it. They complain that this simply is more work with no valuable end, other than to get the board of education "off our backs." The assistant superintendent is very patient and even offers to provide a summer stipend for teachers willing to write the quarterly tests. Of course, this would necessitate that all teachers teaching the same course would have to agree on what is tested and would have to use the tests.

After the meeting, you approach the assistant superintendent and express interest. She indicates that she really was hoping for the math or science departments to take on the initiative because those quarterly tests would be easier to write in a multiple-choice, optical scanner format. You indicate that you'd like to present the idea to your department and that you feel that quarterly tests could be written in that format in your content area as well. You and the assistant superintendent agree that the English department members need an opportunity to discuss this and that you will get back to her after the department explores the concept.

At your next department meeting, you present this idea to your faculty. Some of the teachers like the idea but are reluctant to volunteer to be the first department to do it. As you probe their concerns, you find that they are worried about the data being used to evaluate their performance. They are quick to point out that each class is composed of different personalities. Also, some classes are slower to learn than others. "Who would want to teach the slow learners?" "If I teach the slow learners and they don't perform as well as others on the test, will this be held against me?"

On the other hand, they recognize the benefits of having common, quarterly tests in terms of curriculum alignment and the possibility of mapping the curriculum. Also, the diagnostic benefits regarding differentiation of instruction are quite valuable. The teachers also like the idea of getting a stipend to work in the summer, but they are skeptical if all this work can be done in the summer. There also are some teachers who are opposed to the idea and won't even consider its feasibility.

You don't want to lose the momentum expressed by some of the teachers, and you want to answer the concerns of all of the teachers, but you're not sure exactly how to lead them through this initiative and to make the timelines reasonable. Also, you want to get the nay-sayers to buy into the idea, realizing that this not only would be a benefit to help teachers differentiate instruction, it also would help the English department to gain more respect in the school.

Develop a bulleted plan of how you would ensure ownership on the part of your faculty while addressing their concerns. Be sure to align your plan with ISLLC Standard 2: *An education leader promotes the success of every student by advocating, nurturing, and sustaining a school culture and instructional program conducive to student learning and staff professional growth.*

Ethical Considerations

The department chair has to be careful not to let the opportunity of helping the English department overshadow the genuine concerns of the teachers. Also, the teachers have to be careful not to let the incentive of summer curriculum pay drive their decision to become involved in this initiative. The decision to embark on this project has to be grounded in what's best for students.

On the other hand, this is an opportunity to be the first department to write the quarterly assessments. Assuming it will be successful, the expectation will be for all departments to comply in the future. To be the forerunner with this would be an advantage in that the department could shape the direction that other departments will have to follow. Also, the teachers' use of the data will definitely set a precedent for other departments' use of the test data.

When considering all these points, the department chair has to be careful to engage all the teachers. Ownership plus empowerment equals success. Conversely, to mandate this with only partial support from the department is a formula for failure. The dissenters have to be heard, and they have to be led to a point where they recognize the value of the initiative. Despite the fact that the assistant superintendent wants this to begin in the summer, the process of getting buy-in can't be short-circuited.

4-9. THE SPEECH TEACHER'S PERSONAL AGENDA VS. THE INSTRUCTIONAL PROGRAM GOALS (ISLLC STANDARD 3)

You are the English department chair at a suburban high school of 2,500 students. The assistant superintendent for curriculum calls you into his office to talk about the new standards being required by the state department of higher education. One of them states that students have to have four years of English in order to qualify for admission to the state public universities. Your response to him is, "We're in good shape; we require four years of English for graduation from our high school." The assistant superintendent corrects you. "We say that we require four years of English, but really we require three and a half years of English and a semester of speech." You are surprised that he is "splitting hairs" over whether your school considers speech an English course. He goes on to explain that the state department of higher education has specifically addressed this situation in their requirements. The board suggests that speech become part of the English curriculum and not a stand-alone, semester course.

You recognize this as more support for the whole-language approach that has overtaken the "feeder schools." The assistant superintendent agrees with your analysis, but he is quick to point out that you don't have a choice here. You either do away with speech or incorporate it into each English course. He suggests that other high schools have moved to an English I, English II, English III, and English IV program. He also tells you that you cannot say that you're moving to this configuration, but then earmark a semester of one of the courses as a speech course. According to the state department of higher education, speech has to be integrated into all four years of English.

Knowing that all your teachers are certified to teach English, you recognize that there are no certification issues. But only one of your teachers is certified to teach speech, and she has had all the speech courses. This means that she will have to teach English and that the other teachers will have to incorporate speech into their courses. She is a rather outspoken person and frequently has bragged about being friends with the superintendent and his family. The superintendent never has said anything to you about granting her a special schedule, nor have you seen any favoritism on his part.

Fortunately, the effective date for this is next year. In other words, you and the department have this school year to work on this. It is October, and you have until next

August to implement the change. That should be adequate time to revise the curriculum. You also recognize that all English teachers have an oral report component to each of their courses. To earmark that these oral reports take on a certain theme is not hard. The freshman could do informative oral reports, the sophomores could do expository oral reports, the juniors could do persuasive oral reports, and so on.

Much to your surprise, your department is not at all happy with the new requirements of the state department of higher education, and they see this as a major undertaking. Despite your attempts to quell their fears and to explain to them that it doesn't have to be a major disruption, they just won't agree. Finally, you indicate the reality, "We don't have a choice." Of course, the department's opposition is not based on their perceptions of difficulty of the task. The opposition really is about the speech teacher. They are backing her, because she doesn't want to teach English. That's what it's really all about. Over the next two months, you involve the department in finding out what other high schools have done. It is quite clear that the majority of them have moved to an English I, II, III, IV program. Not only have they done this to satisfy the requirements of the state department of higher education, but they also have shown that it gives the students a more balanced approach to learning public speaking. Their reasoning is that one speech course during the sophomore year is not as effective as giving the students multiple speaking opportunities over a four-year period. When teaching a unit on persuasion, teachers would have the students read persuasive position papers, write a persuasive essay, and deliver a persuasive speech, all supporting the persuasion unit, but exposing students to different ways of self-expression.

You also have seen that the speech teacher really doesn't have the same workload as the other English teachers. She has no papers to grade, and her preparations are quite limited when she has five students giving speeches each day. With 25 students in her class, that would take five days for each type of speech. That means for five days, she has no preparations and no papers to grade. Multiply that by the number of types of speeches (informative, expository, persuasive, argumentative, visual-aids, and so on), and she really doesn't have much to do in terms of preparations and grading of papers.

After working with the department on analyzing their research results of what other schools are doing, you are relieved to see the department working together to revise the program to include speech activities in each of the four years. They seem to be excited about the opportunity to integrate reading, writing, speaking, and listening. Things seems to be going quite well, and you even hear some of the teachers mentioning that for once the speech teacher will really have to teach. Overhearing that comment, you smile to yourself. Things are going quite well, for once. . . .

Then, in December, the speech teacher notifies you that the state speech teachers' association has been bombarding the state department of higher education with complaints about their four-year English requirement and that the state department of higher education has rescinded its requirement. She goes on to say, "Now we don't have to worry about teaching speech in all four years. I can have my speech classes back. After all, that's what I'm really good at doing." You check with the assistant superintendent, and he verifies what the speech teacher has told you. However, you're not sure that you want to go back to the old way of putting speech into a one-semester speech course. In light of the way that students learn, you believe that an integrated approach of teaching the various oral reports/speeches in conjunction with reading and writing is a better way.

As the supervisor, what would you do? Would you honor the speech teacher's request, knowing that it's been like that for years? Or would you try to improve the system despite the speech teacher's complaints and her personal connection with the superintendent? Explain your plan in a bulleted approach aligned with ISLLC Standard 3: *An education leader promotes the success of every student by ensuring management of the organization, operation, and resources for a safe, efficient, and effective learning environment.*

Ethical Considerations

Sometimes even though a problem seems no longer to be a problem, it still is. This is one of the cases. Although the state department of higher education might change their opinion about minimum requirements, do you want your program to uphold only the minimum standards? If the department members (except for the speech teacher) agree to improve the instructional delivery and curriculum, and if it is better for students, then why wouldn't you want to continue with the plan? The answer is that the speech teacher wants you to stop the plan. But should her personal interests take precedence over those of the students? The answer is obvious, but the crux of the problem might rest with your belief that the program needs to be improved and her belief that the program already is very good and doesn't need to be improved any further.

A power struggle could occur, but you will win because of your authority position in the chain of command. Needless to say, that isn't the best approach to use when trying to resolve this issue. Not only will she resent you for pulling rank, but also she will feel that you don't value her expertise or her opinion. Dissension in your faculty isn't a good thing, and it can become contagious. A better approach would be to try to reason with her. Of course when one's personal schedule and daily teaching practice is subject to radical change, emotions usually usurp any attempt at rational thinking.

Whether the assistant superintendent agrees with you isn't as important as the fact that your faculty agrees with the change. You don't want to squelch their enthusiasm and willingness to improve the English curriculum. However, you also have to recognize that teachers have a strong bond of camaraderie, and the speech teacher could be viewed by them as the victim. If that were to happen, you not only would lose the opportunity to improve the program, but you also would be viewed as a bully in the teachers' eyes. So you need to approach this with tact and diplomacy, but also in a way that capitalizes on the teachers' initial enthusiasm about the proposed change of the program.

Another factor to consider is the equity of work. If the speech teacher has been taking a too-easy route to teaching speech, you probably should have been addressing this sooner than now. Her professional growth as an effective teacher should have been part of annual evaluation goals. If your observations noted an overly simple approach to teaching certain lessons, you should have asked her what she was trying to accomplish, what she thought the students were learning, and how well the students were meeting her expectations. By focusing her on the outcomes of each lesson, you could have been helping her to improve and not allowing her to slip into complacency. Good supervision prevents such problems.

CHAPTER 5

Supervision of Personnel

One of the most important aspects of educational leadership is that of supervision of personnel. Just as teachers are responsible for the success of their students, direct supervisors (most often principals and department chairs) are responsible for the success of their faculty and staff. In the past, the concept of supervision was more of an industrial model, which basically assumed that employees had no interest in the organization other than as the means to earning a paycheck. If a supervisor believes that the employees have no interest in the organization's mission or goals, then that supervisor will look upon supervision and evaluation of personnel as a way to criticize the employee's work or performance. The intent behind the criticism is twofold: to improve performance and to reinforce authority over the employee.

Of course, schools aren't factories, and industrial management doesn't work well with faculty and staff. Instead, empowerment and having the necessary resources to perform well are the keys to good supervision in a school setting. Teachers typically aren't motivated by extrinsic rewards; rather, they choose their profession out of a sense of responsibility to help others. Various studies have been done over the years to investigate the feasibility of merit pay for teachers, only to find that teachers aren't motivated by pay. Of much more importance is empowerment and responsibility to teach a classroom of students. The reality is that once the classroom door is closed, the teacher is responsible for implementing the appropriate instruction and utilizing the curriculum of her or his choice for the success of the students, regardless of how an evaluation of performance might be written. Although the pressure to hold teachers accountable to improve students' test scores continues to be exerted, teachers are expected to differentiate instruction and to make accommodations to the curriculum as deemed necessary by the teacher. In other words, the teacher is responsible, and an industrial model isn't going to work here.

For this reason, supervision resulting in self-assessment of performance relative to good instructional practices is of paramount importance. Even if a supervisor were to observe a teacher's classroom and make suggestions for improvement, those suggestions are taken out of the context of a much longer lesson. Questions about how the teacher determined that this lesson is appropriate, how the students' learning is measured, what the students are expected to do both during and after the lesson, and what interpersonal dynamics have been at force in the classroom all need to be taken into consideration before any suggestions can be made. The popular evaluation system known as the clinical supervision model can address these questions and provide pertinent feedback to teachers, if it is done correctly. Unfortunately, most supervisors are so pressed for time due to management situations demanding immediate response that they don't or can't take the time necessary to make the clinical supervision model work well.

Instead, the supervisor will hold a cursory preconference at which the lesson is explained briefly and a mutually agreeable time for an observation is determined. On the day of the observation, the supervisor often arrives late to class due to "management fires" that had to be put out. Because the supervisor arrived late, there is no frame of reference regarding how the lesson was introduced, how expectations were set, or what questions the students might have had. Instead, the supervisor observes the actual lesson in a vacuum, and often leaves after about 30 minutes (due to other management issues beckoning him or her away from the classroom). Needless to say, the supervisor doesn't see how the teacher is assessing the status of the students' learning, what still has to be taught, what guided practice is given, what work is given to reinforce the day's learning (homework), and what is planned for tomorrow.

The supervisor then draws conclusions about the limited observation and usually compares the teacher's lesson delivery to how the supervisor would have taught it. Unless the teacher is a clone of the supervisor, there will be some suggestions for improvement written out for the teacher to employ. These suggestions are quickly explained during the postconference, but there is no opportunity for the supervisor to find out how the unit ended. Remember, the observed lesson is only one component of a much larger unit.

Fortunately, some school districts have begun to move away from the traditional clinical supervision model by building in steps for analysis of the data collected during the observation and for self-reflection on the part of the teacher. Also, some school districts have adopted a goal-setting model, and others have adopted a peer-coaching approach. These models emphasize the importance of self-evaluation and professional growth. While there might be a very small percentage of teachers who need a more direct approach, the vast majority of teachers will grow in their performance if their work is valued by the supervisor and if they are given the opportunity to take risks and to draw their own conclusions as to how well the risk worked. Teachers in other countries such as Japan try new lessons and critique the effectiveness of the lesson. Teachers in the United States try new lessons, but the supervisor critiques the teacher's delivery of the lesson. With this approach, there is little incentive to attempt new lessons because if they don't go well, the teacher is blamed. In Japan, if the lesson doesn't go well, it is reworked until it is successful. The teacher's delivery is expected to be professional and appropriate to the students' abilities.

With this in mind, it is important that today's and tomorrow's educational leaders not only be up-to-speed with current supervision techniques and models, but also that they recognize the importance of allocating sufficient time to providing resources and assistance to teachers in an attempt to help them to grow, and not to criticize their risks. The case studies presented in this chapter are intended to pose a myriad of challenges to the supervisor of tomorrow. They present situations that will help the future educational leader analyze his or her philosophy of leadership. They also provide a sense of reality as to what the supervisor faces when working with a faculty of unique individuals. The expectation of this chapter is that tomorrow's educational leaders will recognize the importance of differentiated supervision aimed at promoting professional growth through self-evaluation. Through the ethical considerations, tomorrow's educational leaders can get a sense of the various forces at work during an evaluation. It is hoped that what's best for teacher growth and ultimately student success will win out.

In addition to scenarios related to teacher evaluation, this chapter also includes case studies about the interpersonal relationships and challenges that occur among administrators. There is a certain level of competition among principals as well as among central office administrators. How does the educational leader manage within an environment of competition that might result in one's having to negotiate shark-infested waters? Again, the ethical considerations following these case studies are intended to help tomorrow's educational administrators as they define their philosophy of leadership.

5-1. ASSIGNMENT OF CLASSROOMS TO BENEFIT A NEW TEACHER (ISLLC STANDARD 5)

You are the new English department chair, and you have a staff of 17 teachers to evaluate. You also are responsible for scheduling the teachers and the various courses and sections in your department. Your high school has been growing in enrollment, and you no longer have enough classrooms in your department. In the past, the department chair had his own classroom, even though he taught only three classes per day. Now, with the increase in enrollment, that will have to change. You are willing to travel from classroom to classroom, but with the increase in enrollment, you will have two new teachers in your department. One of them is a teacher from another high school in your district, and she will get the former department chair's classroom. The other teacher is a new teacher—new to the school and a first-year teacher. She also is the only African American teacher in your department. You hired her, and you are happy not only to provide students with some ethnic diversity, but also because she seems to be a very good teacher. Shareeta did some long-term substitute work for you last year, when one of your teachers had undergone surgery and was out for nine weeks.

Unfortunately, the rest of your staff was not very accepting of Shareeta last year. You suspect that their lack of acceptance is racially motivated, because Shareeta has excellent interpersonal skills, and she relates well with other faculty members outside your department. Last year, during department meetings, Shareeta always was cordial to the other members of the department. She brought an upbeat perspective to the meetings and was willing to offer suggestions, but not in an overbearing manner. She always began with, "I know I'm just a sub, but here's an idea." The rest of the department would politely listen, but wouldn't really move with Shareeta's suggestions. You were troubled by this and realized that the department needed someone like Shareeta—not only because of her race, but also because she provided a fresh, new perspective to a group of teachers who have been together for many years. When the opportunity arose to hire her, you jumped at it. The principal expressed gratitude for your recommendation to hire Shareeta, because he had heard good reports about her when she was subbing in your department. You involved two teachers from the department in the interviewing and selection process. They also agreed that Shareeta had been the strongest candidate.

Now you have the challenge of trying to schedule 17 teachers into 16 classrooms! The most obvious way to do this would be to schedule Shareeta into five different classrooms. Each teacher's classroom is unused for one period per day, when that teacher has a prep and planning period. The teachers typically come to the department office during their prep and planning periods, and the classrooms sit empty during that period. By scheduling Shareeta into whatever classroom is empty during those respective periods, you wouldn't disrupt anyone in your department. But is that the best situation for a new teacher? Granted, Shareeta has some experience, but that's only nine weeks or one quarter of the last school year. She still is a beginning teacher.

You struggle with this, because in your heart, you know that first-year teachers need their own classroom more than veteran teachers do. Because first-year teachers have so much to learn both about teaching and about classroom management, having to move from room to room would only complicate her life. As you work on the room usage schedule, you realize that you could schedule each teacher in one room for the morning and a different room for the afternoon. No one would have to move more than once; each teacher would have two classrooms. You are delighted with this solution. Certainly no one would mind having to shift classrooms once during the day, especially if this is done to help a new colleague.

You mention this to some of the department members, and you are shocked to hear their reactions. One of them said, "I've paid my dues, and I deserve my own room. Let her pay her dues, too." Another said, "That's part of being a first-year teacher. You take what's left." A third teacher replied, "The only reason you're doing this is because she's Black. If she were White, you wouldn't be so concerned about accommodating her schedule." You are very disappointed with these responses, and you try to explain that this is not only about helping a first-year teacher to be successful, but also about helping students to have the best teachers that we can give them. Why would we want to place undue hardships on a new teacher just so she can "pay her dues"? You further ask, "What about the students? Don't they deserve a teacher who can concentrate on teaching and not have to worry about moving to five different classrooms?" Of course, your comments have fallen on deaf ears.

The next day, you share your dilemma with the assistant principal, who is a friend as well as a supervisor. He agrees with you, but cautions that some of your staff members are quite vocal in the union ranks. Ultimately, the power of assignment and scheduling rests with you as department chair. He assures you that he will support your decision. As you continue to ponder the best solution, you realize that you have to follow your heart. We've all been first-year teachers, and we all know how important it is not only to have the support of one's colleagues, but also to be able to concentrate on teaching and classroom management without the added strain of having to move to five different rooms. You also see this as an opportunity for your veteran teachers to become more open-minded, especially when the student population is 20% Black, but there are no Black teachers in the English Department. The more you think about the situation, the more you affirm your decision to create a schedule in which each teacher has two classrooms: one in the morning and one in the afternoon.

After creating the schedule, you begin to strategize how you will introduce this to all the department members. Of course, you strongly suspect that those who have opposed this idea already have "poisoned the well" with the other department members. Nevertheless, you decide to meet individually with each department member, share the schedule, and explain your rationale. You believe the personal approach will allow you not only to appeal to each person's sense of compassion for newcomers, but also will give you an opportunity to address first hand any concerns that person might have.

After meeting with each department member individually, you are disappointed by some of the reactions, especially from those who had your trust and confidence. You begin to feel that you are alone with little support from your department. Even those who didn't really mind sharing classrooms clearly have been influenced by one veteran teacher who now has made this her mission in life. She has filed a grievance against you. Although you and she both are members of the teachers' union, in your role as evaluator and scheduler, she feels, you have violated her rights of seniority. You read and re-read the contract and can't find any seniority provisions for assignment, much less scheduling rooms.

The next morning, you receive a surprise visit from the union president who makes it very clear that he wants you to rescind the schedule. He agrees that there are no grounds for a grievance because you have not violated the contract. But, in the interest of respecting the seniority of union members, he is asking you to give the new teacher five classrooms and to leave the other teachers in their respective classrooms. You ask him if he intends to recruit the new teacher into the union. His response is, "Yes, of course." You then ask about her rights as a new union member. His answer sickens you. "She isn't a member yet, and she won't protest her schedule because she wants a job."

You tell the union president that you respectfully disagree with him and that your understanding is that the union president should represent *all* members, including you and the new teacher. He tells you that you will regret this decision and abruptly leaves your office. Shortly after, you get a phone call from the principal. He wants to meet with you regarding the schedule. Remembering the support the assistant principal pledged to you, a certain level of confidence fills your soul.

Much to your surprise, the meeting with the principal includes the union president and principal, but not the assistant principal. You are surprised by this because the assistant principal is the one who puts the master schedule together after receiving the proposed schedules from each of the department chairs. The meeting begins with the principal asking you to explain your rationale for the English Department schedule. His tone and choice of words immediately makes you feel that you are on the defensive. He listens carefully and then indicates to the union president that he needs to take this under advisement. He dismisses the union president, but asks you to stay.

After a heart-to-heart talk, the principal confidentially tells you that he agrees both with your rationale and with your willingness to stand firmly behind your decision. He also tells you that he will support you, but that the union will continue to scrutinize every move you make in the future. As you leave the principal's office you feel a sense of victory in that you know the proposed schedule is all about what's right, but you also feel a sense of fear about what might lie ahead. You are hopeful all this will calm down during the summer.

The next fall, you realize that most of the teachers are willing to try the two-classroom schedule, except for the one who filed the grievance last spring. She still "has her nose out of joint." The second day of school, she comes storming into your office, complaining about what Shareeta left on the chalkboard. She asks you to go into the classroom to see for yourself. As you enter the room, you notice a number of sentences written on the chalkboard. There are cross-outs and edit marks written on the chalkboard. The complaining teacher points out to you that Shareeta has a grammatically incorrect sentence written on the board. She also questions if Shareeta has a good grasp of grammar and if she is able to teach English. She continues to explain to you that Black people have their own way of writing and speaking, and that way does not contain correct grammar. You ask her not to make such prejudiced statements and not to draw such generalized conclusions. You assure the complaining teacher that you will find out why a grammatically incorrect sentence was left on the chalkboard.

When you talk to Shareeta about it, her explanation is simple. She asked the class to give her a sentence that they could correct as a class project. The sentence was purposely written as a grammatically incorrect sentence so the class could then copy it and revise it as a written homework assignment. You suggest to Shareeta that it would be a courteous gesture to erase the board for the next teacher who will be using the room. You also begin to wonder if your plan to help the veteran teacher to become more open-minded will ever work.

When you explain to the complaining teacher the real reason for having a grammatically incorrect sentence on the board, you are very discouraged by her response. "Do you actually believe that excuse?" she challenged. "If I were caught making such a mistake, I would make up some crazy excuse like that, too!"

As a supervisor, what would you do? Develop a bulleted plan of action that aligns with ISLLC Standard 5: *An education leader promotes the success of every student by acting with integrity, fairness, and in an ethical manner.*

Ethical Considerations

An interesting dynamic sometimes occurring with employees in any field is their willingness to keep their personal beliefs to themselves if one of their peers has different beliefs. In this scenario, each of the teachers agreed with the plan to share classrooms when asked individually, but in a group they would not try to convince the complaining teacher to look at things differently. Needless to say, this put the supervisor in a difficult position of knowing that the faculty agreed with him behind the scenes, but also knowing that they wouldn't support him in front of the complaining teacher. If the supervisor were to cave in on his position, the teachers would most likely lose respect for him, but if it appears that he doesn't support one of them (the complaining teacher), they will be quick to criticize him in her presence.

Furthermore, because of the racial undertones involved in this situation, more is at stake than being fair to a new teacher. The issue of racism cannot be ignored nor can it be tolerated. It must be addressed directly. What the supervisor doesn't know is if the other teachers might also harbor some latent racism. When he confronts the complaining teacher about her racist comments, he also could lose the support of the other teachers. They could align themselves with the complaining teacher on the basis of shared racial attitudes. Although the loss of their support would be detrimental to the supervisor, not to address the racial issues would be unethical. Needless to say, unethical behavior ultimately results in loss of support.

5-2. THE DYNAMIC READING PROGRAM EQUALS A RECIPE FOR SUCCESS? (ISLLC STANDARD 2)

The state test scores are becoming more and more significant in your school district. The board of education is concerned about competing with other school districts; the superintendent sees the test scores as an indicator of his success; and the press has taken it upon itself to create comparisons and lists of scores as a week-long investigation of the public schools. The school district has a 25% mobility rate and a 48% low socioeconomic rate. Although the success on the state test has a direct but inverse correlation with the socioeconomic rates of districts, the press has chosen to ignore this important fact.

The teachers in George Washington Elementary School attend a summer workshop about the new "Dynamic Reading Program" that is sweeping the nation with its promise of increasing state reading test scores. These teachers are tired of having their school's scores at the bottom of the district ranking, so they have taken it upon themselves to seek a "magic potion" that will solve their problems. The principal has not provided them with much instructional leadership, primarily because she is overwhelmed with the influx of new students and the egress of current students as families in the area are laid off work and move away to find new jobs, and other families move into the area, attracted by the lowered housing costs caused by the egress of the recently unemployed families.

The following summer, upon reviewing the spring reading scores on the state test, Dr. Stephanie Miller notices that Washington Elementary has more student scores in the state "meets standards" category than does any other school in the district. While she is happy for their success, she suspects what the superintendent will do with this information. Dr. Miller knows that the faculty of Washington Elementary have attended the "Dynamic Reading Program" and that they have worked together to plan lessons and curriculum mapping around this program. It is a good program, but Dr. Miller, the curriculum coordinator, realizes that no single program can guarantee such success for all students. She also realizes that the success of any program rests with the commitment of the teachers implementing it. This one was successful because the teachers in the school all worked together on implementing it across content areas and grade levels.

At the next principals' meeting, the superintendent congratulates the principal of Washington Elementary and asks her for the secret to the school's success in reading. The principal proudly states that the teachers all attended a "Dynamic Reading Program" the previous summer and that they all worked very hard to implement it across content areas and grade levels. Expecting the superintendent to be pleased with the teamwork and planning of her faculty, the principal embellishes upon the great work of her staff. Unfortunately the superintendent didn't listen to the explanation about the teachers' involvement. Instead, he launches into a scolding of the other principals for not being innovative enough to implement such a successful program. He then turns his anger to the curriculum coordinator and asks why, if she knew of such a successful program, she didn't mandate that all the schools use such a program.

The superintendent then does just that; he mandates that all the other principals implement the "Dynamic Reading Program" in their respective schools.

Analyze this situation from the perspective of management and leadership theories.

- What would you do if you were the principal in one of these schools?
- Will this program be successful if it's mandated of the teachers?
- Being principal and having been commanded to implement the program, how would you break this news to your staff?
- How can you ensure the success of the program?

Using these questions to frame your thinking, develop an action plan of how you would handle this situation from a principal's perspective. Kindly align your plan with ISLLC Standard 2: *An education leader promotes the success of every student by advocating, nurturing, and sustaining a school culture and instructional program conducive to student learning and staff professional growth.*

Ethical Considerations

Unfortunately, there is a certain level of competition among principals in the same district. Although some might argue that competition is healthy, when it results in the other principals being blindsided, it is not good for the district or for the students. Certainly, for the principal who was lucky enough to stumble onto some good fortune, the perspective is different than for the other principals. There is no doubt that the superintendent's criticism of the principals and the district curriculum director is not the best way to manage people, but out of a sense of frustration with the state scores, the superintendent probably feels justified in treating his administrative staff in this way.

It is important to understand the superintendent's motivation if the principals are going to maintain their credibility and self-confidence. If they allow the superintendent's scolding to erode their self-confidence, their leadership undoubtedly will suffer. No one likes to be ordered around; it is disrespectful to them both as professionals, but also as people. The same is true for the teachers; they won't want to have a mandated program thrust upon them. Knowing this, the principal has an interesting challenge to face.

While it might be easy to simply blame the superintendent and explain to the faculty that they must learn and implement the "Dynamic Reading Program," that's probably not the best way to achieve success with the program. Human nature would prevail, and the teachers would not buy into the program. Without their buy-in, the program will fail; consequently, this approach is not a good one for teachers or for the students.

Probably the best approach would be for the principal to get excited about the program and to infect the teachers with that excitement. This is a difficult approach, because the principal most likely will feel resentful about having to implement the program. On the other hand, if the principal were to reject the mandate, not only would the principal appear to be against programs that might help the students, but she or he would be jeopardizing the working relationship with the superintendent. That would not be good for anyone.

So how does a principal become excited about a mandated program without appearing to be a hypocrite? Should the principals work together to develop a common strategy for introducing this to their respective faculty members? There would be some logic to that approach, but would it also alienate the principal who piloted the reading program? They might want to do that due to their having been blindsided, but that ultimately would not benefit anyone. Perhaps the other principals could learn from the principal whose faculty piloted the program. Most likely the ethical approach would be to put their personal feelings aside and to work together (with the principal whose faculty piloted the program) to ensure its overall success as well as the success of their students.

5-3. THE FIRST-YEAR TEACHER AND THE SUPERVISION PROCESS (ISLLC STANDARD 2)

You are a new principal. During your first summer, you hire five new teachers, due to retirements. Even though you always involve the appropriate division chairs and a teacher from the department, you sometimes wonder if they really take the hiring process seriously. Do the division chairs really feel responsible for the success of their staff? Your belief is that once the school hires a new teacher, there are a number of people who must assume responsibility for that teacher's success, especially during his or her first year of teaching in the school. The thought has crossed your mind that some of the division chairs seem to be more concerned about textbooks and curriculum than they are about the actual teaching and learning in their content areas.

Recently you and the division chair for English, social studies, and foreign languages, an English teacher, interviewed Laura Smith for the English teacher vacancy. Laura was not the most shining example of a new teacher, but she was better than the other candidates. After reaching consensus that she would be offered the job, you asked both the division chair and the English teacher to provide Laura with whatever support she needed during the first year.

In accordance with the contract, the division chair is responsible for conducting the first observations and evaluation, using a clinical supervision model consisting of a preconference, observation, and postconference. During this process, the division chair concludes that while Laura has some classroom management problems, she certainly is "coachable." Relieved to hear this, you thank him for keeping you informed. It still is early in the school year, and you are trusting the division chair's ability to work with Laura to ensure her success.

A week later, however, your assistant principal notifies you that Laura Smith has been generating an inordinate number of discipline referrals. He further tells you that she still has not submitted her classroom management plan to his office, which is required of all teachers. When he asked her for the plan, she flatly refused. The assistant principal shared this information with the division chair, who assured the assistant principal that Laura was just jittery about her first year of teaching and that he would get her to comply with the request to submit her classroom management plan.

Upon hearing this information, you talk with Laura about the importance of having a classroom management plan that the assistant principal can use when supporting her discipline referrals. She agrees and says that she needs help developing a plan. You suggest that she work both with her division chair and the assistant principal. They will help her with the plan. You then follow up with a communication to them. Not hearing anything from either of them, you are confident that Laura must be working with her division chair and the assistant principal.

Early in January, you invite Laura in to a preconference with her, prior to your observation. You ask her how things are going and how she is adjusting to the role of teacher. She assures you that everything is fine and that she couldn't be happier. When you broach the topic of classroom management, she explains that she misunderstood the expectation and that she will take care of it immediately. You then go into the normal preconference questions about lesson planning, the intent of the lesson you're going to observe, where it falls in the scope and sequence of the course, if there's anything in particular that you should observe, and so on.

During the actual classroom observation, you are disappointed with Laura's interaction with the students. She has little control of the classroom, and there seems to be a mutual disrespect between teacher and students. You take copious notes so that you can share your observations with her.

During the postconference, you ask Laura how she thought the lesson went. She responds that the lesson was very effective. You then ask her how she feels about her relationship with the students. She explains that there are very snooty students in the high school, and she has never experienced anything like this in her student teaching and even in her own high school. In other words, she blames the students for everything. As you offer her suggestions about how to develop a working relationship with the students, she feigns interest, but it's obvious to you that she is not going to take your suggestions seriously. She also indicates that the division chair agrees with her that the students are at fault.

You then have a conference with the division chair. He sides with the teacher and asks for more time for her to acclimate to the school. You explain to him that you and he need to work together for the success of both the teacher and the students. He agrees wholeheartedly.

One month later, the assistant principal again mentions that Laura's discipline referrals are consuming a lot of his time. He further explains that he is "up to his eyeballs in alligators" and she demands that he give her referrals a quicker response. According to him, Laura is not following her own classroom management plan, which makes it difficult for him to provide her support. You again meet with Laura and talk to her about how things are going, especially in the area of classroom management. She says everything is going well. You broach the topic of excessive referrals, and she again blames the kids and their lack of morals and manners. You set a date with her for the next preconference.

During the preconference, you ask specific questions about students that she anticipates will upset the lesson. You ask her how she plans to engage them. She is completely oblivious to your questioning and asks if you are making excuses for the students' lack of behavior. She then launches into blaming the assistant principal for not backing her up when she sends students to the office. You ask her how many students she sends to the office on a daily basis, and she admits that she typically sends at least two students to the office during each class period. You try to work with her about the reasons she sends the students to the office, what interventions she has tried, how many parent contacts she has made, and so on. Her response is that her job is to teach, not to discipline students. Regarding parent contacts, those are the responsibility of the assistant principal, and not hers.

At this point, you are very upset about her attitude and her lack of accepting responsibility. As calm and supportive as you try to be, she continues to argue and blame. Finally, you explain to her that your expectations are that teachers handle classroom management problems themselves and that only the serious infractions and multiple violations should be sent to the assistant principal. You again explain the importance of a classroom management plan that students and parents understand.

During the next classroom observation, you see the same behavior as you did in the first observation. In other words, Laura has not taken any of your advice nor has she taken the advice of your assistant principal. Prior to the postconference, you explain to the division chair that you are not going to recommend Laura for continued employment next year. As a first-year teacher, she is not going to be renewed for next year. The division chair agrees with you that this is a good decision. You ask him not to mention this to her, as it is your job as principal to deliver such bad news. He again agrees.

When you meet with Laura in the postconference and go through the usual questions of how she perceived the lesson, she begins to cry and to vent at you about how you haven't supported her during her first year of teaching. She goes on to say that the division chair told her that you're going to fire her and that he doesn't agree with your decision. You are surprised that the division chair has told her of your plans, especially since you asked him not to say anything to her about this. You attempt to do some damage control with Laura by explaining that you have offered her many suggestions and that the assistant principal also has offered her many suggestions. You also explain that according to the contract, the division chair is the front-line person for support and that he has been keeping you apprised of her success or lack thereof. She calls you a liar and demands a meeting with you and the division chair. You explain that as a first-year teacher, she's not even entitled to a reason for her lack of renewal and that you have gone way beyond the norm in explaining to her the reasons for her not being renewed. She bursts out of the office in an emotional state of crying and shouting at you.

You sit there calming yourself and reflecting on what just happened. You wonder how you're going to support her and her students during the next four months, until the end of the school year. Just then, the division chair appears at your door and asks why you treated Laura so rudely. You invite him into your office and attempt to explain the series of events, but he already has formed an opinion that you are completely at fault for this. When you remind him that he has not been entirely truthful with you about his observations of Laura, he becomes defensive, saying that you had determined when you first hired her that she wasn't going to be successful. You listen patiently and then explain your disappointment in his role both as her immediate supervisor and as a team player, especially in the area of doing what his principal (you) asked him. You are referring to his telling her about your plan not to renew her contract. He admits that he shouldn't have told her, but in light of how she alleged that you cruelly evaluated her, he had to provide her emotional support.

- How would you deal with the first-year teacher?
- How would you deal with the division chair?

Using a bulleted format, develop a plan of action in which you specifically address ISLLC Standard 2: *An education leader promotes the success of every student by advocating, nurturing, and sustaining a school culture and instructional program conducive to student learning and staff professional growth.*

Ethical Considerations

When a principal hires a new teacher, I believe there is an obligation on the principal's part to do everything possible to ensure the success of that teacher. Principals sometimes forget that they still are teachers. A parallel comparison can be drawn between the teacher and the students, and the principal and the faculty. Just as the teacher is responsible for his or her students' learning and growth, similarly the principal is responsible for his or her teachers' learning and growth. Far too often principals look upon nontenured teachers as dispensable. If they don't work out during the first year, we just throw them away and find someone else to replace the new teacher. Not only is this unethical when one considers the impact this can have on an individual's job, family, income, and self-esteem, but it also raises the question of whether the principal also views students in the same way.

If principals truly believe in the inherent potential of each individual (students and teachers), then good learning will occur. But if the principal believes that some individuals can and should be tossed away, what does that say about his or her belief that all students can and will learn? Sometimes principals don't realize that their ability to hire and nurture new teachers is up for scrutiny if they are quick to release nontenured teachers.

What complicates matters related to good supervision of teachers' professional growth is the competition of urgent matters for the principal's attention. Far too often, the urgent matters win out, and the supervision and nurturing of teachers becomes second in terms of priority and importance. In high schools, often department chairs or instructional leaders who possess an administrator certificate conduct most of the evaluations of their teachers, and the principal does a pro-forma evaluation in accordance with the terms of the teachers' negotiated agreement (contract). Because the department chairs or instructional leaders are considered to be experts in their content area, they are given the bulk of the responsibility for evaluating new teachers in their departments. The principal will assume that the nurturing of the new teachers is being done at the department level, but it might not be. Department/division chairs or instructional leaders typically have teaching assignments in addition to their supervisory duties. Once again, the supervision and nurturing of teachers takes second priority to the other duties of the department chair or instructional leader.

To expect a new teacher to be fully seasoned and an expert in classroom management is quite unreasonable. Good teaching is learned and developed over time. All too often, principals are quick to dispose of new teachers rather than taking the time to work with them and to help them grow.

Another ethical consideration is that of handling insubordination. While you have an obligation to help the new teacher, she also has an obligation to grow and to learn. Her insubordination, especially in her refusal to develop a classroom management plan, must be addressed. Although dismissing the teacher can be very injurious to her career, to her financial situation, and to her mental health, if she will not cooperate with you, how can you expect her to carry out the mission of the school? Are the children in her classroom receiving the educational opportunities they deserve? Would you want your own children in her classroom? These are questions you have to consider when deciding if she is "salvageable."

In this case study, it is obvious that the principal had placed more trust in the division chair than that person deserved. There is an obvious problem in the division chair's execution of his duties. If he perceives himself as an insulator or protector of the teachers from the administrators, there is a big problem. One might question how this person has continued in this role if he has assumed such a mission of protection from the administration. Typically, department/division chair or instructional leader positions are annual appointments by the principal. Perhaps the principal should pay more attention to the supervision of the division chairs in this school? This is especially important if the division chairs conduct the majority of the supervision and nurturing of new teachers.

As is true in just about any leadership challenge, politics can seriously impact the decision making. If this division chair had become a legend in the school, it certainly would be more difficult to remove him from the position. Just as the supervisor has the responsibility for the professional growth of teachers, the principal also has the responsibility for the professional growth of the division chairs. Before just tossing this one away, some serious conversation should occur about what went right and what went wrong with this situation. How could it have been avoided if we could turn the clock back?

5-4. FOUR INTERNAL CANDIDATES DON'T GET THE ADMINISTRATIVE JOB (ISLLC STANDARD 6)

You are a high school department chair, and you are interested in pursuing a move into administration. In your district, the route to becoming an assistant principal is by having been either a department chair or a dean of students. Because you have served in your present role of department chair for 10 years, you are confident that you are positioned well for the next assistant principal vacancy. Of the two schools in the district, yours has had a new assistant principal every two years. The other school has had the same assistant principal for the past 15 years.

Your current assistant principal just announced that he has accepted a principalship in another district, and the resulting vacancy has been posted. You and three other internal candidates apply for the position. One of the internal candidates presently serves as dean of students. Another has been a teacher for 20 years, but has not been either a department chair or a dean. You and the other internal candidate are department chairs who have served in that capacity for a number of years.

Each of the four internal candidates gets an interview, and yours goes very well. You are confident in your performance during the interview, and the gossip around the school is that you are the front-runner for the position. Typically, candidates are notified of their status rather quickly after the interview. Oddly, none of the internal candidates hears anything for a month. It now is the summer, and school is out, but still no news about the assistant principal position.

During the second week of June you receive a newsletter in the mail announcing to the faculty the name of the new assistant principal. He is a former elementary school principal from another city. The new assistant principal has not been a high school principal and has spent his 10-year career in the same elementary school district, two years as a junior high school assistant principal, and one year as an elementary school principal. You and the other internal candidates are shocked by the announcement. Not only are you surprised by his lack of high school experience, but also by the way in which the announcement was made. You know that the superintendent should have had the courtesy to at least notify each of the internal candidates personally before they read about it in a newsletter.

As you and the other internal candidates talk with each other about this, the re-actions of your colleagues are surprising to you. One of them suggested that the four of you protest at a board of education meeting. You quickly respond by explaining that the filling of the position seems as if it might have been influenced by the board. This does not seem like the superintendent's normal manner. Another of your colleagues expresses such disappointment that she vows never to apply for another administrative position again. The third one is going to refuse to do any extra duty as a sign of protest. All three of them also indicate that they will not give the new assistant principal any help whatsoever. "If he's so good as to be hired instead of us, then let him fend for himself."

What would you do? Develop a plan of action, taking into consideration your future goals as well as your sense of professionalism and ethics. Kindly align your plan with ISLLC Standard 6: *An education leader promotes the success of every student by understanding, responding to, and influencing the political, social, economic, legal, and cultural context.*

Ethical Considerations

It's easy to let one's emotions take control, but that most likely isn't the right way to align oneself for future consideration. As far as boycotting any assistance to the new person, not only is that immature behavior, but it also borders on being unethical. Once again, what's best for students is of primary concern. Our personal ego games cannot stand in the way of achieving the overall goal of helping students.

On the other hand, there is some credibility to letting the superintendent know about the internal candidates' displeasure with the way they were treated. One has to ask how the superintendent will interpret this. Will he respect them for standing up for their beliefs, or will he see them as standing in the way of progress? If his hand had been forced by the board, he never will admit that, but for future administrators not to recognize that political dynamic might cause him to reconsider their administrative potential.

To refuse to do any extra duties or to simply withdraw from any future consideration probably verifies that this person is not the right choice to serve in an administrative position. This really is an opportunity for the internal candidates not only to show that they are team players, but also that they are resilient and can bounce back from difficult times.

5-5. JAKE'S CLASSROOM MANAGEMENT (ISLLC STANDARD 2)

Jake Johnson is a 25-year veteran who has been teaching vocational education all his life. He fondly remembers the days when students wanted to learn about metals and woods. Back in the early days of his teaching career, he didn't have any discipline problems in his labs. Unfortunately for Jake, today's students aren't the same as he remembers from 25 years ago. Jake never misses an opportunity to express his displeasure with today's students. He complains that the students don't respect him and that they don't care at all about learning. Having this attitude is not something that Jake can suppress. Students know that he doesn't like them and that they're not living up to his expectations.

Given the slightest opportunity, the students typically play jokes or pranks on their teacher. Because Jake's classroom is the shop (metals and woods), students have a lot of freedom. Whether they unplug tools and then ask Mr. Johnson why the tool won't work, or they toss things at each other behind his back, or make gestures when he isn't looking, it's obvious to Jake and to any observer that there are problems in Jake's classes. Thus far, there haven't been any serious threats to the safety of students, and although the students' antics infuriate Jake, students have been able to successfully make their wooden birdhouses and metal toolboxes.

You are the new assistant principal, and within the first month, you can't help but notice the large number of discipline referrals that Jake sends to you on a daily basis. According to the handbook, you dutifully assign after-school detentions, but that really hasn't had an impact on student behavior in Jake's classes. Of course, Jake comes in at least once a week to complain to you about how little respect today's students have for teachers. As you have analyzed both his complaints and his discipline referrals, there doesn't seem to be anything of real substance, just a cranky teacher who hasn't adjusted to a changing society. Nevertheless, you are determined to help him. You tell him that you will visit his classroom to see firsthand what the kids are up to. He welcomes your offer, but he also reinforces his belief that today's kids are not as good as yesterday's kids. "You'll see what I mean! These kids just don't want to learn! How can I teach them when they don't care about learning?"

The next morning you visit Jake's class, and you notice little childish acts going on behind the teacher's back: students looking at each other and rolling their eyes at what the teacher says, students passing notes and giggling, students doing homework from another class, and so on. The room is set up with workstations/tables at which four students sit. Of course, there are various stations containing power equipment. During today's lesson, Jake is instructing the group at the beginning of the period. Then Jake dismisses the students to go to the various equipment stations. The students quickly move to their stations in a rowdy and noisy manner. Jake flashes a look at you, almost to say, "Do you see what I mean?" Of course, Jake does nothing to alter the students' noisy behavior. You also notice that when students are working on their projects, they make a game of calling the teacher to help them. Of course, he can only answer one at a time, and then the others use this as a reason not to work until he gets to them. You also notice that when Jake works with individual students, he turns his back to the other students. You wonder why he has to lean over the student's back, instead of facing the student (and the class). As some students finish their projects earlier than others, they simply wander to other stations, presumably to watch their classmates' progress and to offer help. The reality is that they engage in horseplay, which inevitably slows the progress of those students who aren't done with their projects. You spend most of the period in Jake's class, and then leave about 15 minutes before the end of the class. Jake is free during the next period, so you plan to visit him and talk about what you saw.

Needless to say, Jake makes a big deal about how terrible today's kids are, and he pays little attention to your suggestions that he not turn his back on the class when working with individual students. You also suggest that if he were to give clearer instructions and then ask students at random to explain what they're supposed to do, that might eliminate the game of everyone asking him for help at once. He seems oblivious to your suggestion. You tell him that students should not be allowed to wander around the shop when they finish their projects. Jake's response is, "What am I supposed to do, chain them to their tables?" At the end of your conference with Jake, he tells you that the students' behavior got even worse when you left the room. You smile and ask, "Jake, do you expect me to stay in your classes every day, all period long?" Jake's response surprises you. "Yes, I expect you to support me. How can I teach when the kids won't behave? Your job is to maintain discipline in this school so the teachers can teach." You reply that Jake's job is to teach *and* to maintain discipline in the classroom, and your job is to handle things that he can't. You also remind him that there are 75 teachers in this high school. If they all had this attitude, you wouldn't possibly be able to be in 75 classrooms every day. Jake becomes very upset and storms out of the room.

Just after Jake leaves your office, you get a phone call from the superintendent asking you to come to his office, which also is in the high school. The superintendent is in his second year in the position and at the school. Prior to his coming to this school, he was assistant superintendent in a large high school district. Prior to that, he was a department chair in that same district. Your current principal does not speak highly of the superintendent and has often mentioned that the superintendent doesn't have a clue about building leadership because he has never been a principal. You have a good relationship with the superintendent (he thought enough of you to hire you), and you don't see things the same way that your principal does.

Upon reaching the superintendent's office, you quickly learn that a board member has been questioning the superintendent about Jake's classroom management. You not only can tell that the superintendent is irritated by the board member's interference in school matters, but you also can tell that the superintendent isn't going to challenge the board member. The superintendent asks you to begin keeping a log of the discipline issues stemming from Jake's classroom. You inform the superintendent of your plans to continue to visit Jake's classes and to offer him suggestions for improvement. The superintendent replies that it might be too late for that, but for now, be sure to keep good records. The superintendent also explains that he understands that you are overwhelmed with your workload, but this has to be a priority. You agree, but you also wonder how you're going to handle all your responsibilities plus this new duty of frequently visiting Jake's classroom. The superintendent also explains that he is going to ask the principal to visit Jake's room, and that you and the principal need to coordinate your schedules so that one of you is in every one of Jake's classes. You don't have to spend the entire period, but you do have to be sure to be in there for a short time each period.

As you leave the superintendent's office, you reflect on this morning's visit to Jake's room and his response during your attempts to help him. You wonder if Jake isn't his own worst enemy. Furthermore, you wonder where this situation with the board member is going. Will you be able to help Jake to turn things around? Why the record-keeping? You suspect that the superintendent is beginning to build a case. As you reach your office, the principal is sitting there waiting for you. He's already been given orders by the superintendent to observe Jake's classes, and he wants to build a schedule of visits with you. While you and he determine who's going to observe which classes, the principal expresses concern for Jake's mental status. He explains that five years ago, Jake had a "nervous breakdown." The principal is concerned that all these visits might trigger another breakdown, and he blames the superintendent for that. You explain to the principal that the board member really is the source of the observations, but the principal continues to blame the superintendent.

The next morning, you again visit Jake's first-period class, and you see many of the same behaviors that you saw yesterday. Jake has not taken any of your suggestions to heart; he continues to turn his back on the class, and students still walk around when they finish their projects. His directions to the class are better than those he gave yesterday, but they could use more clarification as indicated by the number of requests for help. You wonder if making metal toolboxes is so difficult that the students have to ask so many questions. You also wonder if Jake has given too much detail to his directions, thereby creating confusion. It seems to you that a sample of a completed toolbox or birdhouse might be a good thing to show them at the beginning of the unit. Of course, Jake is very particular about what constitutes an "A" toolbox. After class, you ask Jake what determines an "A" toolbox, and what determines a "C" toolbox. What you really want to know is if the students understand the difference between an "A" and a "C" toolbox. Jake's response is shocking to you. He explains that he knows the difference, and he expects the kids to know the difference. When you ask to see the rubric for evaluating toolboxes, he stares blankly at you. You quickly find out that he has no rubric!

During the third-period class, the principal is scheduled to observe Jake's class. You are in your office, processing discipline referrals with two students who got into a "teddy bear fight," when you see Ralph, the director of buildings and grounds, waiting outside your door. You finish with the students and ask Ralph to come in. He tells you that while the principal was observing Jake's class, someone tossed a firecracker into the wastebasket. The principal didn't see it until it blew up and started a fire in the wastebasket. One of the custodians heard the noise and ran to the metals shop; he quickly grabbed the fire extinguisher off the wall and put out the wastebasket fire. Your first thought is, "Wow, Jake really is in trouble now."

Not surprisingly, the superintendent phones you and asks that you provide him with a detailed list of every discipline referral that Jake has written so far this year. He also explains that the board member's son phoned his dad to tell him about the wastebasket incident, and that board member wants Jake removed from his teaching duties for safety reasons. The superintendent further explains that the only way he could calm the board member was to assure him that either you or the principal would continue to be in every one of Jake's classes. He also gives you the latitude to assign a guidance counselor to watch Jake's classroom if you can't make it.

You are reluctant to put a counselor in this position, but you have to be at a special education cooperative meeting tomorrow morning, and the principal can't cover the class either. You call in your most senior guidance counselor and ask him to help out. He agrees, and tells you that he's already heard about the wastebasket incident. Like you, he wants to help Jake, but he's afraid that things might be too far down the road.

After a week of having you or the principal (or an occasional counselor) visit Jake's classes, things have calmed down significantly in the metals and wood shops. While you resent having to spend so much of your valuable time "babysitting," you also recognize that kids are learning instead of misbehaving. One morning the superintendent comes to your office and informs you that Jake no longer will be with us, that he has accepted a "buy-out." As he gives you the details, you learn that the association has agreed to a three-year severance package for Jake. You are sad that it has come to this, but you also realize that this is beyond your control.

Just after the superintendent leaves your office, Jake comes in. You tell him how sorry you are about the way things happened, but that you would keep your eyes and ears open about vocational teaching jobs. You also suggest that perhaps a fresh start in another district would give him a chance to establish himself. You are very surprised when Jake blames you for "setting him up." He believes that the list of his discipline referrals that you forwarded to the superintendent is what caused all this trouble for him. He resents that you compiled that list, and he tells you that you have destroyed him and his family. Before you can say anything, he storms out of the room. Knowing that you tried to help him, and that you were following orders from the superintendent, you are quite troubled. You wonder if there could have been a way to prevent this outcome.

From a supervision perspective, consider the following:

- Could this situation have been prevented? If so, how?
- Hindsight is always better than foresight. Even though you are a new assistant principal, is there anything that you should have done differently?
- Should the superintendent have reacted differently to the board member's demands?
- How would you handle a teacher who is oblivious to your suggestions as well as to what he is doing wrong regarding classroom management?

Create a plan of how you would have handled the situation. You may use bulleted statements, but be sure to align your plan with ISLLC Standard 2: *An educator promotes the success of every student by advocating, nurturing, and sustaining a school culture and instructional program conducive to student learning and staff professional growth.*

Ethical Considerations

The first question one might ask is, "How did things get to this point?" Had Jake been properly supervised and guided throughout his 25-year career, this situation most likely would not have happened. How can a principal not notice that one of his teachers is not staying abreast of current trends in his content area? How can a principal not know about the discipline situation that continues to erode in the teacher's classroom? Most likely, the principal was not doing a good job of visiting classrooms, of getting to know what's going on in the classrooms, and of providing true guidance and supervision of teachers.

The assistant principal, being new to the job, is learning a lot and seems to have the right focus by trying to help this struggling teacher. But how much will a veteran teacher listen to a new assistant principal? Because the teacher's evaluations have not reflected any problems, nor have they offered any suggestions for improvement, the teacher assumes that his teaching is fine. In the absence of any help to the teacher, one can understand why he believes that the students are at fault. It can't be the teacher who needs to change, because his evaluations have not indicated any need for change.

The assistant principal is in a very tough position, because whatever he does or says certainly shows the principal's prior negligence of supervisory responsibilities. On the other hand, because he is new, he wants to please the superintendent, even if the superintendent might be micro-managing the situation. The assistant principal would like to offer help and guidance to Jake before giving up on him. The superintendent wants to placate the board member by getting rid of the teacher. It's easy to recognize that the teacher is not doing the job he should be doing, but it's also easy to understand why. He has not been given appropriate guidance and supervision in the past. What is the ethical course of action? Should the teacher be given an opportunity to grow and change, especially in light of his 25-year tenure at this school? Doesn't the school have an obligation to help its employees?

On the other hand, is it ethical to put students' safety in jeopardy while the teacher is learning to improve? Of course, short of simply removing the teacher from the classroom, he most likely will remain there until the end of the school year. Isn't the safety of the students in jeopardy for the next few months? Couldn't the teacher be assigned to a mentor who would co-teach with him, thereby helping the teacher and providing a safe environment in the classroom? Wouldn't this be more fiscally responsible than paying legal fees to get rid of the teacher? These are ethical questions that the superintendent should be considering, but while the assistant principal might be thinking about them, the reality is that things are well beyond his control at this point.

Knowing that the superintendent is building a case against the teacher, does the assistant principal refuse to collect the necessary data? While that might make him feel better, the data can be acquired with or without the assistant principal's help. He would be putting his own job in jeopardy, but he would not be able to affect the outcome of the teacher's future. It seems to be a sure thing that the teacher's job already is lost. Perhaps the best thing the assistant principal can do is to offer advice to the teacher regarding classroom management in the hope that Jake will be able to take that advice with him in his next job.

Because the superintendent also is new, he doesn't have either the confidence or experience to diffuse the situation with the board member, or he has a need to flex his muscles to show his authority. One might suggest to the superintendent that he needs to be less of a micro-manager, but in light of the fact that his principal is a lame duck waiting to retire and the assistant principal is a rookie, the superintendent most likely feels a justifiable need to be very directive in situations like this. We shouldn't be too quick to judge the superintendent until we understand his motivation and whatever pressures he faces from the board members.

5-6. THE OUTDOOR EDUCATION PROGRAM THAT GOES BAD (ISLLC STANDARD 6)

You are a middle school principal in a suburban town. Your school has approximately 650 students, and it is one of three middle schools in the district. There has been a tradition of running an outdoor education program every fall. Within a three-week period, each middle school uses the same campground for the outdoor education program, but they stagger their schedules so that only one middle school is at the campground at the same time. The event takes place on a Thursday evening, Friday all day and night, and Saturday morning. The students are bused home after lunch on Saturday.

The program includes many team-building and leadership activities, all of which are intended to set a positive tone of respect and high expectations for the school year. The student participants are sixth graders. The seventh and eighth graders already participated when they were sixth graders. One of the goals of the program is to introduce the sixth graders to their new environment: middle school. The outdoor education program has become a tradition to which students look forward. It is a "rite of passage" from elementary school to middle school.

The sixth-grade faculty have assumed the outdoor education program as part of their responsibilities, and they willingly organize and coordinate the daily activities. They also act as chaperones in each of the cabins, which accommodate approximately 20 students. To help with the supervision of the cabins, the library aides and teacher aides often volunteer their services, especially those aides whose own children are participating in the program. The teachers and aides don't receive a stipend for supervising students and conducting the various activities, even though the program does encompass two evenings and a Saturday morning. It is considered part of their daily work, and the evening and weekend supervision is considered professional service. This is consistent with the district's value and belief that teaching is servant leadership.

All in all, it has been a very successful program, and one that receives positive comments from students, parents, and faculty alike. As principal, you are proud of your faculty and students as they participate in this important event. On the day before the outdoor education program, you receive a phone call from a teacher's aide who is very concerned about tomorrow's events. She proceeds to inform you that the scuttlebutt around the faculty lounge is that once the students are asleep in their cabins, some of the teachers are planning to visit a local bar for some "rest and relaxation" after a hard day of leading and supervising various activities of the outdoor education program. The teacher's aide explains that this not only leaves her and the other aides behind to supervise the students, but it also presents an unsafe situation in that the cabins wouldn't be covered by a sufficient number of adults. Furthermore, if word gets out to the students, this would create a negative impression on the very students whom they're trying to teach school values of respect, leadership, and trustworthiness.

Needless to say, this is most disturbing to you. First of all, you are extremely disappointed in your faculty members. Second, you feel that your trust in them has been betrayed. Third, you realize that it really is too late to cancel the outdoor education program. Too many students and parents have been looking forward to the event with eagerness and high expectations. You are faced with a serious dilemma.

How would you solve it? Explain your action plan in a bulleted format aligned with ISLLC Standard 6: *An education leader promotes the success of every student by understanding, responding to, and influencing the political, social, economic, legal, and cultural context.*

Ethical Considerations

As mentioned previously, the outdoor education program is an important rite of passage for the students. It also sets the tone for their next three years in your school. They are taught values, and they get to know students from the other elementary schools that feed into your middle school. The bonding, collaboration, and induction to your school are extremely valuable. As much as you'd like to cancel or at least postpone the event, you realize that such a decision most likely would be counterproductive.

Also, how would you handle the explanation? Do you go public with the details? To do so would be detrimental to the reputation of your school and your faculty in general, as well as to the sixth-grade teachers in particular. On the other hand, if the teacher's aides know about this, can you trust them to keep it to themselves? How much information will leak out to parents or, even worse, to the media? These are tough questions that you must take into consideration as you make a decision.

Another question is about the reliability of your source. Would she make this up? How can you further investigate this before making any accusations? On the other hand, if you take too much time to investigate the situation, it might be too late even to stop the teachers' plan to leave the cabins. Do you immediately hold a meeting of the sixth-grade teachers, presumably to do some last-minute checking on the details, and then confront them with what you've heard? If you use this approach, would you be unknowingly implicating your source? Would the sixth-grade teachers figure out who reported this to you? Or, even worse, would they accuse the wrong person, thereby causing serious division and disharmony among the sixth-grade team?

Should you let things go as planned and then do a surprise visit to the cabins? If you choose this plan, would you conduct such a surprise visit one night? If you do that, would they simply move their bar plans to the next night? Does that mean that you would make two surprise visits? Although you don't mind giving up two nights to make these visits, what message does this send to your teachers? Do you convey interest in their program, or do you convey a message that you don't trust them?

Ultimately, there is a safety concern, and you must make sure that the cabins are adequately supervised. Also, there is the problem related to values and being a role model to the students. Simply stated, the teachers are jeopardizing their credibility with students and parents alike. They also are jeopardizing the school's credibility with the camp personnel and whoever might see them at the bar. If this gets out to the public, they also are jeopardizing the school's and the district's credibility with their stakeholders.

5-7. THE MOVE FROM ASSOCIATE CHAIR TO DEPARTMENT CHAIR: HOW TO EVALUATE MY PREDECESSOR (ISLLC STANDARD 3)

You are an associate department chairperson in a suburban high school. Because the school has two campuses, which serve a combined total of 2,500 students, each content area department has an associate department chair and a department chair. Basically, the associate department chair does the same duties as the department chair, with each of them being placed in one of the campuses. Those duties include setting and managing the department budget, scheduling the the department courses and its teachers, leading the teachers in a textbook review and adoption process, and evaluating the teachers. The associate chair is evaluated by the department chair and reports to that person in the chain of command. Of course, the building principal is ultimately in charge of all teachers including the associate department chairs or the department chairs who are assigned to his or her building.

You are serving as the associate department chair and have enjoyed the past six years in this position. You work well with the department chair, who has given you complete supervisory responsibility over the department at your campus. In other words, you are in charge of the department at your campus, and he is in charge of the department at his campus. Even the department meetings are held by campus, and rarely do all the department members ever meet together.

Recently, you notice that the department chair has been making several mistakes regarding communicating with you, sending you the appropriate allocations for the budget, and maintaining a positive tone. You understand that he is having some personal problems unrelated to school, and you suspect that he has been resorting to alcohol as a way of handling his problems. During this semester, some of the students from your campus are taking courses at the other campus. This is due to available space and specialized electives that are offered at one campus but not the other. For this reason, you have to designate a teacher who will split the day between the two campuses. As you ask around your department, no one really wants to do this, but they all agree to do so if you need them to travel.

You decide that you will assume the traveling teacher duties for the first semester. This not only will show that you're willing to pitch in and take a turn, but also it will give you an opportunity to meet with the department chair on a daily basis. This probably isn't a good thing for him, however. You can't help but notice that the department chair shows a disproportionate number of movies to his classes. The appropriate way to use movies in a classroom setting is never to show them from start to finish as entertainment. Not only is this in violation of copyright regulations, but it also is not the best way to utilize them as educational tools. The correct way to utilize movies is to show a short segment that emphasizes the topic or lesson for the day. Furthermore, in this era of learning standards, teachers rarely have time to give up to a movie.

The department chair clearly hasn't prepared his lessons for the day and has resorted to movies as a way to entertain the students. To make matters worse, as the other teachers see the department chair doing this, they too are beginning to show movies from start to finish as a way to entertain the students. You can't help but worry about how well the students will perform on the state test, especially when the teachers aren't using their classroom time wisely to prepare students for the test.

You mention this to the department chair, but he clearly doesn't care to hear about your concerns. He quickly pulls rank on you by reminding you that he is the department chair and you report to him. This is so "out-of-character" for him that you are shocked by this response. As much as you try to reason with him and to determine how you can help this person who once was a very effective teacher, it becomes very obvious to you that your words are falling on deaf ears. Later that evening, you receive a phone call from the department chair who apologizes for being rude to you. He sounds as if he has been drinking, and his sentences are not always coherent as he speaks with you. Then you hear the clinking of ice cubes in the background, and you realize that he is drinking while he's talking to you. Unfortunately, there isn't a clear purpose to this conversation other than a simple apology for being rude to you.

You now suspect that the reason the department chair isn't prepared for his lessons each day most likely is due to his drinking at night. He clearly needs help, and he doesn't want your help. But his students are not getting the proper instruction that they should be getting, especially prior to the state test. Also, the department chair's behavior is having a negative impact on the department members as their teaching is declining in effectiveness. After much deliberation, you decide to go to the building principal of that campus and seek his advice.

He thanks you for affirming some of his suspicions. You are relieved to know that you're not the only one to notice the department chair's need for assistance. The principal agrees to approach the department chair with an offer for help through the district's employee assistance program. A few days later, the principal calls you into his office to explain that the department chair has not agreed to take advantage of the employee assistance program. Specifically, he has rejected any suggestion that he might need counseling. The principal further explains that he has decided to remove the department chair from his supervisory duties and that he would like to appoint you as the department chair. Your position of associate department chair will be posted as a position for which the other department members may apply.

The principal tells you what you already know, that the department chair will need careful supervision as a teacher, and he expects you, as department chair, to provide that careful supervision. You realized this when you accepted the position. It will give you an opportunity to employ your best leadership skills.

Knowing the former department chair's feelings toward your offer to help, how would you provide supervision that hopefully would result in an improved attitude and more effective teaching? Also, what would you do about improving the attitudes and teaching of the other department members? Develop an action plan in a bulleted format aligned with ISLLC Standard 3: *An education leader promotes the success of every student by ensuring management of the organization, operation, and resources for a safe, efficient, and effective learning environment.*

Ethical Considerations

From the former department chair's perspective, you're the one who snitched on him. He doesn't think he needs any help, and he might even suspect that you did this just to get his job. Handling his supervision and improvement requires a very delicate and tactful approach. If you use a directive approach, which he needs, he most likely will reject your attempts to help and might even challenge your authority over him. On the other hand, if you don't give him specific direction, he probably won't improve. Somehow you have to win his confidence and get him to realize that he needs to change his teaching behaviors.

You are in a tough position, because not only is the former department chair willing to challenge your authority, but the rest of the department members at that campus also are willing to challenge you. After all, you're the one who is questioning their teaching practice of showing so many movies. You not only have to win the confidence of the former department chair, but also theirs as well. They also might see you as having purposely dethroned the former department chair for personal gain. Because you haven't directly supervised them in the past, you have very little credibility with them.

5-8. A NEW ASSISTANT SUPERINTENDENT IS CHOSEN OVER AN INTERNAL CANDIDATE (ISLLC STANDARD 3)

You have applied for an assistant superintendent's position in a suburban school district. Specifically, the position oversees the curriculum, instruction, and assessment programs of the school district. Because the school district is well known for being on the cutting edge of instructional technology, you are extremely happy to be called for an interview. Upon arriving at the school district central office, you are greeted cordially and offered coffee or water, and you immediately have a favorable impression of the school district. The interview goes quite well, and you are impressed by the questions, most of which focus on mission and vision. You are told that you are one of three people being interviewed and that the committee will decide upon two of the three to be called back for a second interview.

A day later, you receive a call to come in for your second interview, and you have a very good feeling about your possibility of being hired in this district. The second interview begins with the original committee, and then you are taken to a room in which the curriculum and instruction directors and the secretary are present. This portion of the interview also goes quite well, and you leave with a very favorable impression.

Two days later, the superintendent phones to explain that he would like to meet alone with you to talk more specifically about mission and vision. But he would like you to plan on spending the entire day in the school district. One of the principals will take you on a tour of the district and show you each of the schools. You also will spend time meeting two elementary school principals and two junior high school principals in their respective schools. They will take you on a personal tour of their buildings, and they will report back their impressions of you to the superintendent. You know that this is an important step in the interview process, and you know that they are quite interested in you. Also, you find out that there is one other semifinalist who is going through the same process of tours.

On the day of your scheduled meeting with the superintendent and the tour of the district, there is a bad snowstorm. You successfully make the commute, but it does take a little longer than you expected. You phone the superintendent when you are about 10 minutes away just to let him know that you are coming despite the snowy weather conditions and bad traffic. He explains that he is impressed by your fortitude in making the commute. Apparently, there was some talk about whether he should have cancelled the interview because of the weather. He chose not to cancel, and he is pleased that you have successfully made the journey to the district.

The interview and the tour, along with the meetings with the principals, all go quite well, and again you are convinced that you have a very good chance of getting this job. The next day, the superintendent calls to offer you the job, but he wants to meet with you over lunch to discuss salary and benefits. That meeting also goes well, and the salary package is very much acceptable to you. The superintendent gives you a day to think about it, but you quickly counter by telling him that you don't need any time to think about it. This is the job you want, and the salary package is fine with you. He then explains that the other candidate for the position was an internal candidate. You are experienced enough in the world of administration that this doesn't faze you.

The superintendent admires your self-confidence, but he cautions you that she is one of the curriculum directors (language arts) in your department. She will report directly to you in the chain of command, and he suspects that she will not be easy to work with when she finds out that she did not get the position. He assures you that he will take care of notifying her and that he will get back to you about how she receives this news.

The next day, the superintendent phones to say that the language arts curriculum director did not take the news well and that she even threatened to quit her position. Knowing that she usually overreacts to situations (which is one of the reasons she wasn't chosen for this position), he gave her some time to cool off. She then withdrew her threat and said that she would like to continue in her current position for the time being. Nevertheless, she isn't a "happy camper." To placate her, the superintendent is willing to offer her a slight promotion, but he wants to run that idea past you. He would like her to be in charge of some of the grants as well as her content area. This added responsibility would give her a slight increase in salary to match her additional duties. He asks you to consider the idea and to get back to him next week. If you agree to it, you can meet with her and offer her the position. You recognize that this could be a way to win her over and to develop a smooth transition for your coming into the department and leading it.

After giving it some thought, you agree that this would be a good idea. Not only would it possibly ease some ill will with the curriculum director, but also it would show the superintendent that you are willing to accept his ideas and to implement them. How would it look if you told the superintendent that you didn't like his idea? As agreed upon, you set up a meeting with the curriculum director to talk about the idea. She prefers to come to your present district office rather than having you drive to your new office. You find this interesting, but agree to it. You are very surprised when you offer her the new position to find that she isn't happy and that she needs time to think about it.

A few days later, she phones to say that she will accept your offer of the new position. You are concerned that she still doesn't sound very happy, but you realize that she probably hasn't gotten over her feelings of rejection. You explain to her that you sense some sadness on her part and that you also have had that experience in the past. But you are looking forward to working with her and the other members of the curriculum and instruction department. You attempt at being understanding isn't very well accepted by her, but she remains polite with you. When you phone the superintendent to tell him that she has accepted the position, you also explain her reaction. He then tells you that she isn't a very happy person by nature and that she will need your guidance and support. You begin to wonder how she made it so far in the interview process, if the superintendent knows that she has a sour personality, but you suspect there must be some political reason.

When July arrives and you begin your new job, you spend time getting to know each of your staff members. You have three curriculum coordinators, one of which also holds the title of assessment director. When you explain to him that the language arts curriculum coordinator also will be responsible for some of the grants, you can't help but notice the pained look on his face. You ask about this, but he simply says that you will learn a lot about your staff as time goes on. He also assures you that he will do whatever he can to help you make the transition into your new job.

When you meet with the language arts curriculum coordinator, you still sense some ill feelings on her part. As she explains her plans for one of the grant applications, you are astounded. She is planning to include an expectation that you know is not reasonable. You question her about this, and she is quick to criticize your questioning her, saying, "If I don't set high expectations, what message are we sending to the students and their teachers?"

You try to explain that setting high, attainable expectations is great; but setting high, unattainable expectations sets everyone up for failure, including her. The grant requires an evaluation component along with anticipated results. She wants to write in that 100% of the students will show at least one grade level increase by the end of the school year. You know that many children are already above their grade level, but they won't necessarily make a full-year gain by the end of the year. In other words, if a sixth grader scores at the seventh-grade level at the beginning of sixth grade, that student might not make a full-year gain to eighth grade by the end of the seventh-grade year. The student might make a half-year gain, which still would put her above the normal grade level expectation for sixth graders. The student would end the year with a mid-seventh grade score, which still would be six months ahead of the norm. You are afraid that stating every student will show a full-year gain not only isn't attainable, but it also could jeopardize future funding of the grant.

She persists in arguing that her expectations are reasonable and that you haven't been in the district long enough to know what's reasonable. She then makes some insulting comments about your previous district and that this district has much smarter students than you had previously. Not only do you dislike her attitude, but you certainly don't appreciate anyone making such comments about your previous district.

How do you handle this situation? You not only are dealing with academic issues, but also with personal issues. Explain, in a bulleted manner, your plan of action. Be sure to align with ISLLC Standard 3: *An education leader promotes the success of every student by ensuring management of the organization, operation, and resources for a safe, efficient, and effective learning environment.*

Ethical Considerations

Knowing that the language arts curriculum director is setting up the students, teachers, and the grant for failure makes vitally important that you do not allow her to write unattainable expectations into the grant. Trying to be collegial by appealing to reason and common sense isn't working. It is obvious that regardless of your personal leadership style preference, you have to become very directive when dealing with this person.

On the other hand, you also know that once you use a direct approach and tell her not to set such high expectations, she undoubtedly will run to the superintendent (and whoever her political power base might be) and boldly state that you are against setting high expectations. This won't bode well for you in your position as a district leader, second in the chain of command. Because you are so new, you haven't had the time to prove yourself and to establish your credibility. Furthermore, if she complains that you used a very direct approach of command with her, you also realize that this won't speak well of your leadership style. This certainly wasn't the style you communicated in your interview.

To complicate matters, you also know that if you allow the language arts coordinator the latitude to try her expectations, there is a great likelihood that the students won't reach those expectations, and the grant could be lost. Needless to say, this would come directly back to you. If the grant were to be lost, not only would the district lose money, but the reading specialists whose salaries are covered by that grant could lose their jobs. You also could lose your job if the superintendent were to view this situation as your negligence in supervising your staff.

This situation obviously tests the ethics of the new assistant superintendent. While there could be an allegation that the language arts coordinator has purposely set you up for failure, you have no proof of that. She might really believe that she's doing the right thing. You also haven't yet found out what political base she has, but you strongly suspect some political support if the superintendent even granted her an interview for your position. Although these unknowns could alter your decision, ultimately, you have to keep the best interests of the students in mind.

5-9. THE SCIENCE TEACHER'S SENIORITY VS. THE INSTRUCTIONAL PROGRAM (ISLLC STANDARD 5)

You are the assistant principal of a large, suburban high school. One of your responsibilities is the master schedule. The process that has been in place for years includes the department chairs creating schedules for their respective departments and then submitting them to you, meshing these schedules into a master schedule that not only meets the needs of the departments but also ensures a quality program for all 1,300 students. The process has worked year after year, but not without a lot of negotiating with the department chairs. Although some of your predecessors have taken a less collegial and more bureaucratic approach, they either left the district or left the position and returned to the classroom. You are convinced that the only way for your career to survive this process is to barter with the department chairs and to grant them as much of their recommendations as you possibly can.

As you examine the science department schedule, you notice that the department chair has scheduled one teacher with all the biology courses and another teacher with three biology and two general science courses. While you question why he didn't more equally schedule the "plum assignments" of biology between the two teachers, you don't want to challenge his recommendation. Upon further scrutiny, you find that the teacher with the general science courses is not certified to teach them. The teacher who is being recommended to teach all the biology courses is certified to teach both biology and general science, but the other teacher only has the biology endorsement. What do you do?

One option is to go back to the department chair and tell him that you've changed the schedule to match the teachers' certification. Another option is to kick the schedule back to the department chair and tell him that he has to fix it. Knowing the tenor of the department chairs, you choose the second option.

You are shocked when the department chair returns the schedule to you without any changes except that the name of the teacher assigned to biology and general science has been deleted. You ask him to explain, and he tells you that he is going to release the biology/general science teacher because she is not certified to teach next year's schedule. You reply by reminding him that he could flip-flop the two schedules and not have to release anyone. You add that the teacher in danger of being released has had excellent evaluations. The department chair agrees with you that she is an excellent teacher, and he tells you that he doesn't really want to release her, but without proper certification, he can't schedule her to teach general science. Obviously, he's dodging the real issue, so you bring it out into the open.

"Why don't you give her the full biology schedule, and give the other teacher the biology–general science schedule?"

His response is disappointing. "Barb has more seniority than does Sally. I asked Barb if she'd be willing to teach Sally's schedule, but Barb refused. I'm going to honor her decision."

You pursue this deeper by explaining that Sally is a single mom and needs a job as much, maybe more than Barb does. You ask the department chair how he can turn someone loose, take away Sally's job just because Barb doesn't want to teach general science. The department chair replies, "Barb worked hard to get certification in both areas of biology and general science. Sally only pursued biology. It's not my fault that she didn't have the foresight to expand her marketability by taking general science courses."

As the supervisor, what should you do? Should you "pull rank" on the department chair to ensure that both teachers keep their jobs, or do you support the department chair's recommendation even though it will result in the dismissal of an effective teacher? Create an action plan in a bulleted format aligned with ISLLC Standard 5: *An education leader promotes the success of every student by acting with integrity, fairness, and in an ethical manner.*

Ethical Considerations

For any supervisor to willingly dismiss a good teacher doesn't make any sense. However, one has to understand the dynamics at play in this situation. Union leaders have an obligation to protect the rights of their members. Also, seniority is a bone of contention between administration and teachers. Administration maintains the right of assignment. Teachers are hired to teach in the district, but not necessarily in any particular school. In a high school, teachers are hired to teach a content area, but they can be assigned to teach slow learners or advanced learners. It all depends on the enrollment and other scheduling complexities. Union leaders want to support their membership by pushing hard for rights of seniority, but the only legal requirement regarding seniority is to use a seniority list for RIFs (reduction in force not related to performance.)

Because the science department chair also was a union leader, he might not have been able to view the situation objectively. He most likely was looking at the seniority issue as a priority. The administrator, on the other hand, was able to see a bigger picture related to retaining good teachers as well as what might be in the best interests of the students. This is not to say that the department chair wasn't interested in what's best for students, and he probably would argue that by supporting his union members, he was ensuring quality teaching in the classroom.

For the assistant principal to overturn the department chair's scheduling decision could be misinterpreted as micro-management. On the other hand, not to overturn it would result in the dismissal of a good teacher. Hopefully the two could reasonably discuss this and come to a mutual understanding of what's best for students and teachers. If this discussion cannot occur, the assistant principal would have to exert his authority. Not to do so would not only result in losing a good teacher, but it also would set a precedent regarding personal preference over the general good of teachers and students. All too often, supervisors can lose sight of the importance of trying to nurture and support their teachers. Teachers should not be considered as dispensable items, but rather as valuable assets to the school.

CHAPTER 6

School Community Relations and Strategic Planning

An often over looked area of importance in the role of an educational leader is that of school community relations and strategic planning. Actually the two are inseparable; an educational leader can't expect to have a good relationship with the school community unless he or she has been involved in the school's strategic planning process, and the strategic planning process can't be effective unless it is steeped in good school community relations. The public supports our schools through tax dollars as well as through moral support, volunteer service, and outright donations. Unfortunately, the public doesn't really know much about its schools. What the public does know is based either on news stories from the media or on hearsay from students, employees, and parents. Often the information shared by these groups is the result of some negative experience with the schools. While the news media will occasionally report about the positive activities and the successes of students, these stories typically don't make the front-page headlines.

Consequently, the public supports an institution about which it knows little. From this perspective alone, the educational leader can grasp the importance of good school community relations. But another complicating factor is the nature of "business" conducted by schools. Because the public tends to be grounded in the corporate and industrial principles of accountability related to profit and loss, they tend to view schools in the same light as they do corporations and industries. One major difference is that schools don't have a manufactured product that eventually goes on sale. Schools can't control the quality of the raw materials before they enter the system, but a factory can. The varied developmental stages and potential of students often is assumed to be standard or the same for everyone. When the corporate and industrial models of accountability are placed on the schools, the uniqueness and creative aspects of individuals are lost.

In the absence of understanding the nature of work in schools, the public has developed its own understanding of what they think should happen in schools. With good public relations and including the involvement of the public in strategic planning, educational leaders can bridge the chasm of misunderstanding and forge powerful relationships with the community they serve.

Needless to say, whenever human emotions are involved, tact and diplomacy must be utilized when attempting to solve problems. Over the years, schools have met with much criticism, resulting in a lack of public confidence. When students are disciplined, parents and the public often side with the student instead of supporting the school's efforts to teach good appropriate behaviors.

The case studies presented in this chapter are intended to help our future educational leaders to understand the complexities related to dealing with the public. They also are intended to help future leaders to understand the intricacies of marketing the positive aspects of schools.

6-1. THE BAND BOOSTERS AND A TRAILER: A SCHOOL COMMUNITY RELATIONS DILEMMA (ISLLC STANDARD 4)

John Smith is the new principal of a small, blue-collar-town high school. The marching band has 21 students who are hard-working, but their performance isn't appreciated by the fans at the football games. The band typically plays during the first quarter and then leaves. John Smith is puzzled by the community's lack of concern for the band program. No one even talks about it.

One day, the band director comes into John's office indicating his desire to retire. John is grateful for the many, many years of the director's service, and he puts together a nice retirement ceremony. But he also is relieved to know that he now can begin to do something to improve the band.

A new director is hired through a process involving parents and faculty members. One of the first things that the new band director does is to form a band boosters group to fund various costs that the district has not had to absorb in the past. Needless to say, there is a lot of enthusiasm among parents and students who sense a new spirit in the band. Within a one-year period, the band grows from 21 to over 100 participants, some of whom are football players who participate during half-time, then quickly go to the locker room for half-time adjustments.

The band participates in competitions and is quite successful in bringing home awards and honors. But as numbers have grown, more buses are needed for the kids, and there no longer is room for instruments in the back of the bus. Although John has budgeted for band buses in the past, the number of competitions and the number of buses needed are really putting pressure on John's budget. The superintendent's response to John's request for additional transportation money is for John to be "creative and to think outside the box."

The boosters aren't willing to wait for budget discussions to be resolved, and they take it upon themselves to conduct fund-raising to purchase a trailer and tow it with a parent's vehicle. The band director has kept John Smith apprised of this endeavor, and the principal makes sure to be present when the trailer is delivered to the school. The trailer has the school name on it, but it needs to be licensed. Who owns the title? Who carries the insurance? Is the parent's insurance responsible for the trailer? These are questions that suddenly pop up as John shares the good news with the superintendent.

The school district seeks advice of attorney and learns that the boosters are an agent of the school. They have been operating as a free agent, but they realize the need for school district protection in the form of liability insurance, vehicle insurance, and licensing of the vehicle. This raises another question—shouldn't the school district provide the towing vehicle? The only one available is the maintenance pickup truck, which is used by the custodians for Saturday work around the grounds (plowing snow, hauling debris from cleaning the grounds, etc.). Furthermore, the director of buildings and grounds is concerned that if something were to happen to the vehicle while it is towing a trailer (parents might not be as careful with the vehicle as the staff are), this could hamper the Monday through Friday maintenance work that requires the use of the truck.

The only reasonable option is for the district to acquire a vehicle specifically for towing the band trailer. One of the band parents is willing to donate an old Chevy Suburban with 90,000 miles to the program, but only under the condition that the vehicle *not* be used by the maintenance staff. Once again, budgetary issues present themselves.

John Smith is very pleased with the involvement of the boosters, and he wants to support them, but he also understands the superintendent's concerns about what appear to be spiraling costs related to the band program. The boosters are willing to do more fund-raising, but they would like their efforts to go more toward improvement of instruments, new uniforms, and competition-related costs. They see the trailer and the towing vehicle costs as the responsibility of the district.

From a public relations perspective and from a communications perspective, what should John Smith do?

Use a bulleted format to explain the steps of a process that John should follow. Be sure to align your plan with ISLLC Standard 4: *An education leader promotes the success of every student by collaborating with faculty and community members, responding to diverse community interests and needs, and mobilizing community resources.*

Ethical Considerations

There is an old story about a person who receives a free elephant. He declares, "What a great gift! Look at how big it is! Now where do I keep it, and how do I feed it?" To a certain extent, the trailer is like the proverbial elephant. It is a great gift, but now the school has to license, insure, maintain, and tow it. Of course, the band parents had the best of intentions when they donated the trailer. It is needed for the program, and the school cannot afford to buy a trailer. This really is a great gift. The principal has to be thankful and supportive of the band parents. In addition to the trailer, they provide a tremendous service resulting in such a successful program for the students of the high school.

On the other hand, there are some missing pieces in the process. The band director should have known about the band parents' intentions as they were doing fund-raising for the trailer. He should have kept the principal apprised of the plans. Sometimes it's better to seek forgiveness afterward than permission beforehand, and that might have been the case here. Perhaps the band director had been afraid that the idea would be shot down, so he opted to keep quiet until it would be too late to stop the process. Based on the reaction of the superintendent, that very well could have been the case, and who would blame the band director for taking that approach?

From a public relations perspective, the trailer is a large billboard advertising the school and one of its programs. It will be used at contests and parades, which will have good exposure for the school. Also, the band parents are just that—parents. They can spread lots of good news about the school, or they can complain about how unsupportive the school is to their program. A wise principal will recognize the benefits associated both with the gift as well as with the generosity of the band parents. Furthermore, when the trailer arrives, it will be a tremendous photo opportunity and press release for the local news media.

The realities of insuring, maintaining, and licensing the trailer are rather small in contrast with the size of the school's budget. To add a nonmotorized vehicle to the school district's insurance policy would be an insignificant cost. Of greater concern is the towing vehicle. The maintenance staff certainly has a legitimate concern about letting the band parents use the school's pickup truck. That vehicle is not only critical to their daily work, but it could also be needed on a Saturday when the band parents would have it. To rely on the school's pickup truck to be the towing vehicle is not a good plan.

While the donated vehicle has a lot of mileage on it, that does not necessarily mean that it will be an expensive vehicle to maintain. Its use would be limited to parades and contests. Not many miles would be logged on the vehicle if it were reserved solely to tow the band trailer. That could set a precedent for other programs to want their own vehicles, but each request could be handled separately. The need for a vehicle to tow the band trailer is very clear. Also, the concern of the band parent donors that the vehicle would be misused by the maintenance staff and not be available when the band needs it is a legitimate concern. Even though it might be hard to hear that, the principal has to admit that maintenance vehicles are put to hard use.

This is a situation in which diplomacy and tact are key elements of good communication with the band director, the band parents, the maintenance staff, and the superintendent. There is a lot to be gained if the situation is handled well. Conversely, there is a lot to be lost if it is handled poorly.

6-2. THE CENTRAL OFFICE SNITCH (ISLLC STANDARD 3)

You are an assistant superintendent for curriculum and instruction, and you are a former assistant superintendent for human resources in the same district. Recently, you changed positions to acquire a more diversified background in the central office administration of the school district. You hope someday to become the superintendent when the present one retires. There is no desire on your part to rush him to retire; rather, you just want to get as much experience as you can so you will be ready for the position when the time is right.

The practice in your district is for the superintendent to meet with his cabinet every Monday morning. The board of education meets on the first and third Monday of every month, and the focus of the cabinet meetings on those days is that evening's board of education meeting. Not only are the three assistant superintendents (business, human resources, and curriculum and instruction) part of the cabinet, but also included are the special education director, the bilingual education director, and the district grant administrator. Usually, the cabinet meetings are rather lively because the superintendent is not in a good mood on Mondays. His usual practice is to pick on one of the cabinet members throughout the meeting. There doesn't seem to be any pattern as to who is picked for verbal abuse during the meeting. Most likely it is determined by whatever issue seems to bother the superintendent that day. If it's an issue related to money or expenditures, the assistant superintendent for business will catch some criticism. If it's an issue related to staffing, the assistant superintendent for human resources will be criticized. If the issue is regarding test scores, the assistant superintendent for curriculum and instruction will be picked on. Each of the cabinet members has been the victim at some point.

Today, the district grant administrator is the victim. She must have sensed that she was due for this because she is trying to sidetrack the superintendent by sabotaging you. She issues a series of complaints about the district's recent curriculum revisions in the area of reading. But the superintendent becomes angry with her for trying to sidetrack him and launches into a tirade about how the evaluation measures that the district grant administrator had written into a particular grant were unreasonable. He is concerned that the district might lose future funding through that grant if the evaluation measures weren't met. Despite her attempts to defend herself, the grant administrator cannot convince the superintendent to not be concerned about future funding.

Instead, the superintendent begins to raise his voice and pound his fist on the table for emphasis. At one point, he accuses the district grant administrator of not listening to what he is saying to her. The argument continues for more than 20 minutes, and neither person will back down. You and the other assistant superintendents are embarrassed for the grant administrator, but each of the assistant superintendents wonders why the grant administrator doesn't offer to amend the grant evaluation measures, which is what the superintendent seems to want. She persists in arguing with him. You know that her actions will infuriate the superintendent, because he can be a very stubborn person, but so can she.

As you and the other assistant superintendents are making eye contact, each of you notice that the veins on the superintendent's neck are protruding more and more. You are wondering if they're going to pop, and you suspect that same thought is crossing the others' minds as well. You and the other assistant superintendents smile and sheepishly look away for fear of his seeing your smiles. Finally, the arguing stops and the meeting agenda is addressed.

Four hours later, it is noon, and the meeting ends. The superintendent quickly leaves the room as his secretary signals to him that he has an important phone call. You ask the other cabinet members if they'd like to join you for lunch at a nearby restaurant. They agree, except for the district grant administrator. During lunch, the conversation turns to the cabinet meeting. You and the others laugh at the superintendent's veins and how they were popping during the heat of the argument. No one says anything derogatory about the superintendent. The laughter is about his veins. As the food arrives the conversation quickly changes to other topics. Everyone has an enjoyable lunch, especially after such a grueling meeting.

Two days later, the superintendent calls you into his office. He is very upset and tells you that he heard that you were making fun of him at lunch the other day. Of course, you and the others weren't making fun of him, but you were laughing at his veins. You tell him this, but he convinced that you were making fun of him. After he gets this off his chest, his disposition returns to normal, and he talks to you about school district business. All seems to be normal.

As you leave the office, you reflect on the situation. Who would have told him this? As you replay the lunch conversation in your mind, you remember that the bilingual education director wasn't laughing when the others were. You go to the office of the assistant superintendent for human resources to share with him the recent allegation by the superintendent. The assistant superintendent for human resources informs you that the bilingual education director had been complaining about the way that the group made fun of the superintendent on the way back from the restaurant. The group had gone in two cars and she was in the other car than the one in which you were riding.

This information along with your suspicions leads you to believe that she is the one who badmouthed you to the superintendent. Knowing your future aspirations to the superintendency, would she be sabotaging you? Until the superintendent retires, it is important that all of the cabinet members work together. How is this possible when one of the cabinet members is back-stabbing another member? Judging from the way that the superintendent prejudged you based on false information, you realize that going to him with this would be fruitless. What should you do?

Develop a bulleted plan of action explaining how you would handle this political situation. Kindly align your plan with ISLLC Standard 3: *An education leader promotes the success of every student by ensuing management of the organization, operation, and resources for a safe, efficient, and effective learning environment.*

Ethical Considerations

Certainly, the actions on the part of the director of bilingual education weren't very ethical, but she apparently either is unhappy, or she is trying to advance herself at the expense of others. This behavior is not unusual at the senior management level of educational or corporate organizations. There is an old adage, "Two wrongs don't make a right." It is most appropriate here. For you to counter her actions with equally divisive actions might initially make you feel better, but in the long run, you wouldn't be any better than she is from an ethical perspective.

You might want to confront her about this, especially because you are her direct supervisor, and she has just done an "end-run" past you to the next person in the chain of command. That certainly is not protocol in any organization. On the other hand, in trying to understand her motivation, you have to ask yourself if you conveyed any indication that you might be trying to erode the superintendent's authority. There is a chance that she misunderstood your laughing at his actions as being insubordination. In that case, she could feel very justified in running to the superintendent with this information. Furthermore, even though the assistant superintendent for human resources told you that she was complaining about how everyone had been laughing about the superintendent's behavior, you don't know for certain she is the one who ran to the superintendent with this information.

How you confront her is very important. If you do so in a questioning manner as you attempt to better understand her, she most likely would be less likely to run back to him and to accuse you of bullying her. If you confront her as having broken the protocol regarding the chain of command, she most likely will feel that you are bullying her as the authority figure. You can rest assured that the superintendent will be told about that, too. Of course, you are her supervisor, and you have to address the issue of her going around you to the superintendent. You can't have her continuing this behavior, as it is counterproductive both to the organization as well as to your ability to supervise her. Ultimately, you are responsible for supervising her and helping her to be successful. How can you be effective if she continues to report directly to your supervisor?

This is a delicate situation, insofar as it has to be addressed, but only in a manner of diplomacy and tact, if you expect good results. Often supervisors who are faced with a similar situation will resort to their authority in the chain of command to get their point across. While this might seem like a good short-term solution, it most likely will have disastrous results over time. Disgruntled employees are a threat not only to their direct supervisor, but also to the organization. The ethical approach is to seek to understand her motivation, and to try to work with her in understanding yours. Good communication is the key.

6-3. CRISIS MANAGEMENT: A STUDENT FATALITY (ISLLC STANDARD 5)

You are a principal of an urban high school of 2,500 students, 63% of whom are Hispanic. Most of these students are the children of immigrant parents who are new to the United States and are trying to establish a good life for their families. As a result, many of your students work either part-time or full-time jobs to help the family establish itself in the United States. You are proud of your students and recognize their strong work ethic.

It is seven o'clock Thursday morning. You usually arrive at the office early because it is a time during which you can try to catch up with the "loose ends" and paperwork that often get pushed down on the priority list. Your secretary is not required to come in until seven-thirty but she also likes to get to work early. Just as you are sorting through the pile of work left over from yesterday, your secretary tells you that Juan Gomez's parents are in the office and they want to speak with you.

Knowing that their English is very limited, as is your Spanish, you are apprehensive about this meeting, especially because your bilingual teachers are not yet here to assist with any translations. You welcome Mr. and Mrs. Gomez into your office and ask how you can help them. You notice that both of them have tears in their eyes and are visibly upset. They explain to you, in broken English, that their son Juan died a little after midnight in a car accident as he was coming home from work. Apparently the body is at the county morgue, and the parents don't know what to do next. As your mind races to find an answer to their question, you realize that Juan was a very popular student who not only was on the honor roll, but also was a talented member of the high school soccer team. You wonder how many students know about this tragedy. You also begin to strategize how you're going to handle this crisis with faculty and students. But back to the immediate concern—what do you tell the parents? Where can you find assistance for them with funeral arrangements?

As you excuse yourself to check with your secretary about who can help them, she hands you the morning newspaper. You see the headlines telling of Juan's death—the result of his car being hit head-on by a drunken driver who crossed the center line.

Explain, in bulleted format, your plan for handling this tragedy. Include steps of how to deal with the parents, faculty, and students, both today and tomorrow. Please align your plan with ISLLC Standard 5: *An education leader promotes the success of every student by acting with integrity, fairness, and in an ethical manner.*

Ethical Considerations

Whether this is a reasonable expectation of the school to find funeral assistance for the parents is irrelevant. The school is here to serve, and these people need help. One could criticize the school for selecting one funeral parlor over another, and the principal should have some criteria for determining whom to call. Furthermore, the principal has to put into place a plan to handle the emotional fallout that inevitably will occur throughout the day. Faculty and students alike will need some guidance and emotional support.

On the other hand, students will be coming to school and expecting their day to proceed as normal. Shutting down the school is not an option. Holding students in school with nothing for them to do is a potential time bomb. The day must continue as normal, but some of the faculty will be unable to do so. Obviously additional resources are needed.

Of paramount importance is meeting the needs of all involved in the school.

6-4. THE DUMPSTER INCIDENT: INTERNAL AND EXTERNAL PUBLIC RELATIONS (ISLLC STANDARD 6)

It is March and you have had a good but challenging first year of your new principal-ship. There have been many areas needing your attention, ranging from a neglected curriculum to equity issues between boys' and girls' sports, and you're trying hard to make a good impression on everyone. One area in which your predecessor fell short is that of public relations with parents and with the neighbors whose homes border school property. You've already gotten phone calls from owners of new homes being built along a wooded area just past the end zone of the football field. You agree that they have a legitimate gripe, and what once was just an overgrown field now is an eyesore. You promise them that improvements will be made and that you will include them in the planning process. You then meet with your head custodian to strategize what can be done. He agrees to utilize college workers who will be hired both during spring break and summer vacation. He also suggests that you include this in the updating of the soft-ball field, which is one of the sports equity issues that you are facing. The boys' baseball field is far superior to the girls' softball field in terms of drainage, outfield grass, and bleachers. You and the head custodian draw up plans for beautification of the strip of land that borders the new homes and extends along the end zone of the football field, the outfield of the baseball field, and the outfield of the softball field.

A few days later, you and the head custodian walk the area making notes about just how to improve it. It is supper time, and some of the new neighbors are just com-ing home from work. They see you and walk over to talk with you. Everything is going quite well as you explain to them the ideas about cutting out the "scrub trees" and trimming the mature trees. You also explain that there is a drainage stream hidden by the scrub trees, and that your plans are to improve its appearance as well. There is a small clearing surrounded by some trees, and you'd like to make that a picnic area both for the baseball and softball fans as well as for the neighbors. They are very pleased by this. You and the head custodian walk away feeling really good about the public relations you have built with the new neighbors. The head custodian tells you that he will order a dumpster for the scrub trees and branches, and that he will ask the custodians if they'd like to earn some overtime on Saturday by beginning to trim the trees and scrubs.

On Monday, the head custodian comes to your office, very upset. He explains that the custodians accomplished quite a lot of work, filling the dumpster with branches. You are pleased, and wonder why he's so upset. He them informs you that there are load limits on dumpsters and that the one he ordered is for tree branches and yard waste. It is not to be used for building materials. You are puzzled by this, because building materials were never part of the discussions you and he had last week. Then the head custodian gets to the meat of the problem. On Saturday, while the custodians were cutting and trimming trees and placing them into the dumpster, they saw a neighbor from the other side of the field (not one of the new neighbors) building a deck on the back of his house. He was putting the scrap lumber pieces in the school district's dumpster! Apparently, one of the custodians said something to the neighbor and he told them to mind their own business. Your head custodian further explains why this is such a problem.

The yard waste dumpster is for branches only, not for building materials. Even if the branches could hide the deck lumber in the dumpster, when it is dumped, the landfill operator could be fined for allowing treated lumber to be mixed with yard waste. Inevitably this will come back to the school district in the form of a fine and a clean-up fee. The only option is to pull a custodian from his regular duties and have him empty the dumpster piece by piece, separating the treated lumber from the branches. Then he'll have to refill the dumpster with the branches. That will leave a pile of treated lumber for which you'll have to order another dumpster. Needless to say, this is becoming an expensive venture. In light of the fact that the beautification of the land wasn't originally budgeted and you're cutting other line items to cover its cost, this new development will be costly.

Of course, you want to know who the neighbor is that so boldly placed his scrap lumber in your dumpster. You are shocked to find out his identity. He is a prominent citizen and the president of the board of education of the elementary district that feeds into your high school! You know what you have to do.

You phone the neighbor and explain to him the situation about the dumpster and the costs involved. He rudely tells you that it's not his problem and that when the school district leaves a dumpster out in the open, it is fair game for anyone to use it. You try to calm him down and explain the situation about beautifying the property for the new neighbors and that you can't afford the additional costs associated with his scrap lumber. He tells you that he resents your accusing him of dumping materials in the high school dumpster. "How dare you accuse me of doing this? Do you know who I am? Do you really think that I, the board president of the elementary district, would do this to the high school?" You remind him that your custodians were working on Saturday and that they not only saw him, but also asked him not to put materials in the dumpster. You are shocked by his response. "So, you take a custodian's word over a board president's word? You really are naïve as a new principal, aren't you?"

What would you do? Explain, in bulleted format, a process for handling this public relations challenge, aligned with ISLLC Standard 6: *An education leader promotes the success of every student by understanding, responding to, and influencing the political, social, economic, legal, and cultural context.*

Ethical Considerations

A lot is at stake with this case study. The custodians are waiting to see if the principal is going to back them up. The board president of the elementary school district is waiting to see if the new principal has the courage to confront him, or is the new principal a pushover? The neighbors are waiting to see if the new principal is going to allow the school property to be misused by the public. Of course, word of this situation will spread through the faculty and staff as well as the community as those directly involved begin to talk about how the situation was handled.

The new principal has to establish his credibility, but he also has to be sure not to burn any bridges so early in his career. Working with the elementary school board is important for a high school principal in a small community. The parents of students in the elementary schools will be sending them to the high school in a few years. The parents' impression of the high school will be formed before their students get to high school. From a public relations perspective, it is important that the principal establish a good working relationship with the elementary school districts feeding into his school.

On the other hand, the principal has an obligation to protect the high school's fiscal resources and to use them wisely. To close his eyes to the misuse of the dumpster has a cost attached to it. In addition to any fines that might be assessed for mixing construction lumber with landscaping waste, the dumpster is full and a new one has to be ordered. The high school is liable for additional costs because of a neighbor's misuse of the dumpster. Legally, the principal could file a complaint with the police department, but that might be considered extreme. The best route is to contact the neighbor directly. This isn't based on some far-fetched allegation. The neighbor has a new deck; no one else has one. The lumber scraps in the dumpster match the new deck. The gate to the school grounds was locked, and the only access to the dumpster that weekend was through the neighbors' property.

Of course, no one appreciates being accused of a misdeed, even if the person is guilty. The principal does run the risk of making a bad first impression, but lack of action also runs that risk. The manner by which the principal addresses the situation is key here. A professional and nonaccusatory approach must be used. The principal should be understanding but focused on the real issue. The high school now has to pay for another dumpster. Even if the neighbor/board president were to argue, the principal has to maintain his "cool" and stick to the real issue.

On the other hand, the principal could recognize the misuse, talk to the neighbor/board president, and let it go. That wouldn't remove the extra cost, but it would avoid conflict. To take that approach most likely would send the wrong message to the custodians and to the neighbors. They could easily deduce that it's permissible to do things that will cost the high school additional money. Perhaps trying to avoid the initial conflict with the neighbor/board president would result in even more conflict later.

6-5. GRADUATING STUDENTS' FAMILIES GET INTO A FIGHT IN THE SCHOOL PARKING LOT (ISLLC STANDARD 4)

You are the principal of a large suburban high school. Graduation ceremonies traditionally are held in the school gymnasium, and in years past, there have been problems with parents running up to the stage to hand their graduates bouquets of flowers or balloons. Through vigorous communication with the graduates and their parents, as well as through a restructuring of the seating arrangements, including using cordons to block visitors' access to the stage, this problem has been rectified. Also, there have been some problems with loud and obnoxious behavior on the part of the guests. You have learned that it is not wise to put your faculty in a position in which they have to remove parents or guests from the ceremony. To address this issue, you have hired professional uniformed ushers who not only collect the tickets at the door, but also maintain quiet and respect during the ceremony. Mostly, their presence has been a preventive measure, but occasionally they will have to remove someone who won't quiet down.

You are feeling good about this year's graduation because you think all the problem areas have been addressed. Your guidance counselors agreed to monitor the graduates while they put on their gowns to make sure no one is smuggling in noisemakers or other disruptive devices. You and your assistant principal have arranged the seating chart so that potential trouble-making graduates are sitting near a faculty member on the main floor of the gym. Parents and guests have seating in the bleachers, and there is a special section for videotaping. In addition, professionally done videos as well as individual photos of each graduate receiving the diploma will be available. There is no reason for anyone to leave his or her seat. Also, bouquets of flowers or balloons are prohibited, and the professional ushers will enforce that at the door.

During the ceremony, all is going well. The graduates are behaving properly, and the parents and guests are not being disruptive. About half of the graduates' names have been announced, and prior to the ceremony everyone was asked not to applaud until after all the graduates had been announced and had gone up to the stage to receive their diplomas. This is to make sure that no one's name gets "stepped on" by fanfare. Suddenly, when one of the graduates walks up the stairs to the stage to receive her diploma, a loud noise emanates from the bleachers. Someone has set off an air-horn. The ushers quickly identify the person and remove him from the ceremony, and the ceremony goes on with no other disruption.

After the ceremony, you are mingling in the crowd, congratulating graduates and meeting parents, when one of your faculty comes up to you. "We have a situation in the parking lot. Please come immediately." As you run out to the parking lot, the teacher explains that members from two of the graduates' families have squared off and are ready to fight. As you enter the crowd of potential fighters, you hear, "When you blew off that air-horn you stepped on my son's name. We waited four years to hear his name announced as a graduate, and you wrecked it." Apparently the uncle of one of the graduates was shouting this.

"Shut up! My granddaughter's graduation is something we've waited for, and we're celebrating. I have every right to blow off an air-horn." Obviously this was the grandmother of one of the graduates shouting back.

Other members of the two families are shouting and complaining to each other about the same thing. As you position yourself in the middle and try to stop this behavior, one of the family members tells you to get out of the way.

You now have a decision to make. Do you continue to try to resolve this? Do you call the police? Do you walk away in the hope that the situation will die out, assuming that your presence might be fueling it by giving them an audience to impress?

Develop a bulleted action plan, aligned with ISLLC Standard 4: *An education leader promotes the success of every student by collaborating with faculty and community members, responding to diverse community interests and needs, and mobilizing community resources.*

Ethical Considerations

All three of the choices—to try to break this up, to call the police, or to walk away—could be the right choice in terms of shutting down the conflict. But there are other considerations, one of which is the overall safety of all those present. Another is your credibility as a principal. Also, your role in establishing good public relations with the parents and other guests is at stake. This is a situation that could escalate on various fronts.

To try to break this up probably is what most administrators would do impulsively. That's what would be done in a school setting. But in school the principal is known and respected as an authority figure. These people might not even know who this person is that's trying to break up the situation. Also by positioning himself between the two groups, the principal could be putting himself in personal danger.

To call the police probably is the safest thing to do. The police know how to handle these situations, and their presence will be recognized as authority figures who also have the power to arrest if necessary. On the other hand, the principal could be viewed as a bully who has called the police on guests of the high school. From a public relations perspective, that is not a good idea. Undoubtedly, the parents and guests will talk about this situation and will enhance it beyond what really happened. This could result in negative public relations for the principal and the school. Or, the opposite could happen. The other guests might be grateful if the police were to come in before the situation gets worse. Family members might be afraid of the embarrassment that would come from a fight between the two families.

To just walk away most likely would not be the best solution. Although there is a chance that the argument would die out, there is an equal chance that it would escalate. For the principal to walk away would convey mixed messages, one of which might be lack of ability to lead; another might be lack of care and concern for the safety of guests of the school. Furthermore, there is the role model perspective that will be viewed by graduates and current students. It would not look good for the principal to walk away from this situation.

6-6. LET MY SON GRADUATE EVEN THOUGH HE FAILED TWO COURSES (ISLLC STANDARD 5)

You are the principal of a small-town high school. This is the month of May and graduation is two weeks away. Students who were in jeopardy of not graduating due to failing grades were notified several times since January. The school has a policy that allows students to walk across the stage if they are short one course, but any more than that would prohibit them from participating in the ceremony. You have mixed feelings about this policy, and you've checked with other high schools regarding their policies. Some have a zero-tolerance policy, which allows students to walk across the stage only if they have completed all their requirements. Others allow students to walk across the stage if they are three courses short of the graduation requirements. Of course, in that scenario no diploma would be issued until the student successfully completes the necessary courses. Your high school is in the middle of the range, with a one-course allowance. Your board of education is adamant about this, and some of the board members feel that the current policy is too liberal.

This morning, you receive a phone call from the parent of one of the students who is in jeopardy of not graduating. This student is failing three courses and is not showing signs of being able to turn this around in the next two weeks. The parent explains to you that she has invited family members from other states to come to the graduation. Motel accommodations have been made and airline tickets have been purchased. Not to allow her son to graduate would be a tremendous burden on the family.

You respond with the hope that her son can complete the missing assignments and bring his grades up so he will be able to graduate. You tactfully and kindly inform her that she should be having this conversation with her son. His future is under his control. But she continues on with excuses as to why her son is in this situation. "He's a good boy, but he just doesn't take school seriously. We want him to graduate so he can get a job."

You listen attentively and express concern about the motel and airline reservations. The parent goes on to explain that while she is hoping her son can turn his grades around, no one will know that until right before graduation. That would be too late to cancel the reservations, according to her. She then boldly asks if you can make an exception for her son and allow him to walk across the stage regardless of how many courses he might pass or fail. She merely wants the relatives to see him participate in the graduation ceremony. They don't have to know if he really graduates or not.

Your heart goes out to her, and you understand the embarrassment that she would feel if she had to cancel the family's plans at the last minute. But you also know how strongly the board of education members feel about the current policy. To not abide by that policy would never be acceptable to the board members. You would be jeopardizing your own career with that decision. But the parent begins to cry, and you really feel bad for her. She's right about her son. He isn't a bad kid; he just doesn't take school seriously.

What should you do? Develop a bulleted plan of action regarding how you would handle this from a public relations perspective. Please align your plan with ISLLC Standard 5: *An education leader promotes the success of every student by acting with integrity, fairness, and in an ethical manner.*

Ethical Considerations

While his heart goes out to the parent, the principal knows that he can't violate the board policy. On the other hand, the only ones who would know about it would be the student's guidance counselor, the registrar, the student, and his family. If he were to allow this one to slip by, would they all be silent about it? Or would the principal be setting a precedent for other such cases? On the other hand, can the principal let this slip by without appearing to be unethical? Isn't it his responsibility to uphold the policies set forth by the board of education for the good of all students?

From a public relations perspective, the principal probably wants to keep all the parents happy. This parent's concerns about family are real and could have embarrassing repercussions for her and her son. But isn't this all the result of her son's not taking school seriously? Ample warning and guidance have been given for quite a while. Neither the students nor the parent have been able to turn the situation around. Who owns the problem? On the other hand, is there any harm in allowing a student who has completed four years of high school to participate in the graduation ceremony? These are tough questions.

6-7. LOCAL FLORIST COMPLAINS ABOUT THE DATE OF THE PROM (ISLLC STANDARD 4)

You are the principal of a high school in a suburban setting. There are two local florists in town, and they enjoy a lot of business from the students at prom time. The two florists also have offered discounts to students having an A average on their report cards. You are grateful for the positive public relations between the high school and the local businesses.

The determination of a prom date is based on when various spring athletic competitions take place. In other words, the prom is scheduled so as not to conflict with baseball, softball, track, or band state-level competitions. Also, the student council sponsors the prom, and they typically choose a site about a year in advance. Availability of the facility is another consideration. While all these factors are taken into consideration, sometimes conflicts still occur even with the best of planning.

This year's prom is being held on a Friday night in May. As usual, the florists are getting most of the requests for prom flowers. Also, this year's date doesn't conflict with any of the state-level sports competitions, although there are some events being held the next day, on Saturday. You and your assistant principal both typically attend the prom not only for supervisory reasons, but also to show interest in the students. It is refreshing to see them dressed up and acting in a grown-up manner.

The Monday after the prom you get a phone call from one of the local florists. He is very angry with you for holding the prom last Friday. You're not understanding the problem as he rants and raves about how busy he has been this weekend. You're thinking to yourself that a local florist should be elated that business was so good. As the florist continues to complain, you stop him and ask why this is a problem. He goes on to explain that yesterday was Mother's Day, and that in addition to doing the prom flower orders for the students, he also had to complete Mother's Day flower orders for the public. He had so many orders that he had to bring in extra help. Knowing that the prom flower orders should have been completed on Thursday and Friday and would not conflict with any flower orders on Saturday, you're still not understanding the problem.

The florist then tells you that he and his staff were very tired after completing the prom orders and that they barely had the energy to complete the Mother's Day flower orders on Saturday. Then he felt the need to be open on Sunday for any last-minute orders. If the high school had been more considerate of him and his staff, the prom never would have been scheduled on the same weekend as Mother's Day. Despite your attempts to reason with him and to explain just how the prom date is chosen a year in advance, he persists in criticizing the high school. He also states that he will no longer give a discount to the students who earn A's on their report cards. You thank him for his past support, and you caution him that such action would not be well received by the students. They might opt to go to a florist in a neighboring town. He misunderstands your attempt to reason with him as a threat and hangs up the phone.

What should you do to restore a good relationship with the florist? Should you initiate a call to the other florist in town, or do you assume that his feelings are the same as this one's?

Develop a bulleted public relations plan aligned with ISLLC Standard 4: *An education leader promotes the success of every student by collaborating with faculty and community members, responding to diverse community interests and needs, and mobilizing community resources.*

Ethical Considerations

Although the principal's first reaction might be to tell the florist how lucky he is to have such a great weekend from a business perspective, that might not be the right thing to say at that time. Perhaps that comment would be best reserved for a later time when calmer heads prevail. Often when a person is so upset that reasoning is impossible, it is wise to listen and to empathize, but to get back in touch with the person later to attempt a resolution.

On the other hand, to attempt to buy some time to think this through and to let things cool down might be misinterpreted as not taking the issue seriously. It is difficult to determine the right course of action unless the principal can gauge the florist's ability to reason and to understand. The fact that the prom really didn't conflict with the flower orders for Mother's Day, but rather simply occurred right before is hard to digest. What business person would complain that his business is too good? This just doesn't make sense. Of course, from the business person's perspective, if the orders could have been spread over two weekends, things would be better for him in terms of ordering and storing the raw materials needed to complete the flower orders.

The bottom line is that the high school is being viewed as a villain, and there's nothing that can be done at this point, short of turning the clock back a couple of days, which is impossible. A strong attempt at rebuilding public relations is very important. The likelihood of students boycotting the florist if he refuses to continue the discount is great, and that would have a negative impact on the florist's profits. Needless to say, the high school would again be accused of being the villain in that scenario, too.

6-8. MEDIA SCOOPS AND THE SCHOOL'S PUBLIC IMAGE (ISLLC STANDARD 4)

You are a high school principal in a small town, which is served by a weekly local newspaper and a large city newspaper that has various editions for the suburbs that it serves. You have established a relationship with the editor of the local newspaper, but because her children are still in the elementary school district, she really doesn't have much of an interest in covering high school events. You notice that the elementary school district gets more positive coverage in the paper, and the high school only gets negative, critical coverage. On the other hand, the big city newspaper reporter assigned to your geographic area is very interested in providing positive, personal interest coverage to high school events.

It is the day before graduation, which is a big event in your small, suburban town. Families typically take their graduates out to eat in nearby cities to celebrate tomorrow's graduation. This is the last day of final exams, followed by graduation practice. Once practice is over, the seniors are free to leave the school grounds. This is a special privilege for them, as the juniors, sophomores, and freshmen still have exams to complete during this day. Practice with this particular group of seniors has gone very well, and you are especially proud of this graduating class. For the most part, they are very sensible and act maturely. You are hopeful that the graduation ceremony will be problem-free.

On the morning of graduation day, you arrive at the office early to make sure that all the graduation ceremony details are addressed properly. You make sure that the gym exhaust fans have been running all night to ensure a cool and comfortable environment. As you are checking the microphone, your secretary pages you. When you return to the office, you learn that one of the graduates was in a car accident last night. Her family was just leaving the restaurant parking lot when the dad pulled out in front of an oncoming car. The mom was taken by ambulance to one hospital, the graduating daughter was taken to another hospital, and the dad and son were examined and released. You feel very sad for this family, and you contact the superintendent so that he will be apprised, just in case a board member were to mention it. As you and the superintendent are talking you both get the idea of going to the hospital room of the graduate after the regular graduation ceremony. You make arrangements with the dad to confer his daughter's diploma at a special ceremony at the hospital. The superintendent makes arrangements for the board vice president to join you and the superintendent in this special ceremony.

After the regular graduation ceremony, you, the superintendent, and the vice president travel to the hospital and confer the diploma in the presence of the immediate family (the mom is still in another hospital, but recovering nicely). The girl is very grateful and very surprised by this. The family thanks you many times. Upon leaving the hospital, the vice president mentions that it's too bad that the newspaper wasn't there. You explain to him that it all happened so quickly that you didn't have time to contact the press, but you will write up a press release and send it out tomorrow morning.

You send it out to both the local newspaper and the big city newspaper. Two days later, the big city paper contacts you for more information, and the reporter tells you that he's going to contact the dad to get permission to photograph the girl with her diploma. You are very happy about this and you also call the dad to tell him that he will be getting a phone call from the paper. He is very excited about this. Unfortunately, you don't hear anything from the local newspaper. Later that week, the major newspaper runs the photograph and a very well-written article, which definitely casts the school in a warm and caring light. You make sure that the superintendent has a copy of the newspaper for inclusion in the next board meeting packet. You're very pleased with both the good deed that you have done for this graduate, as well as for the positive press that the school is getting.

But your bubble is quickly broken when you receive an irate phone call from the local newspaper. The editor asks for an immediate meeting with you to discuss why you "scooped" them by leaking a news story to the big city paper without giving the local paper a chance to publish it. You agree to the meeting, but you are puzzled by the allegation. You did send a press release to the local paper, and it wasn't acted upon. When you meet with the editor, you explain this to her, but her response leaves your head spinning. She explains that because her paper is a weekly one, she didn't have the time to act quickly on it. You listen empathically, but you then ask her to see things from your perspective. You explain that you did mail it to both newspapers on the same day. Because her paper comes out on Wednesdays, and your press release was mailed on a Saturday, you believe that she had ample time to act on it. She doesn't see things that way. According to her, the Wednesday paper is already put together on Friday of the previous week. She goes to demand that in the future you not send anything to the major newspaper for at least a week after the local paper has had it.

What would you do? Explain, in bulleted format, a process for handling this public relations challenge, aligned with ISLLC Standard 4: *An education leader promotes the success of every student by collaborating with faculty and community members, responding to diverse community interests and needs, and mobilizing community resources.*

Ethical Considerations

The principal certainly has the best interests of the students at heart when he goes to the hospital to present the diploma to the accident victim. How could the local newspaper be critical of that? But, in the highly competitive world of newspapers, large urban papers often target their marketing efforts to the suburbs. They even make special editions customized for particular suburbs. Needless to say, this has put a lot of pressure on the little weekly gazettes that at one time were the only purveyor of local news. Even local businesses, while they might want to buy advertisements in the local weekly paper, recognize that the readership of the large urban paper is much larger, and an advertisement in that paper has much greater potential of attracting more customers. The small paper is swimming upstream to fight for its survival. For a touching story about the local high school to appear in the large newspaper before it appears in the local paper is a serious blow to the editor.

On the other hand, the principal has an obligation to promote the school in the news media. Good public relations are sorely needed in all schools. This is a tremendous opportunity to cast the school in a kind and caring light. Furthermore, the principal did send the press release to both the large urban and the small local newspapers. If the local editor didn't read her mail on time, is it the principal's fault? Of course, we also know how much mail people receive in today's busy society. Perhaps the principal should have made a phone call indicating that he had a touching story to share? Maybe this would be good public relations with a community business? While the principal can say that he treated both papers equally and fairly, perhaps the local paper should have been given an advantage. This is not to say that the principal would hold the story, as suggested by the local editor, but rather that a phone call or e-mail sent as a "heads-up" would have been appropriate because the local newspaper supports the school through its taxes, whereas the large newspaper doesn't.

6-9. A PARENT'S CONCERNS ABOUT THE TECHNOLOGY CURRICULUM (ISLLC STANDARD 4)

You are a junior high school principal in a suburban school district that serves students from preschool through junior high. Your school has 900 students in grades six, seven, and eight. Your curriculum is a typical junior high program including a technology-based exploratory course. This course consists of computer-assisted modules that promote hands-on learning through discovery. The modules include rocket science, plastic-injection molding, wood crafting, bridge building, architectural design, interior design, screen painting, robotics, and so on. Each module has a tutorial component that ends with a quiz. If the students pass the computer-based quiz, then they can proceed to the hands-on portion of the module.

Students from each of the three grade levels spend nine weeks (one quarter) of each school year in this program. They can complete three modules in each nine-week course, resulting in the completion of nine modules by the time they graduate from eighth grade. Some students actually complete more than that, and there are a total of 15 modules available to them. The modules have no textbook and no homework. Rather, all learning is done with the tutorial and the hands-on lab projects. At the end of each module the students take another computer-based assessment, which addresses what they learned from both the tutorial and the lab portions of the module. The teacher's time is spent facilitating their learning by providing individual and group assistance.

Most of the students enjoy this approach, and their test scores are indicative of success. There are some students who don't do well in this environment, however. They need more structure and direction and don't do well when their learning is left up to them. The teacher usually can identify these students rather quickly and provides a more direct approach with them, but the bottom line is that they have to complete the computer-based assessments on their own.

This morning, a parent comes to your office to lodge a complaint about the technology-based exploratory program. According to him, he has requested written information from the teacher as to exactly what his son is learning in this course. The teacher has been unable to provide the requested information to the parent. You explain how the program works, and you invite the parent to accompany you on an impromptu visit to the lab. The parent stops you and says, "I know how the program works. I saw a demonstration during curriculum night. I'm concerned that my son isn't learning as much as he should through this approach."

You ask if the parent has had an opportunity to speak with the teacher, who can give him a status report regarding his son's accomplishments. The parent thanks you, but explains that he already has met with the teacher and that his concerns were not addressed. Instead, the teacher referred him to you. This is troubling to you because the teacher never mentioned this, and you don't appreciate being "blindsided" like this. However, you maintain your calm and assure the parent that you will be happy to address his particular concerns.

The parent goes on to explain that he doesn't want to interfere nor does he want to complain, but he knows his son all too well. According to the parent, his son will take advantage of situations. He tends to be lazy and does not work well independently. The parent simply wants a copy of the curriculum so he can reinforce it at home. This sounds very reasonable to you, and you again assure the parent that you will work with him on this issue. You would like to talk with the teacher and then get back to the parent.

When you meet with the teacher you discover that there is no written curriculum to accompany the modules. Apparently, they were purchased before you got to the district, and there was no written curriculum purchased along with the modules. As you begin to explain the situation about the parent, the teacher stops you in mid-sentence. "I've met with him many times. He's crazy!" You counter by explaining that while the parent might appear to sometimes be crazy, he has a legitimate concern and resulting request. To this the teacher responds, "I don't have a written curriculum to give him. Everything we do is on the computer. There is nothing the parent can do at home with his son. Furthermore, that parent needs to learn to let go. His son is in sixth grade already."

What would you do as the principal? Develop a bulleted plan of action aligned with ISLLC Standard 4: *An education leader promotes the success of every student by collaborating with faculty and community members, responding to diverse community interests and needs, and mobilizing community resources.*

Ethical Considerations

Although it might be tempting to dismiss this parent as an annoyance who just won't go away, he really does have a legitimate request. Isn't it refreshing for a parent to ask for ways by which he can support his son's learning at home? Even though this parent has taken much of your time and that of the teacher, he can be an asset to you and the school. Of course, he also can be a complainer if not handled appropriately.

On the other hand, the teacher's comment might initially seem calloused and cold, but perhaps he is correct about the parent's being overly concerned about his son. Maybe the parent's alleged overprotective nature could be causing the student to slack off when on his own. Maybe he has been programmed only to perform well when his father is right there, hovering over him. While these suppositions might be true, there is no factual evidence to support them. From the principal's perspective, a parent has asked her for help so he can assist his son's learning at home.

Another concern is that of the missing written curriculum. This program was purchased before the principal's arrival in the district, but nevertheless, now that she has discovered the absence of a written component, this has to be addressed. If the vendor didn't provide one originally, perhaps it can be provided now? If not, wouldn't it be something that the teacher could develop and find useful? Isn't it sad that this is the first parental request? Perhaps a written explanation of the learning goals for each module should be given to all parents? Wouldn't that be a great way to encourage parental support at home? Also, wouldn't that be a positive public relations tool?

6-10. THE PRINCIPAL BANS THE LOCAL NEWSPAPER EDITOR FROM THE SCHOOL (ISLLC STANDARD 4)

You are the principal of a small rural high school of 450 students. The English department chairperson in your school also serves as the editor of the local weekly newspaper. Although he hasn't really gone out of his way to showcase the school events in the newspaper, you recognize the potential and you are comfortable with his being the editor. Unfortunately, the superintendent is not comfortable with this arrangement. While there is no contract violation, and the school district cannot prohibit the department chair from holding this part-time job, the superintendent is concerned that the English department chair might have too much inside information about the school and that he could use that information to cast the school in a negative light.

You remind the superintendent that the opposite has been true. The department chair hasn't even given the school much coverage, perhaps because he doesn't want to be accused of favoring the high school over the elementary and junior high schools, which are in a separate school district. Nevertheless, the superintendent takes it upon himself to discuss his concerns with the department chair. As a result of this conversation, the department chair announces his retirement from the editor's position, indicating that he will be retiring from the high school in two years and that now is the time to leave the newspaper so that he can finish his career at the high school with less stress.

This seems like a logical explanation to the readership, and a new editor is chosen. Unfortunately, the new editor is not experienced, and she needs a lot of assistance and guidance from the former editor. They have found a mutually agreeable time to work on the paper, but it is during the school day. The department chair has a prep and planning period and a department chair period, which leaves him with three periods in which to teach. He has blocked his two released time periods together and is using that block of time to coach the new editor.

This arrangement is okay with you, the principal, because you recognize that the department chair arrives at school early and stays late to get his work done. As far as you are concerned, he merely is shifting his time around, but he is meeting his responsibilities. The superintendent, however, does not see it that way. He does not want the new editor in the school for the same reasons that he didn't want the department chair to be editor of the newspaper. The superintendent believes that too much inside information would be available and subject to being printed in the newspaper. In other words, he doesn't trust the local newspaper.

The superintendent has ordered you to forbid the department chair to meet with the new editor during school time and at the school. He would like them to meet at the newspaper office during nonschool time. This seems logical, but you recognize the potential for negative public relations with the local newspaper. To you this seems more dangerous than welcoming the new editor into the school. The superintendent does not agree with your take on this and persists in his order that you stop their meeting immediately.

Recognizing the public relations issue at stake here, develop a bulleted action plan of how you would address this. Kindly align your plan with ISLLC Standard 4: *An education leader promotes the success of every student by collaborating with faculty and community members, responding to diverse community interests and needs, and mobilizing community resources.*

Ethical Considerations

This is a difficult situation from a couple of perspectives. First of all, the superintendent is micro-managing, and he should be leaving the supervision of faculty to the principal. Unfortunately, because this is such a small district, the superintendent's office is in the school, and he is very visible. In some respects this is good, but in other respects, this is not good because it is very easy for him to fall into the trap of micro-management.

Another perspective complicating this situation is the potential for bad public relations with the newspaper. In the past, the department chair was able to separate his role of editor from the school, and while there were times the principal wished he would provide more coverage of school events, there also were times when the principal appreciated his lack of coverage. The principal probably suspects that the department chair's recent announcement about retiring from the editor position might have been coerced by the superintendent. That combined with the prohibiting of his working with the new editor during school time could be the proverbial straw that breaks the camel's back.

As indicated in the case study, the superintendent is not open to discussion about this topic. One would hope that administrators could agree to disagree and perhaps learn to see each other's perspectives, but that isn't always the case. The principal could hope that this will go away and that after the new editor learns the ropes, she will stop needing to meet so often with the department chair, but that probably won't happen any time soon.

From a public relations perspective, this has a lot of potential to backfire, and the principal most likely would like to smooth things out with the former editor and the new editor in an attempt to build a good relationship with the newspaper. This will depend on how the principal delivers the message. Of course, if they try to negotiate with the principal, there is no room for that, due to the superintendent's directive. But, if the principal explains the directive, the superintendent most likely will be upset, and the principal will appear to be a puppet, thereby eroding the principal's authority.

6-11. STUDENTS AGAINST DRINKING AND DRIVING: A GOOD IDEA GOES BAD (ISLLC STANDARD 3)

You are the principal of a small, suburban high school, which has had some challenges related to students' drinking after leaving athletic events, dances, concerts, and so on. You have appointed a faculty member to resurrect a Students Against Drunk Driving chapter, which had fallen apart due to lack of interest. The faculty member is very excited about this opportunity and is doing a fantastic job of recruiting students to join. She has initiated some awareness activities, which have received strong support from the faculty.

It is the spring, and the prom is about a week away. In the past, students have gotten in automobile accidents as a result of drinking after the prom. To heighten awareness, the club sponsor asked you if she could contact a local towing company to place a wrecked car on the front lawn of the school. Signage would warn students that this could happen to them if they drink and drive. You think it is a good idea, and you notify your buildings and grounds staff about this. They have pledged their support to help with the placement of the vehicle and with making sure that the battery and fuel tank have been removed so as not to present a fire hazard.

The next morning, the wrecked car is delivered and placed strategically to attract appropriate attention. The student members have made signage, and the custodians have helped to secure the signs. The display is impressive, and you are proud of the student chapter's work.

Later in the day, you receive a phone call from an irate citizen. She is extremely upset about the wrecked car in front of the school. As you explain the rationale, she becomes even more upset. Not understanding the root cause of her distress, you probe with questions. Eventually, you discover that a relative of hers had been driving that car when it was struck by a drunk driver. The relative is in the hospital, in stable condition. The upset woman is concerned that others might recognize the car and accuse her relative of being the drunk driver. She does not want the car to be displayed on the school property, and she resents what she interprets as an accusation that her relative was at fault. You assure the woman that you will investigate the situation and get back to her, but she wants the car to be removed immediately.

You contact the towing company and learn that the car had been in an accident two weeks ago. The insurance company totaled it because the damage far exceeded the value of the car. The towing company purchased the car from the insurance company for parts, and prior to stripping it, offered to provide it for the club display. You also learn that the previous owner (the caller's family member) lived in another town about 20 miles away. The accident occurred in that town. There is no connection with your school's town, except that the caller happened to drive by on her way to work.

Although you sympathize with the caller's concerns, the car no longer belongs to her family. There is no allegation or indication that her family member was drinking. The car merely suggests that drinking and driving could result in an accident. It is intended to drive a message home to the students.

- What do you do?
- Should you call the towing company and have the car removed?
- Should you leave the car on the school lawn until after the prom?
- How do you respond to the caller?

As principal of this school, what would you do? Explain, in bulleted format, a process for handling this challenge, aligned with ISLLC Standard 3: *An education leader promotes the success of every student by ensuring management of the organization, operation, and resources for a safe, efficient, and effective learning environment.*

Ethical Considerations

Putting a wrecked car on the school grounds prior to the prom is a standard practice that has been occurring for decades. No one wants to see students getting hurt, but often the adolescent mind is far too willing to take risks by dismissing any related danger as happening to someone else. The shock factor of seeing a wrecked car is intended to jar the adolescent mind back to the reality of "Hey! This could happen to me!" Certainly there is no intent to accuse the driver of the wrecked car, but rather the intent is to show what could happen if one were to drink and drive.

When the wrecked car is recognized by the family of the driver of the car, the school does not want to appear to be insensitive to them, but it is not a simple matter to remove the car. First of all, the towing company has paid the truck driver to deliver the car. That cost is not borne by the school; it is a donation from a community business. Second, in order for the car to be displayed on the school grounds, it cannot represent a safety hazard. Fluids have to be drained from the gas tank, radiator, brake lines, and so on, and the battery has to be removed. This work also represents a cost either to the school by its own employees' time that could be spent doing other work, or to the towing company. To honor the family's request to remove the car immediately would mean that these costs would have been encumbered for no result. The shock factor message would not be sent to the students because of the premature removal of the car.

In addition, the goodwill of the towing company would be strained, and the efforts of the club sponsor will be for naught. In other words, there are personal investments in the school community relations "bank account" that would be compromised. The towing company might become negative toward the school and its employees could begin badmouthing the school. The club sponsor could become discouraged and become reluctant to undertake such projects in the future. This could result if people feel that their efforts aren't appreciated.

On the other hand, the family does have a valid concern if the car were to be recognized by students as belonging to the family member. Whether the driver had been under the influence is not important in the displaying of the car, but the family's worry that their relative might be falsely accused is important. The risk of bad public relations is equally as strong with the family as it could be with the towing company. In other words, this situation could become a loser regardless of the decision of how to resolve it.

The educational leader has to be sensitive to the concerns of both parties: the family and the towing company. The leader also has to be aware of the possible negative public relations from this situation. Because the family who originally owned the car lives 20 miles away, there is a likelihood that none of the students would even recognize the car as having belonged to that family. Furthermore, car manufacturers make many cars that are painted the same color. Why would anyone connect this car to the family? Perhaps the family was reading too much into this? While there always is a chance that complaints can end up in the letters to the editor section of the local newspaper, in this case the family most likely would not want to call any more attention to the situation because of the possible conclusions that could be drawn about the driver. It seems that the best option for the educational leader would be to attempt a sensitive and sincere dialogue with the family.

6-12. STUDENTS DRINKING IN FRONT OF THE SCHOOL AND THE POLITICAL IMPLICATIONS (ISLLC STANDARD 6)

You are a new high school principal in a small middle-class, blue-collar town. Most of the people in town are employed at a refinery or its related industries. It is a closely knit town, and anyone not born there is considered to be an outsider. You were hired in the summer, and you've gotten to know some of the locals. It is a charming little town, but it also represents some close-minded thinking when it comes to tolerance and acceptance of any form of diversity.

It is the first day of the school year, and you are just getting to know the building, the faculty, the students, and the community. The first bell has just rung and you are finishing your rounds and are heading back to your office. One of your faculty members who also is a part-time police officer on weekends comes running toward you. He explains that he just saw two of your students parked in a car in front of the school, and they are drinking beer. Because they are in a car parked on a public street, you quickly ascertain that this is a police matter, and you tell the faculty member that you will call the police. He stops you. "One of the boys is the son of the police chief. I just want you to know that before you call the police."

You recall a conversation you had with the superintendent a few weeks ago during which he told you that the school district and the local police had had some rough times in the past. Apparently the police would ticket parking violations, and the former principal would phone to ask them to cancel the parking tickets for certain people. The police chief became upset about this and at one point refused to have his department patrol the school parking lots. This action caused some board of education members to make some public comments about the police department's alleged lack of support for the school. Because these comments had been made in a public board meeting, the press picked up on the issue and made a big deal about it on the front page of the local newspaper.

After much negotiating and diplomacy on the part of the superintendent, the district now enjoys a good working relationship with the police department. Recently, the chief agreed to take to his board a recommendation to provide half-salary for a police liaison to be assigned to the high school. As the superintendent told you this, her pride was obvious.

This conversation runs through your mind as you debate what to do. Should you call the police? It is against the law for anyone to have open liquor in a car. These are minors, and they are your students. If you don't call the police, they could drive away and cause an accident, maybe even a fatality.

On the other hand, if the faculty member hadn't seen them, you wouldn't have known about the situation. Other than marking them absent, the school really wouldn't have anything to do with them because the students hadn't come to school. If they were to park elsewhere, you wouldn't have any responsibility or knowledge regarding their drinking. Should you notify the police and risk destroying the relationship that the superintendent worked so hard to build?

But if you don't call the police, what message are you giving the faculty? You know the faculty member who reported this to you will tell others about it. What you decide to do will be judged by the faculty. Of course, the faculty also knows about the proposed police liaison. What if the police chief withdraws his recommendation, and the faculty blames you for not using good discretion? They are looking forward to having police support in the school.

As principal of this school, what would you do? Explain, in bulleted format, a process for handling this challenge. Kindly align your plan with ISLLC Standard 6: *An education leader promotes the success of every student by understanding, responding to, and influencing the political, social, economic, legal, and cultural context.*

Ethical Considerations

This certainly is a dilemma for the new principal. While it might seem prudent to keep this quiet, situations like this never can be kept quiet. For the new principal to appear to be unethical would not be a good way to begin his career in this high school. The old saying "Honesty is the best policy," holds true in this situation.

On the other hand, all the bridge-building with the police department that has been done by the superintendent could be jeopardized by this report. From a larger perspective, the principal should consider the credibility of the police chief. Would the chief want to be accused of covering for his son and friend? This could be detrimental to the chief's career as well. If not his career, it could be detrimental to his credibility with the police force if word of this spread through the ranks. Because the teacher who discovered it also is a part-time police officer, one can assume that the gossip line will quickly spread this information. To worry about the relationship between the high school and the police department is a valid concern, but there is a much bigger picture to consider when making the decision.

The impact that this situation will have on the student body is another concern. What message is being sent to them if the situation were to be swept under the rug? Similarly, the question can be asked if the situation is reported to the police department. The students can learn from seeing their classmates having to accept consequences for their behavior.

There is another element to consider in this case study. If the police chief wants to cover this up internally, that would be his choice. The school really shouldn't have to worry about whether to report a crime. It is everyone's civic duty to do so. School officials are role models for the students and for the community. Ethics have to win with this one.

6-13. A STUDENT VISA: A NEIGHBORING DISTRICT CHARGES TUITION (ISLLC STANDARD 4)

You are an assistant superintendent in a large, urban school district that is located in an impoverished area. It is a unit district, serving students in preschool through high school. This area once was an industrial powerhouse, but over time, factories closed or relocated and the district's tax base diminished. Also, the area was the victim of decreasing home values as many residents moved to the suburbs. The large, old homes in the district were priced very low, and immigrant groups moved into them. The result is that the school district became very culturally and ethnically diverse.

You are proud to serve in this district, even though your salary is low when compared to what assistant superintendents are paid in other districts. The same is true of all employee groups in the district, but there is a strong sense of dedication to helping the students to be successful. That intrinsic motivation is very obvious among all involved with the school district, from the board of education members to the administrators, the teachers, and the classified staff.

Your district takes pride in helping its students, and you are especially pleased when the high school principal notifies you that a new student from a war-torn country has been enrolled in the school. The principal also explains that the student is living with a host family who lives in the school district. A local church group has made it their mission to find host families for victims of war. The high school staff has made the new student feel very welcome and has assisted with his acclimation to the high school. You thank the principal for the information, and your pride at being a member of the district's administrative team is quite evident as you share the story with the superintendent.

You are quite shocked when you return to your office and receive a phone call from the assistant superintendent in a neighboring school district. She explains to you that there is a host family in her district who has taken in a student from the same war-torn county as the one in your district. Her board of education has taken the stance that this student resides in the school district solely for the purpose of attending school in that district. Consequently, he is not considered a foreign exchange student, nor does he have the correct visa to be a foreign exchange student. She goes on to explain that the board is charging the student tuition and that the board has acquired legal support for its opinion.

You try to dismiss the legal support as being conjecture and not supported by case law, but she counters by saying that the board sought legal counsel from the state department of education. The assistant superintendent went on to say that she would fax you a copy of the official statement from the state department of education. You are crushed by this. Knowing that the host family of the new student in your high school can't afford to pay tuition, you don't quite know how to approach this situation.

After reading the legal opinion from the state department of education, you and the superintendent realize that you have no choice but to notify the host family that they'll have to pay tuition. You contact them, and they are very determined to keep the foreign student in their home. They ask if you can give them some time to raise the tuition. This tears at your heart, and you agree that they don't have to make an immediate payment, but they will have to make a payment within the next month as per board policy.

The host family asks if you will go with them to local service clubs to seek tuition assistance, and you agree. Although the idea sounds great, and you know that the local service clubs are very generous, when presented with the request, they cannot understand why the school district would be charging tuition to this student. Regardless of how hard you try to explain the legalities, their take on it is that the school district is trying get money from someone who cannot afford to pay it. This troubles you from a public relations perspective, as well as from a humanitarian perspective. You know that the superintendent doesn't want to charge this student tuition any more than you do, but you don't have a choice.

After spending some time thinking about this dilemma, you come up with an idea. You ask the superintendent if you can appeal the legal opinion to the state department of education. He agrees that this is worth a try, but he wants you to first present your plan to the board of education. You do this, and your board is shocked that the neighboring board would even push the issue so far as to seek legal advice from the state department of education. They give you permission to pursue an appeal.

After contacting the school district attorney for advice, you put together an appeal and forward it to the chief legal counsel at the state department of education. In your appeal you highlight the details of the case. The student in question did not specifically choose your district to get a free education. His life and that of his family was in danger because his father is a prominent professor in his own country. The opposing forces would like to kill him and his family to send a message regarding their power. The student literally escaped by crawling through sewer lines to avoid recognition. He even had to crawl over dead bodies to get out of the country. When an international relief agency found him, they made arrangements to fly him to the United States, where he was given a visa, but not that of a foreign exchange student. The host family had submitted their name simply to open their home to provide assistance. They had no intention of trying to subvert any school district residency regulations.

After reviewing the details of the case, the chief legal counsel of the state department of education overturned the previous legal opinion and declared that because the primary intention of the student was that of survival and not merely to reside in the district to attend school there, he could attend free of any tuition charges and would be entitled to the same rights and privileges as any resident in the school district.

Although you are very pleased about this, and your district attorney actually has written it up for the legal newsletter, which goes out to many school districts, you also realize that this is a terrible public relations nightmare for the neighboring district. Your board of education wants you to make a presentation at its next meeting, and the local media will be there. How do you explain the situation without making the neighboring school district look bad? Explain your public relations plan in a bulleted manner aligned with ISLLC Standard 4: *An education leader promotes the success of every student by collaborating with faculty and community members, responding to diverse community interests and needs, and mobilizing community resources.*

Ethical Considerations

As stated in the case study, the assistant superintendent certainly does not want to use this situation to make his school district look good at the expense of the neighboring school district. While this might be tempting and even justifiable in one's mind, it ultimately could result in the assistant superintendent's losing credibility. The real issue here has been the educational opportunity for the foreign student. The focus of any presentation to the media has to emphasize that.

On the other hand, the neighboring school district did cause a lot of trouble for both students as well as for the hosting families. In addition, the service clubs now have a less than favorable opinion about the school district that was trying to raise tuition assistance. The neighboring school district certainly caused this school district to lose some ground in the public relations arena. Of course that district also lost in the same arena.

CHAPTER 7

Diversity Issues in Educational Leadership

When public schools were first established in our country, they were intended to teach children how to read the Bible. The issues related to diversity in schools have changed dramatically since then. Today's schools have students from different races, cultures, ethnicities, and religions. Some students have been born in the United States, and others have been born elsewhere. The values and beliefs of various backgrounds all come together in the schools. The Protestant work ethic upon which many of the traditional school policies have been built might not be embraced by all of today's students and their families. The nuclear family of a father, mother, and three children that was typified in children's literature of the forties and fifties isn't the norm in today's society. Biracial families, single-parent families, and same-gender parents are just some of the diverse family structures from which today's students come.

Because our nation's first schools were intended to teach children how to read the Bible, many of their celebrations and holidays were centered around religious practices. Some of those still exist in today's schools, regardless of the religious beliefs of the community served by the schools. Examples include Thanksgiving Day, a national holiday to give thanks to God; Christmas vacation, which has been renamed "winter break" but still occurs in conjunction with Christmas Day on which the birth of Christ is celebrated; Good Friday, which no longer is a national holiday, but continues to be a day of nonattendance for schools recognizing the crucifixion of Christ. These are just some of the holidays that schools recognize by days off and/or by activities and projects. They all are based in religious beliefs. As our schools become more diverse in their student population, and as our country attracts more immigrants from all parts of the world, the traditional religious holidays no longer make sense to many of the students and their families.

Since 1972, when Title IX legislation was enacted to ensure equal educational opportunities and programs regardless of gender, the schools led society in recognizing the importance of equal rights for males and females alike. In the 1960s when federal legislation mandated a free and appropriate public education for all students regardless of handicap or disability, schools had to recognize the diversity of learning abilities, physical abilities, and mental abilities. Programs had to be developed to ensure equal educational opportunity for all. In the 1950s when the famous *Brown v. Board of Education* case resulted in equal educational opportunities for all students regardless of race, schools had to adjust their practices and policies to prevent segregation on the basis of race. Federally mandated programs also ensure that non-English-speaking students have programs to help them learn English. While some states have challenged the federal requirement for transitional bilingual education, the overall intent in all states is that of helping students to become bilingual and biliteral, and schools provide language support to students. These are some examples of the ways in which schools have adjusted to embrace diversity and to ensure fair and equal treatment of all individuals.

Today's schools have challenges related to bullying, sex education, world cultures, world religions, gender, learning styles, learning abilities, and disabilities, all of which fall under the category of diversity. To not only survive, but also to be successful in today's world, students have to embrace the richness of diversity. Unlike their parents or grandparents who might have taken pride in the concept of the "melting pot" of the United States, today's students recognize the importance of uniqueness. Consequently, the term "melting pot" has been replaced by terms such as "mosaic" or "fruit salad vs. marmalade." Valuing the uniqueness of individuals is taught by our schools.

Needless to say, this change in values is not readily accepted by all age groups or communities. Schools have a challenge as they promote acceptance of diversity. Some school districts have banned certain books because of community pressure. These books might depict a family consisting of a same-gender couple, or the books might represent certain religious practices. The American Library Association publishes a list of books that either have been banned by libraries or have been challenged by groups wanting them to be banned. It is interesting to read the list and the reasons. Many of these books are on the required reading lists of schools.

This chapter is intended to prepare future educational leaders for the challenges that accompany schools' attempts to promote diversity and to teach acceptance. Although there has been legislation to ensure fair and equal treatment, the pressures of various values and beliefs present themselves as challenges to educational leaders.

7-1. BILINGUAL ISSUES (ISLLC STANDARD 4)

You are an elementary school principal in a district that serves four villages. One of the villages has a large Hispanic population, many of whom are first-generation immigrants. To address their needs, your school has a large bilingual program consisting of a bilingual classroom in each grade level. The bilingual classes are taught in both Spanish and English as appropriate, but the goal is to transition students into the English classrooms. This means that half of your faculty is covered by a bilingual grant, which has specific requirements for the type of instruction and the evaluation of students. It has been difficult for you to staff the program because bilingual teachers are hard to find. As a result, some of your teachers are more proficient in Spanish than they are in English, but they have passed the state certification exams.

Although you are aware of their comfort level in their native language of Spanish, you are convinced that the teachers are doing a good job of teaching their students English. You also realize that the rate by which students acquire a second language is very much subject to individual backgrounds and abilities. In other words, some kids take longer than others to develop proficiency in English. As a result, some of the students move more slowly into the English classroom than others do. Some students go into the English classroom for reading, but remain in the bilingual classroom for science, because of the terminology.

On the state-level English proficiency tests, your students are progressing into English at an acceptable rate, but some of the board members have expressed concern that the students aren't progressing fast enough. One of the board members has accused your staff of purposely delaying kids' transition into the English classroom to ensure job security. This board member also has expressed concern that students are automatically placed in the bilingual program on the basis of their surnames and not on their ability to speak English. While you have assured the superintendent that your staff is following district placement procedures and transition procedures, you can't help but worry that the superintendent might believe the board member over you.

At a recent board meeting, one of the members declared, "This is America; our students should be taught in English. I went into Ms. Ruiz's second-grade classroom and heard her speaking to the students in Spanish. I think that is terrible!" The board member went on to demand that the superintendent rectify this situation.

You sat in the audience, appalled at this outburst. You've been in Ms. Ruiz's classroom, and you know that she does an outstanding job of teaching her students. You believe that expecting second graders to transition into an English-only classroom is unreasonable, but the board member referenced "immersion" as the way to learn English.

After the board meeting, the press interviewed the board member who said, "Sink or swim. That's the way of our world. When you're in America, you have to learn to speak English. If we allow them to speak Spanish, they'll never be successful in America."

As principal of this school, what would you do? Explain, in bulleted format, a process for handling this challenge, aligned with ISLLC Standard 4: *An education leader promotes the success of every student by collaborating with faculty and community members, responding to diverse community interests and needs, and mobilizing community resources.*

Ethical Considerations

There is no easy, quick way to learn a second language. Most high school graduates have studied a foreign language for two to four years, but they still are not biliteral in that language. Research shows that it takes years to learn how to read, understand, and communicate in a second language. Although educators know this, the general public doesn't. They quickly forget their own high school experience of trying to learn a second language. In addition, some people have assumed a self-proclaimed patriotism by insisting that all immigrants instantly learn English. Interestingly, there is no national language in the United States because the original colonies were inhabited by people who didn't speak the same language.

Educational leaders certainly want their students to learn English as quickly as possible, but learning it means more than simple conversation. Students have to be proficient in reading and writing as well. Native English speakers continue to study English through elementary, junior high, and high school so they can become proficient in reading, writing, and speaking. Often schools are viewed by the public as holding

English language learners back to generate more bilingual grant dollars. The media is quick to criticize schools and the bilingual education programs.

The principal in this case study is facing some of the criticism usually levied by the general public. It is disappointing that a board member would use the public forum of the board meeting to raise this issue. It would have been more appropriate for her to approach this with the superintendent first. For her to use the news media to further her cause is not appropriate behavior for a board member. She clearly has lost sight of the fact that she is an agent of the school district. The principal obviously believes in the bilingual program and its supporting research. The board member has created a confrontational situation between her and the principal, and she just did that in front of the news media.

This is a difficult situation because the principal does not want to discredit the board member, but she also does not want to discredit her faculty. They have worked hard to help students acquire English proficiency. The principal needs to support her faculty and their efforts. On the other hand, the board of education members have direct control over the superintendent. To appear not to support a board member's concerns could be detrimental to the principal's career.

Clearly, this is a situation in which the principal has to appeal to reason. She has to work with the board member away from the attention of a public meeting. Calmer minds have to prevail, and little will be accomplished when emotions are so strong. The superintendent also has a role in trying to address this issue. For years, the school district has embraced the transitional bilingual model of English acquisition. Teachers, parents, and students have embraced this model with success. To move away from that model at the whim of a board member would not be a wise choice.

7-2. THE BLIND ELL STUDENT: WHO'S RESPONSIBLE? (ISLLC STANDARD 2)

You are a principal in an urban high school that has a large Hispanic population. The district's bilingual program is one of the largest in the state, and it has earned state recognition for its effectiveness. Your school has a large mobility rate of 50%, which means that by the end of the school year one half of the students have moved out of the school and have been replaced by another 50%. Each day new students arrive to register and other students check out to move to other areas of the country.

Today, a 16-year-old student is brought in to register. He speaks no English, and his Spanish is very poor. The student has very limited vision and can be considered legally blind. His educational background in Mexico is sparse. There are no records of his having attended any school, and most likely because of his blindness, he was educated at home.

As a program and schedule are being developed for the student, the question arises as to which department is primarily responsible for the student's educational plan: the bilingual department or the special education department. His lack of good language skills in English would make him eligible for bilingual services, and his blindness would make him eligible for special education services. To further complicate matters, his lack of good language skills in Spanish makes it difficult to test his academic abilities. One of the two departments has to assume primary responsibility for developing an educational plan and the other department will have to provide support services in accordance with that plan.

As principal you sometimes are invited to sit in on these meetings at which an incoming student's educational plan is determined, but your content specialists are responsible for this process. They invite you to this meeting because it is particularly complex. You are thinking that the complexity is based on both the special education department's and the bilingual department's wanting to assume primary responsibility, and neither wants to play the secondary role of providing support in accordance with the other department's plan. You are both surprised and disappointed to learn that just the opposite is true. Neither department wants to assume primary responsibility for developing the student's plan, and both want to assume the secondary role of providing support.

As the educational leader who always puts students first in all decision making, you want to shout out, "What about the best interests of the student?" But you refrain and seek to understand more about the situation. Unfortunately what becomes clear is that both departments are feeling overwhelmed and understaffed, and neither wants the additional work associated with this case.

As principal, what would you do? How would you handle this situation? How would you try to get both departments to embrace this student's diversity and to work with him? Develop a bulleted action plan aligned with ISLLC Standard 2: *An education leader promotes the success of every student by advocating, nurturing, and sustaining a school culture and instructional program conducive to student learning and staff professional growth.*

Ethical Considerations

A lot is at stake here. First of all, the principal can easily jump to the conclusion that neither department wants to be burdened with this student. But the opposite might be true. Both departments could be concerned that they don't have the resources to do justice to this situation, and each one wants the other to take the first step with the assumption that the other department is better equipped to provide the primary assistance to the student. Their reluctance to take on the primary responsibility might be because they each have a support plan in mind.

Of course, the opposite could be true, too. When a district has such a big mobility rate, there are many new plans that have to be written. It is frustrating to write up plans only to have the students transfer out in a few months. The faculty could easily become jaded, thinking that the plans don't really make any difference because half of the students won't see them through to fruition anyway. While the principal doesn't want to recognize this possibility, if it is true, he has to work on the problem from a different angle than if each department wants to unveil a grandiose support plan.

When a student has so many factors working against his educational success, one has to wonder how much can be accomplished in two years, assuming the student will leave high school after he turns 18. As educators it is important that we believe in the potential of each student. One never really knows how much hidden potential lies waiting for us to uncover. But we also have to balance that hope with capacity and reality. Of course, neither can be properly measured.

So, this is a complicated issue that doesn't rest only with the warring of two departments. There are some philosophical and practical questions that the principal has to address with his faculty, in addition to the motivational ones.

7-3. COMMUNICATION WITH A STUBBORN SUPERINTENDENT (ISLLC STANDARD 6)

Mike is an experienced middle school principal who previously worked in another district. His ethnic background is Caucasian, but he is quite proficient in Spanish. His school is approximately 60% Hispanic, and Mike has developed a strong relationship with the Hispanic students and their parents. There are three middle schools in the district, each of which hosts a district special education program. Mike's school hosts the behavior disorders (BD) program. Of course, few students have only one disability, and those in the BD program tend to have learning disabilities (LD) as well as BD. Knowing that the BD students might have difficulty in making good decisions, the staff has been very supportive of an approach that includes warning students that their behaviors will lead to certain consequences. This approach has been working well.

Of course, one of the steps in the discipline process is to refer students to the principal after the teacher has exhausted various classroom management techniques. Robert, an African American male and one of the BD students, has begun to develop a pattern of coming to school late. After a series of warnings and parental contacts, it was agreed that the next time Robert is late, he will have to see the principal before he can proceed to class. Today, Robert came in late and knowing the consequence, reported directly to the office. Mike knows his students, especially those in the BD room. He understands that Robert comes from a dysfunctional family in which the father has a violent temper and frequently acts as if he were a drill sergeant, imposing some pretty severe punishments on Robert. Mike knows that Robert does not react well to scolding, and actually that can be a trigger to overt behavior. Mike and Robert have a very productive conference during which Robert admits that he is responsible for his tardiness and that he will try to remedy it. Mike works out a plan by which Robert will set his alarm clock a little earlier. Mike also walks Robert through a structured schedule including having breakfast and being out of the house by a certain time.

When Mike finishes, he sends Robert to class with a pass. As Mike makes some notes, he then leaves his office to check with his secretary. She informs him that Dr. Peterson, the superintendent, is in the building. Mike heads down the hall to catch up with the superintendent. Just as he rounds the corner, Mike hears the superintendent hollering at a student. Mike's fears become a reality as he sees Robert walking away from the superintendent, ignoring the superintendent's demand to see a hall pass. When the superintendent raises his voice and again demands to see a pass, Robert turns and lets loose with a barrage of obscenities. Because this is occurring just outside the BD room, the teacher immediately runs to the door and calmly tells the superintendent that she will take care of this matter with Robert. Unfortunately, that's not what the superintendent has in mind, and he again demands that Robert show him a pass. Mike tries to intervene, quietly asking the superintendent to come to his office where Mike can go into detail about this student. Of course, the superintendent is embarrassed to have both the teacher and the principal as witnesses to what he considers a loss of a battle, but he turns abruptly and charges to Mike's office.

Once inside the office, Mike attempts to explain Robert's situation and that his "trigger" is loud demands. Mike also explains that because Dr. Peterson is an African American male who aggressively placed demands on Robert, the student probably was reacting as if Dr. Peterson were his father. The superintendent is not buying any of the explanation and instead accuses Mike of running a sloppy ship. He further demands that Mike suspend Robert for not complying with a reasonable request. Mike explains that because of Robert's disability, he really can't be suspended. The superintendent demands that the boy be suspended, and he further alleges that Mike is coddling Robert. According to the superintendent, Mike does not expect minorities to abide by the same standards as other students.

What would you do if you were Mike, the principal? Explain, in bulleted format, a process for handling this diversity challenge, aligned with ISLLC Standard 6: *An education leader promotes the success of every student by understanding, responding to, and influencing the political, social, economic, legal, and cultural context.*

Ethical Considerations

Making sure that students demonstrate appropriate behavior can be a challenge with any student, but with those having behavior disorders it is particularly difficult. It is a slow process to deprogram explosive and impulsive behavior, and the behavior specialists often see progress one day and regression the next. The student having behavior problems didn't get this way overnight and won't change overnight either. For the superintendent not to recognize this is an insult both to the students and to the teachers.

On the other hand, the superintendent most likely was concerned that if the student treated him with such disrespect, he would treat other visitors to the school the same way. The superintendent certainly doesn't want any visitors to walk away with a negative impression about the schools in his district. From the superintendent's perspective, such student behavior cannot be tolerated, and if not addressed strongly can proliferate. Not only would the superintendent feel embarrassed by the student's rudeness to him, but he also would feel an obligation to address the problem immediately. Also, his pride is on the line as others have witnessed this, and as the leader of the school district, he most likely has the expectation that he can handle any problem that comes his way.

What the superintendent doesn't realize is that teachers don't expect superintendents to know everything about every program in the district. That's why the behavior specialists have a job. They are experts at handling behavior problems, and they want to be empowered to deal with the situations as per their training. Although the superintendent might be trying to appear strong and decisive, he really is undermining the work of his faculty. That not only is insulting to them, but it also can cause them to question his credibility as a leader.

The principal is in a tough position because he has to support his faculty, but he also has to help the superintendent to save face. In addition, the principal's primary focus is on what's best for his students. As is true in most emotional situations, time is needed for a cool down. Problems can be resolved when calmer minds prevail, but only if reason and rationality are possible. Somehow the principal has to buy time in order for the situation to de-escalate. Ideally, he should be able to get the superintendent away from the scene and into his office where they can calmly talk about this. The audience of teachers and student isn't conducive to good problem solving. The teachers need to get the student into their care where they can address the situation in accordance with their training and expertise.

7-4. FACULTY ISSUES RELATED TO GENDER (ISLLC STANDARD 5)

You are an elementary school principal, and your faculty is all female, except for the physical education teacher. As you work with your teachers on the development of curriculum and lesson plans, you begin to notice a subconscious prejudice about expectations for students depending on gender. When you observe classes, you notice that boys are called upon more in science lessons, and that they typically take the lead in the labs and experiments. You also notice that girls are called upon more frequently to answer questions in reading lessons. As the teachers lead discussions about the reading selections, the teachers express an obvious opinion about gender roles in the family. If you hadn't looked at the calendar, you'd think you were in the 1950s, as indicated by some of the comments made by the teachers about the roles of moms and dads in discussions and stories about families. You also notice that boys and girls are disciplined differently at recess. Some of the aggressive behavior that the boys exhibit is not tolerated if the girls exhibit the same behaviors. The teachers seem to dismiss the boys' behavior as "Boys will be boys." But they are quick to criticize the girls by saying, "Young ladies don't act that way."

Although you have a very dedicated and collaborative faculty, you realize that they most likely are influencing student success based on gender. As you look at the state test scores, you notice that the boys score significantly higher in math and the girls score significantly higher in reading. You could dismiss this as typical of the interests of boys and girls at this age, but you strongly suspect that your faculty members might unknowingly be contributing to this achievement gap.

As principal of this school, what would you do? Explain, in bulleted format, a process for handling this challenge. Please align your plan with ISLLC Standard 5: *An education leader promotes the success of every student by acting with integrity, fairness, and in an ethical manner.*

Ethical Considerations

Despite Title IX legislation mandating equal opportunities in educational programs for both genders, and a multitude of studies indicating that both genders are equally intelligent and skilled, many people still hold onto traditional beliefs that boys and girls have innate advantages in specific content areas and consequently should not have equal educational opportunities. Often the expectations that teachers place on students differs between the genders, both in content areas as well as in disciplinary situations. Sometimes social values convey messages that girls shouldn't appear to be too intelligent or that boys shouldn't appear to be too artistic. These attitudes are difficult to break when they are deeply rooted within the community.

The principal certainly has to address the faculty's practices and beliefs, but it must be done in a way that won't cause the faculty to resist his efforts. The risk of causing the faculty to become defensive and resistant to change is high when questioning these deep-rooted beliefs. On the other hand, the principal cannot let such gender-biased practices continue. It simply is not ethical nor is it fair to the boys and girls to ignore these practices. The unwritten expectations conveyed by teachers are powerful, and students are quick to perceive them.

How many boys and girls might have interests and potential in certain content areas, but have had them snuffed out by gender-biased teachers? Although this is a very sensitive topic that requires individuals to question some of their fundamental beliefs, the principal has to develop a plan of action to address this and ultimately to change teacher behaviors.

7-5. HOMOSEXUALITY ISSUES AND A BOARD MEETING (ISLLC STANDARD 5)

You are the principal of a junior high school in an affluent, suburban school district. In this district, principals are required to attend all board of education meetings. As part of the regular agenda, the public are invited to make comments or to ask questions. If the questions are specific to a particular school, the principal is asked to respond to the question. That's one of the reasons the superintendent requires principals to be at the board of education meetings. Usually the questions are rather trivial, such as, "Why does Open House begin at 6:00 P.M. instead of 6:30 P.M.?" or "Why do the school parking lot lights stay on all night?" or "Why do the buses take so long to unload in the morning?"

As you are sitting there listening to the mundane questions, you are jolted from your thoughts when a parent who is quite irate in her tone of voice states that she has a question for you. The tone of her voice alerts you that trouble is on the horizon. She loudly proclaims that Ms. Smith is a homosexual and therefore is a poor role model for the children. The parent continues to state that because Ms. Smith is so well liked by the children, she is conveying to the children that such a lifestyle is acceptable. Religious beliefs enter the parent's verbal attack as she proclaims that the teacher is acting in a way that is contrary to the parent's and the child's religion. She wants to know why you hired Ms. Smith in the first place and what you're going to do about this now.

How would you handle this situation? You have to think quickly, and you don't have time to put together a detailed plan. Explain, in a bulleted manner, how you would respond to this parent. Kindly align your plan with ISLLC Standard 5: *An education leader promotes the success of every student by acting with integrity, fairness, and in an ethical manner.*

Ethical Considerations

The principal's immediate reaction might be to declare that she hires teachers on the basis of their ability to teach and not on their sexual preference or lifestyle. While that would be an accurate statement, the principal has to be careful not to imply that the teacher is or isn't homosexual. That is none of anyone's concern unless the teacher were to try to influence her students regarding sexual lifesyles. Clearly, a public forum such as the board meeting is not the appropriate place for the parent to make such accusations, nor is it the appropriate forum for the principal to go into any detail about the teacher's performance in the classroom. The superintendent and board members might be willing to allow principals to directly answer questions from the public so as to promote the leadership abilities of the principals. In this case, however, the superintendent would be wise to intervene and suggest that the parent contact the principal to set up a private appointment during which they can discuss classroom-related issues.

Should the superintendent not take the lead on this, the principal should treat the complaining parent politely and diplomatically. A request should be made to the parent that she phone the principal tomorrow morning to set up an appointment. At this point, the principal doesn't know if the teacher has been making inappropriate comments in class. One has to wonder what caused the parent to become so upset. The principal needs to do some investigation. Perhaps during the private meeting with the parent, the principal could determine the root cause of the parent's concern. The principal will need time to talk with the teacher and possibly with some students as part of the investigation. While it might be uncomfortable to talk to the teacher about this, she deserves to be kept in the communication loop. The principal would not want the teacher to hear about this second-hand, and then to wonder why her principal didn't have the courtesy to at least apprise her of the allegations.

7-6. PLACEMENT IN THE GIFTED PROGRAM? (ISLLC STANDARD 3)

You are a new principal of an elementary school, and your year has been going quite well. The faculty, students, and parents all like you and your leadership style. Unfortunately, one of the board members, Arlene McDougal, has been making negative comments about your school. She doesn't like the traffic congestion at dismissal time, and she keeps bringing that up at board meetings.

You are aware of the traffic problem and have been working with the police department to come up with a solution. Unfortunately, the layout of the streets prevents any radical changes. The police agree that the current traffic plan is the best that anyone can do. The traffic problems are short-lived, and the neighbors know to avoid the school at dismissal time. Even though you have explained this to the board of education, Arlene continues to make negative comments at the board meetings.

At a recent meeting, when Arlene started to complain about the traffic problems at your school and that you're doing nothing to solve them, she even suggested that perhaps the board has hired the wrong principal if you can't solve problems like this. At this point, another board member, Bob Murphy, spoke in your defense. His comments quieted Arlene, as other board members agreed with him. The next morning you sent an e-mail to Bob thanking him for his support.

Later that day, your gifted education teacher comes to you with a problem. Mr. and Mrs. Bob Murphy requested that their son be considered for the fifth-grade gifted program. The criteria for admission to the program include standardized test scores, teacher recommendation, parental recommendation, and straight A's in all subjects. The Murphy child met all the criteria except the standardized test scores. The minimum is the 90th percentile, and young Murphy scored in the 85th percentile. The teacher explains that because he is the son of a board member, she thought it wise to bring this to your attention. There are 20 students who met the criteria and the gifted class size limit is 20. To complicate matters, there are five other students who scored at the 85th percentile. If you make an exception for young Murphy, you'd have to make an exception for five other children, thereby raising the gifted class size to 26. Obviously, this is way beyond the limit for the gifted class, but not enough to run two gifted classes.

If it were anyone else, you could explain that the child didn't meet the criteria, but knowing that Bob Murphy has supported you complicates matters. If it weren't for Bob, you could be looking for a new job. In the past, the superintendent had been the victim of Arlene's verbal attacks, and now he is reluctant to challenge her. He obviously is afraid of her ability to influence the other board members, and he is not going to put his job on the line to protect yours. You are not sure how Bob will handle the news that his son did not qualify for the gifted program.

What should you do? Develop a bulleted action plan aligned with ISLLC Standard 3: *An education leader promotes the success of every student by ensuring management of the organization, operation, and resources for a safe, efficient, and effective learning environment.*

Ethical Considerations

This case study has multiple situations with which the principal has to deal. The board member's support regarding the traffic situation complicates the issue, but that board member has not used it to pressure the principal. Of course, the principal is politically astute enough to recognize that the "quid pro quo" premise might be at work here. While one situation has nothing to do with the other, the principal most likely is worried that the board member who supported him with the traffic situation might expect a return favor.

Of equal concern is the integrity of the gifted program. Can the principal be sure that the selection criteria are fair? Can he be sure that they truly represent giftedness? Should a standardized test score be used as a determining factor? What if no students scored at the set percentile rank? Would the school then take the top 20 students, even if they didn't score at the 90th percentile? What role do the teachers in the gifted program play in the selection process? Can the principal make a special exception for the board member's son without doing so for the other students with similar scores? How would he explain that to his faculty? If he were to do so, would such a placement hurt the board member's credibility? The principal's credibility?

The principal has to consider all these questions, but most of all he has to ask if the board member's son has the capacity to be successful in the gifted program. Assuming the selection process is grounded on good educational practice, its purpose isn't to create an elite pool of students, but rather to place students who can be successful in the program. Often parents want their children to be in a gifted program for the wrong reasons. Certainly, there is a certain status that accompanies such placement, and there are field trips and other educational opportunities that might not exist in the regular program, but ultimately the students have to meet with success in the program. If they can't handle the expectations and demands of the program, they won't be happy and they won't learn as much as if they remained in the regular program.

7-7. PRIDE AND SNOBBERY BETWEEN SCHOOL DISTRICTS (ISLLC STANDARD 5)

You are the principal of a junior high school in an urban unit school district. Your district is on the south side of the river, and it is comprised mostly of Mexican, first-generation immigrants who have purchased old homes on this side of town. White flight has resulted in these large, old homes having been sold quickly and at relatively low prices as the White residents moved to the west side of the river. The SES (socioeconomic status) is 63% and all 15 of the schools in your district qualify for schoolwide Title I services. This means that in each school, more than 50% of the students are eligible for free or reduced lunch. In other words, their family income levels are at or below the national poverty level.

The issues faced by your district are complicated, because in addition to the struggles that any first-generation immigrant group faces, the financial base of your district has been eroding as a result of White flight. Large corporate bases have moved away to more prosperous areas, leaving your district only with a residential tax base. The tax rate in your district is very high, and there is no hope of seeking a referendum, simply because the taxpayers can't afford it.

Because these are mostly first-generation immigrants, they are willing to work for minimum wages so that they can establish themselves in the United States. They have come here seeking a better lifestyle for their families, and even minimum wage jobs here offer a better lifestyle than that of their homeland. The large, old houses lend themselves nicely to accommodating family members who also are trying to establish themselves in a new country. Consequently, relatives often share a house until they save enough money to purchase their own home. Most of the children in your district come from two-parent families in which both parents have a strong work ethic and a solid base of religion. They are willing to provide support to the teachers, but often a lack of babysitting is an obstacle preventing them from attending PTA meetings or from helping out with after-school activities. They also tend to have relatively large families of four or more siblings.

Your teachers are hard working, and the students are eager learners. Unfortunately, the media doesn't understand the complexities of learning a second language as well as acclimating to a new culture. Although your students are making progress, it does take time for them to become biliterate in English. While many of them can speak English enough to carry on a conversation, being able to read and write in English is considerably more difficult for them. Their foundation in other content areas is quite varied due to the extreme differences in schools in Mexico. Complicating the learning environment is the students' struggle in understanding the slang and allusions that are so prevalent in the English language.

The school district on the north side of the river serves a predominantly white population and receives very little Title I money, which is indicative of the median income level of the taxpayers. Because of the relative prosperity of the west side of town, many commercial enterprises have relocated there, giving the school district a strong commercial base. Needless to say, this has resulted in a lower tax rate for residential property than the residents previously paid when they lived on the east side of town. There is a predominant feeling of superiority on the part of the north siders when comparing their schools and the standard of living with that of the south side.

Because both school districts are in the same city, the mayor and city council have decided to provide financial assistance to programs and projects that could be shared by both of the city's school districts. This necessitates your working cooperatively with principals from the north side school district. You have good interpersonal skills and can work with almost anyone, but you find it difficult to work with people who make derogatory comments about your district. You are fed up with the snobbish attitude of the principals on the north side, but you have to work with them on various projects. You wish there would be some way that they could see your students as children instead of as nameless immigrants. Despite the lack of financial resources in your district, you have excellent teachers who are very dedicated to helping their students. You are proud of them, but the people in the other district don't see it that way. They brag about all the high-tech equipment in their district, while you are happy just to have a computer lab.

These feelings extend beyond the schools and into the service clubs as well. Being a member of Rotary, you can't help but hear and feel the snobbery that is conveyed by the north siders during these meetings. They seem to be focused on showing that their schools and students are superior to yours.

- How do you deal with your own feelings?
- How can you get the principals from the other district to stop being so snobbish?
- How can you get beyond the snobbery and focus on the shared projects?

In a bulleted format, explain your plan of action to resolve this situation. Please align your plan to ISLLC Standard 5: *An education leader promotes the success of every student by acting with integrity, fairness, and in an ethical manner.*

Ethical Considerations

It is unfortunate when competition among schools and school districts results in snobbery and even a feeling of superiority. Educational leadership is a profession of service to the students in particular and the community in general. As each school district serves its constituents with its available resources, other school districts should recognize that we all have different roads to travel. No one is superior because of a large tax base or because of affluent families. One might even argue that the affluent have an obligation to help the less fortunate. As educational leaders serve as role models for the community, it is important that we demonstrate servant leadership and assistance to those in need.

When the less fortunate school district feels snubbed by the more affluent one, it is human nature to feel some animosity toward affluence. From the perspective of educational leadership, the principal has to be careful not to fall into the trap of resorting to harboring negative feelings toward the more affluent district. Not only is that not being a good role model, but it also is counterproductive. Although the principal might feel justified in trying to find ways to bad-mouth the more affluent district, the ancient belief of an "eye for an eye, a tooth for a tooth" doesn't work well in the world of servant leadership.

The educational leaders in the affluent school district obviously need to be informed of the good things that occur daily in the less fortunate school district. They need to view those students and their families with respect, and they need to recognize that intelligence is not limited to the affluent. Despite any ill feelings that might exist between the two districts, it is incumbent upon the educational leaders from both districts to be role models of ethical and servant leadership. If the affluent school district doesn't make the first move toward collaboration, then it's up to the less fortunate school district to do so.

A strong community is one that is not divided, but rather works together for the good of its constituents. Both school districts comprise the community, and both should work together to promote acceptance of diversity and a willingness to help each other. Most likely both districts have specific talents and resources that could be shared with each other. Neither has to be the sole provider or the sole recipient. Cooperative endeavors, partnerships between the two school districts regarding curriculum development, alternative programs, grant applications, and student activities are just some of the ways by which the two districts can share their resources and talents with each other.

CHAPTER 8

Here's What Happened

Each of the case studies is based on true situations, although the identifying details have been altered not only to maintain confidentiality but also to provide meaningful and representative learning experiences for future educational leaders. In some cases, the situations might have occurred in a high school, but they have been cast into an elementary or middle school to provide a balance of administrative challenges to the reader. This chapter contains an explanation of what happened in each of the case studies. Please note that what happened isn't always the best outcome. Readers are encouraged to read these with an open mind as well as with the question, "Is this what I would have done?"

CHAPTER 2: INSTRUCTIONAL LEADERSHIP

2-1. AN ALL-DAY FIELD TRIP IMPACTS THE INSTRUCTIONAL PROGRAM (ISLLC STANDARD 2)

Here's What Happened

The principal tried to engage the department chairs in a collective problem-solving process. None of them would budge from their positions. They weren't willing to seek a third solution, and instead polarized themselves. The English department chair was the "odd man out," in that the other department chairs opposed the Greek Day field trip. The principal tried to get the other department chairs to brainstorm ideas that might allow Greek Day to continue with more supervision or during a half-day, or in conjunction with other content area teachers. But there was no acceptance of this attempt by either the English department chair or the other department chairs.

The principal then explained that despite his attempts to engage all of them in collective problem-solving, they were resistant to these efforts. He expressed his disappointment with their willingness to find a new alternative. Ultimately, the principal made the decision not to approve any future Greek Day field trips during the school day. He explained that the English department had been able to successfully manage an event of this magnitude and, therefore, had to come up with alternate ways to meet the goals of the event without pulling students from other classes.

2-2. KINDERGARTEN AND THE TWINS: WHAT IS OUR VISION FOR LEARNING? (ISLLC STANDARD 1)

Here's What Happened

The principal worked with the three kindergarten teachers to empower them to conduct research about the best practices in effective kindergarten programs. Teachers were given substitute coverage to enable them to visit other schools both in and out of the district to observe different kindergarten programs. The principal emphasized that the focus had to be on the students, and that each of the teachers would have to implement a new program. They either could develop the new program themselves, or it would be determined by others. They opted to conduct research, to visit schools, and to develop a new program. The principal provided them with the necessary resources and met with the teachers regularly to stay apprised of their progress. Because they had ownership of the process and product, and because the principal provided the necessary resources, the teachers enthusiastically developed a new program.

2-3. THE HIGH SCHOOL MATH DEPARTMENT: ARE WE SERVING ALL STAKEHOLDERS? (ISLLC STANDARD 1)

Here's What Happened

The situation didn't end happily. Despite the data, the teachers dug in their heels and refused to own the problem. They insisted that the students were the only ones responsible here, and the teachers had no responsibility other than to teach them and to assign homework. The principal tried, but was unable to rally the teachers into a collaborative team of problem solvers. He was reluctant to mandate change because he was afraid of losing the teachers' confidence in him as a leader. He turned to the central office (the assistant superintendent) for a solution. As a last resort, after trying to reason with the teachers and to empower them to solve the problem, the assistant superintendent mandated that the teachers assign only as much homework as could be done during the last 10 to 15 minutes of the class period. Furthermore, teachers could not issue a failing grade without first presenting a list of interventions that were attempted throughout the semester. The principal would review the list of interventions, meet with a team of teachers, and make a recommendation that the student would either repeat the course or go to summer school.

2-4. PARENTS' AGREEMENT: NO DATA MEANS "GET RID OF IT!" (ISLLC STANDARD 3)

Here's What Happened

The committee couldn't develop a data-collection tool that would be meaningful to the participants and that would yield useable information. Despite attempts by the committee to convince the superintendent that some school initiatives can't be measured by data-collection tools, he flatly refused. The initiative died. Most felt that this was a loss, but the superintendent was on a mission to attach data-driven results to every initiative and program.

2-5. THE PHYSICAL EDUCATION DRESS CODE AND ITS FAIRNESS TO ALL STUDENTS (ISLLC STANDARD 5)

Here's What Happened

The principal met again with the physical education staff and explained, "We have a problem to solve. Too many students are receiving referrals for not dressing for physical education classes. As those referrals accumulate, and the students eventually receive out-of-school suspension, students' attendance, learning, and achievement in other courses is suffering. How do we solve this problem?"

The principal further explained, "We no longer can sit back and place all the blame on the students. We have to find a solution to this problem. We can and should involve students in the solution. This is your charge: to find a solution. Let me know if you need subs so you can visit other schools. If you need to conduct a survey among other schools, we can activate our Internet-based survey program for your use. Let me know what you need. I would like a recommendation within a month."

The teachers really did have the students' best interests at heart, but they were afraid to compromise what they believed to be an integral part of their program—self-discipline. After visiting a number of area schools, they saw not only a more liberal physical education dress code, but also a different curricular approach to physical education. They recommended that the school adopt a lifelong fitness approach to accompany a more liberal dress code. The focus of the new curriculum would be on individual fitness goals. While this new curriculum had an initial capital outlay for computer-based fitness monitoring equipment and exercise equipment, it was an "easy sell" to the board of education.

2-6. THE SOCIAL STUDIES TEACHER AND ETHICAL BEHAVIOR (ISLLC STANDARD 5)

Here's What Happened

The principal investigated the situation and determined that the department chair acted too quickly in trying to solve the problem. The teacher had not been given a clear explanation of why the involvement of the students needed to be changed. Also, adequate support for the teacher, such as help in redesigning the lessons and activities, had not been offered. Just as the principal originally suspected, a schedule was made not with the best interests of the students in mind, but rather with punishment of the teacher in mind.

After finding this out, the principal set up an appointment to work with the department chair in perfecting her supervisory skills. Not only did the teacher need some staff development in creating new and exciting lessons and activities, but the department chair also needed staff development in how to handle such challenges. The principal learned that he needed to be far more vigilant in his supervision of department chairs as well as teachers.

2-7. STATE TESTS AND ETHICS (ISLLC STANDARD 6)

Here's What Happened

The principal entered the classroom and began a conversation with the teacher. Before the principal could even ask why a copy of the State Achievement Test booklet was on the teacher's desk, she volunteered an explanation. "Oh, I'm right in the middle of making sure my students' test booklets are all in numerical order and facing the right direction. You know how kids are. They don't always follow directions. I certainly don't want my class to be the one that causes the processing people to complain."

While the explanation seemed logical, the principal had his suspicions, but in the absence of any real evidence, he reminded her that it really wasn't the teacher's responsibility to pack the test booklets. Teachers should send them to the office, and a secretary would process them for shipping. The principal certainly didn't want to falsely accuse the teacher, but instead made a mental note to remind all faculty of the state's laws regarding teachers' looking at State Achievement Tests. He planned to do that in two ways: a simple reminder that the office would pack the test booklets, and a copy of the state rules placed in each teacher's mailbox prior to future testing dates.

2-8. THE UNCOMPROMISING MATH TEACHER (ISLLC STANDARD 3)

Here's What Happened

The principal very patiently worked with the math teacher to get her to understand the importance of following the student's Individual Education Plan. He also sought the support of the special education teacher to offer some suggestions to the math teacher about how to provide some other challenging activities that all students could enjoy. The math teacher slowly came around, but the principal did have to use a direct and firm approach throughout the process. To ensure compliance, he did observe her teaching during that period, but he didn't merely sit in the back of the room and take notes. Instead, he took an active part as if he were one of the students. He raised his hand and answered questions, as well as asking them. He also tried to bring some levity into the situation by purposely giving wrong answers. After a short while, the teacher recognized that he was there to help her and not to find fault with her teaching.

2-9. THE WALKOUT AND RELATED POLITICS (ISLLC STANDARD 6)

Here's What Happened

Despite the best attempts of the principal to reason with teachers the next morning before school that he was doing all he could to salvage their courses, he only received superficial support. During the first period, the principal met with student council officers to explain the situation to them and to seek their support in trying to head off the walkout. After meeting with them, the principal and the assistant principal went into as many classes as they could to talk directly with students about their concerns.

These steps were partially successful in that only 50% of the student body participated in the walkout. The teachers did stand guard by the doors, but they were unable to prevent students from leaving the building. The students gathered in one of the parking lots, and the principal and assistant principal supervised the area to make sure no mishaps would occur. In an attempt to show superiority in managing conflict, the superintendent somehow acquired a megaphone (was this purchased in anticipation of the walkout?) and tried to speak with the students. They scoffed at him and began leaving the parking lot.

Apparently the media were notified, but it had been a busy news day, and only a newspaper photographer arrived. No television news people showed up or even phoned to ask questions. Teachers did take attendance the rest of the day, and the students who walked out were given a detention for each class period missed, as per the discipline handbook. The walkout occurred on a Friday, and the students who walked out were required to have a signed parent note before returning to school on Monday, again in accordance with the normal attendance and discipline policies.

The superintendent did not show up to work on either Monday or Tuesday, presumably because he was at a conference. His usual practice was to notify the principal when he was going to be out of the district, but he didn't do so this time. When the principal phoned the superintendent to apprise him of how student discipline was being handled, he found out that the superintendent was out of town. Unfortunately, the superintendent blamed the principal for the walkout, and asked the Board of Education not to renew the principal's contract for the next year.

CHAPTER 3: ETHICS AND MANAGEMENT

3-1. AN ALLEGED STEROID USER (ISLLC STANDARD 6)

Here's What Happened

The teacher was reprimanded by the assistant principal. A memo indicating that future acts of misrepresenting his scope of responsibility could result in termination was placed in the teacher's file. This occurred after a conference at which a union representative was present.

After the conference, the teacher admitted that he was thinking of the benefits of the drug assessment, which either could exonerate the student or acquire needed help for him. The teacher offered to phone the parents to convince them to take the student to the assessment. The assistant principal told the teacher that such an offer, while noble in its intent, would only exacerbate his acting beyond the scope of a teacher's responsibility.

Instead, the assistant principal sought another conference with the student and the parents to again explain their options. At that conference, the parents agreed to take their son to the hospital for an assessment. Later that day, the hospital phoned the assistant principal to verify that the student had been assessed and was being admitted into an outpatient program.

3-2. ANOTHER ASSISTANT SUPERINTENDENT FALSELY ACCUSES ONE OF YOUR STAFF (ISLLC STANDARD 5)

Here's What Happened

The assistant superintendent for curriculum and instruction continued to plug along, hoping to change the behavior of the superintendent and his cabinet. Attempts to focus the group on the issues at hand and to dispel the gossip comments were utilized by the assistant superintendent. Just when he thought things were going well, one of his colleagues would drop a "gossip bomb" on the cabinet. This was discouraging to the assistant superintendent for curriculum and instruction. He realized that the superintendent could stop this behavior, but he seemed to thrive on it.

After five years of being the "odd man out," the assistant superintendent for curriculum and instruction decided to take an early retirement. He was quickly replaced by someone who fit in very nicely with the gossip and sniping of the other assistant superintendents. Sometimes the culture of an organization is so strong that it fights any attempts at change. This certainly was the case.

3-3. A BOARD MEMBER'S SON IN A FIGHT (ISLLC STANDARD 3)

Here's What Happened

The assistant principal told Don Anderson, "I don't need to think about this, Don. You and I both know the ramifications if I don't treat both students the same. They both were equally involved in this altercation, by their own admission. I don't have to say anything, but you know how quickly word of mouth will spread if your son gets special privileges. This doesn't bode well for your reputation as a board member."

Don admitted, "You're right. I'm just trying to keep peace in my home, but I understand that this could blow up in my face."

After the assistant principal concluded the phone call with Don Anderson, he notified the superintendent, who agreed that the assistant principal had done the right thing. The superintendent also assured the assistant principal that this decision would not jeopardize his contract renewal.

The board did approve the superintendent's recommendation for contract renewal, and a year later, the assistant principal was appointed to the principalship of the high school. However, the board member continued to remind the principal of this decision for years. At board meetings, he would say things like, "Don't expect to get any break from this principal. He suspended my son for a little altercation." Although the comments were made in jest, they didn't make the principal feel very secure about his job.

3-4. CELL PHONES, A BOMB THREAT, AND A BUILDING EVACUATION (ISLLC STANDARD 3)

Here's What Happened

The principal initially told the parents that the students were safe and that they would be admitted back into school as soon as the police determined that it was safe. The parents wanted no part of this, explaining that they didn't want their students to enter the building if there was the slightest chance of a bomb. Despite his best attempts to reason with the parents, they wanted their students released into their custody. Needless to say, this was their legal right, and the principal could not deny them.

The students were allowed to leave, and parents were required to sign a form releasing them. When the students left the campus, unfortunately, they did so with much noise. They were not allowed to reenter the building to get their books and personal belongings because the police had not yet determined it to be safe for them to enter. This caused some arguing from the parents and students, but the principal really wasn't in any position to allow them to reenter the building. The parents immediately went to the local media to complain. Both the local radio station and the newspaper made a big deal about this the next day. The principal was the recipient of much criticism by both media sources, even though he had acted according to policy.

Once the police allowed students to reenter, about 60% of them were still around. The remaining 40% had left with parental permission. The unfortunate thing is that the teachers could not carry on with the planned lessons because so many of the students were not present, which meant that the lessons would have to be retaught the next day to the whole class.

3-5. DIFFERING PHILOSOPHIES ABOUT DISCIPLINE (ISLLC STANDARD 5)

Here's What Happened

The principal addressed the rift between the two faculty groups at a faculty meeting. She engaged the faculty in a collective problem-solving process intended to clarify and identify the root cause of the problem. From the information shared in this session, the principal developed a plan by which the faculty would conduct research as to what was done in other schools. They would visit other schools, and they would collectively develop an overriding philosophy of discipline. From that specific procedures and practices would be written by the faculty.

The principal also sought opportunities to pair veteran and young faculty together in curriculum projects. At the risk of involving the faculty in too many projects, she recognized that one way to get them to work together would be through curriculum mapping and textbook selection processes. She introduced this idea carefully and deliberately, assuring the faculty that they would have ample time and that the process would take a long time to complete. After two years, the faculty members were working much better together, but it took a lot of nurturing on the part of the principal.

3-6. THE ELECTRICITY GOES OUT DURING THE SCHOOL DAY: HOW TO MANAGE THIS SITUATION (ISLLC STANDARD 3)

Here's What Happened

The principal chose to keep school running as normally as possible. She asked the custodians and maintenance staff to provide flashlight-lanterns for use in the washrooms. She contacted central office and asked any availabel administrators to provide supervision both in the washrooms and hallways. She assured the fire department that she would have either central office administrators or availabel teachers supervising the hallways throughout the rest of the day to report any fire or danger as well as to prevent the same.

The principal, her assistant principal, the secretaries, and the guidance counselor went from classroom to classroom and explained the situation, telling the teachers and students that they would move to the next period at the appropriate time. Also, the students would have the usual five minutes to get to their next class. Teachers were asked to monitor the hallways immediately outside their classrooms to make sure that students got to their next class quickly.

As a follow-up, at the end of the day the principal had her secretary place a thank-you memo in each faculty and staff member's mailbox thanking them for their help with this situation. An explanatory letter was prepared to be sent home to the parents, and the photocopier at the central office was used to make copies for the students to take home. Emphasis was placed on the fact that at no time were any students in danger, thanks to all who provided supervision in the hallways and washrooms.

3-7. ETHICS AND THE PRINCIPAL'S DECISION (ISLLC STANDARD 5)

Here's What Happened

The principal did not allow the students to enter the prom. Instead he followed the policy and notified the parents to come and take their children home. He held his ground, which was witnessed by faculty members who were working the event. The board member also held his ground, despite many attempts to reason with him. He went to the superintendent and demanded that the principal be fired. He also reminded the superintendent of the upcoming board evaluation of the superintendent. This was too much pressure on the superintendent, and he caved under the board member's pressure. The superintendent recommended to the board that the principal's contract not be renewed due to "philosophical differences." Because the principal hadn't been in the district long enough to earn tenure as a teacher, he had a one-year terminal contract. This was in accordance with the district contracts for administrators, which specified that the decision not to renew an administrative contract had to be acted upon by the board prior to March 1st. Consequently, the principal had one year to find a new job, which he did.

During interviews, when asked why he was leaving his current position, the principal told the truth. The interview team in another district was impressed not only by his honesty, but also by his sense of ethics in decision making. They easily decided that they wanted this person to be their principal. He served a number of years as principal in this district.

3-8. MISUSE OF THE RTI INITIATIVE (ISLLC STANDARD 6)

Here's What Happened

The building special education coordinator let things cool down for a few days, and then went back to the principal and tried to reason with him, using ethics as a lever. She asked the principal if he could live with the decision to prematurely exit children and possibly ruin their communication skills for life. She also explained that in her position, she was responsible for ensuring compliance with the state laws. By telling her to exit the children, the principal really was asking her to do something illegal. As much as she loved her position, she was not willing to do anything illegal to keep her job.

After hearing her explanation, the principal reversed his decision and told her to get a half-time speech pathologist. He then used the other half of a resource allocation to hire a half-time intervention specialist.

3-9. A MURDER OCCURS A BLOCK AWAY FROM THE SCHOOL: MAINTAINING A SAFE ENVIRONMENT (ISLLC STANDARD 3)

Here's What Happened

The principal did ask for central office support to help with the supervision of the students. She allowed faculty to leave if they had family obligations, but only after the police declared it safe for them to drive out of the school parking lot. The police gave them a specific route to use as they left the neighborhood. The children were put into the large areas of the school, by grade level. Primary grades (kindergarten and first grade) were put in the gym and given various playground balls and toys to occupy them. The second and third graders were put in the cafeteria and given various coloring books and puzzles to use. The fourth and fifth graders were put in the library and were encouraged to utilize the computers and to choose books and magazines to read.

Those teachers who opted to stay (and there were many of them) divided themselves among the three groups and supervised accordingly. Central office personnel assisted with parental communications as well as with supervision of the students. The police completed their investigation and determined the area to be safe at about five o'clock. The teachers and central office personnel stayed with the students until they were dismissed.

3-10. OFFICE POLITICS: HOW DOES A CONSCIENTIOUS ADMINISTRATOR DEAL WITH THEM AND STILL MAINTAIN A VISION FOR LEARNING? (ISLLC STANDARD 1)

Here's What Happened

When the assistant superintendent for business announced her new program and that she was planning on using the curriculum and instruction account to fund it, the assistant superintendent of curriculum and instruction explained that having 85% of the students meeting or exceeding state standards was an accomplishment that many districts in the state could only hope to make. He further explained that the principals presently were using a standardized test to identify individual students' areas needing help. By addressing the students on an individual basis, not only would the students learn for the long term, but also their scores would rise genuinely, not artificially.

The superintendent did not want to hear any of this. He wanted a quick fix and wasn't interested in genuine learning. He continued to badger the assistant superintendent for curriculum and instruction, and the other assistant superintendents acted like vultures flocking around a dying animal. The assistant superintendent of curriculum and instruction sensed this and sought new employment options.

3-11. DISPOSING OF AN UNDERGROUND STORAGE TANK: LEGALITIES AND POLITICS (ISLLC STANDARD 6)

Here's What Happened

The inspection determined that the tank had a slight leak in its bottom. Only the ground immediately surrounding the tank had been contaminated. No wells had been contaminated yet. But it was only a matter of time before the leakage would continue a journey into the nearby wells. The principal decided to use the capital improvement budget for removal of the underground storage tank, but before committing the money to that project, he decided to contact the state department of education to inquire about any grants that might be availabel either for science lab renovations or for storage tank removal. The department of education referred him to the environmental department, which did have grant money availabel for underground storage tank removal.

The principal and the building engineer wrote the grant application and received money that covered 75% of the cost of removal of the tank. The principal was able to scale back the scope of the science lab renovation project within the amount of money left in the capital improvement budget, after paying 25% of the cost of removing the storage tank.

While the superintendent was pleased with the principal's initiative to find alternate funding sources to solve the problem, he took credit for the decision when he apprised the board of education about the status of the problem.

3-12. THE PRINCIPAL HAS TURNED THE FACULTY AGAINST YOU: AN INTERNAL PUBLIC RELATIONS SITUATION (ISLLC STANDARD 4)

Here's What Happened

The assistant principal tried to speak with the principal about his habit of scolding a faculty member each week. The principal proudly proclaimed it as his way of keeping them on their toes. He actually bragged about how much control he had over the faculty as a result of his scolding them. The principal suggested that the assistant principal learn this technique to control them when he took over. This told the assistant principal that the principal saw the assistant principal as his successor, whether or not he agreed with it.

The assistant principal suggested that he might try a different approach of getting to know the faculty, at which the principal told him that he was a rookie who had a lot to learn. The principal also told the assistant principal that his soft approach never would work, because the principal already had begun to build fear of the assistant principal in the faculty members. The principal claimed to be trying to help the assistant principal by doing this. The assistant principal asked him not to continue to help him in this way and indicated that he would like to build a relationship with the faculty in a different way. The principal said, "Okay, do it your own way."

But the assistant principal doubted his sincerity. After some careful deliberation within his own mind, the assistant principal confided in the superintendent about the situation. The superintendent said that he wasn't surprised, and he assured the assistant principal that getting to know each faculty member was the right way to build a good relationship with them. "Take them prisoner, one at a time," was the advice of the superintendent.

The assistant principal felt relieved that he had brought the situation to the superintendent, and he immediately began using good interpersonal skills to win over each faculty member, one at a time. It was a long and difficult two years, and the principal actually piled more and more busywork onto the assistant principal. But the assistant principal persisted, and the faculty seemed to respect him for that. They still were reluctant to completely trust any administrator, but they were making some strides toward trusting the assistant principal.

Two years later, the assistant principal was appointed to the principalship. Although some of the faculty still didn't trust any administrator, most of them were quite willing to give the new principal a chance to be their leader.

3-13. THE SUPERINTENDENT USES DISTRICT FUNDS TO FIX A DISTRICT CAR, THEN PURCHASES IT: WHAT IS THE ETHICAL COURSE OF ACTION? (ISLLC STANDARD 5)

Here's What Happened

The principal decided to casually mention to the superintendent that he noticed the car and the son driving it. The principal then relayed the story of the superintendent from his previous school district. The superintendent seemed to be unfazed by the story and simply stated, "I didn't do anything wrong." The principal said, "I'm not saying you did. I'm just cautioning you about a similar situation, and I don't want you to get burned by it." The principal then politely dismissed himself from the conversation under the guise of having work to do in his office.

As he walked back to his office, the principal was disappointed by the superintendent's response, but he also knew that he had planted a seed in the superintendent's mind. The principal decided not to go any further with this matter. The superintendent had been made aware of it. The principal thought it wise to give the superintendent time to think about the story of the other superintendent's getting fired for doing something similar. He wasn't sure what the next steps should be if the superintendent were to do nothing about this situation. The principal considered contacting the school lawyer, but he also knew that the superintendent recently recommended that the board of education contract with a new law firm—one with whom the superintendent had previous dealings in another district. The principal decided against the idea of contacting the school lawyer.

The next day, the superintendent came into the principal's office and said, "I overheard talk among the custodians about my purchasing the former district car. Did you say something to them?"

The principal tried to assure the superintendent that he hadn't said anything to anyone other than the superintendent. He reminded the superintendent that others might have read about the other superintendent because the story did appear in a number of area newspapers. Any of the custodians could have recognized the car and might have seen his son driving it. While the superintendent seemed to accept this explanation, the principal couldn't help but wonder if the superintendent really believed him. Of course, the principal hadn't said anything to anyone, but once the seed of doubt had been planted in the superintendent's mind, the principal always would be suspect.

A few days later, the superintendent came back into the principal's office and stated that he had written a check to the school district for the cost of the battery and new tires. He added that he had been in contact with the president of the board of education about this. Apparently, the superintendent convinced the board president that he was a good, ethical superintendent by taking a proactive stance rather than ever bringing any doubts or criticism to the school district.

The following spring, the superintendent delivered an unsatisfactory evaluation to the principal and recommended to the board of education that the principal's contract not be renewed for "performance" reasons. This confirmed the principal's suspicions that the superintendent had been acting with questionable ethics. Although he certainly didn't want to lose his job, the principal also knew that to continue working for an unethical superintendent could have a negative impact on his career. Often when one public leader is suspect, the ethics of those who are directly under that leader also are questioned. Furthermore, who wants to work for and support the mission and goals of an unethical superintendent?

The principal unsuccessfully sought other principalships, and because he had tenure in the school district, he was assigned to the classroom. After a year of returning to his teaching roots, the former principal found a central office position in a large urban district. When asked about the situation, he still admits that he would not have done anything differently. The year back in the classroom actually helped him to be a better administrator, because he had been reconnected with what he calls the "heart and soul of schools," *teaching!*

3-14. A TORNADO STRIKES AT NIGHT: SHOULD I LEAVE MY FAMILY TO CHECK ON THE BUILDING? (ISLLC STANDARD 3)

Here's What Happened

The principal drove to the school and did have to avoid some fallen trees, but he did not encounter any downed power lines. The drive was a bit dangerous in that the traffic signals and street lights were not functional. Upon reaching the school, the principal was relieved to learn that the building had not been hit by the tornado, but there was no electrical power anywhere in the vicinity of the school. He did bring a flashlight with him, and was able to enter the school building and to meet with his custodians. They were checking the windows and doors for any wind damage, and they had reserve flashlights.

Fortunately, the away–sports events had been cut short by the pending bad weather and all the students had arrived home before the tornado struck. The superintendent and the district director of buildings and grounds also showed up and were pleased to see the principal at the school. All three stayed with the custodians until the end of their shift, helping them to check the entire building for damage. At one point the local emergency services agency stopped by to see if the building could be used as a shelter, but then later came back and said they wouldn't need the school after all. The next day, school was cancelled because power still had not resumed.

3-15. TRYING TO IMPLEMENT A "ZERO-BASED" BUDGET (ISLLC STANDARD 3)

Here's What Happened

The principal kept the budgets the same for the next year. He also carefully monitored what each department spent and questioned purchase requests if they seemed to be "fluff." During the year, he also continued to introduce the concepts of zero-based budgeting and calculated risk-taking. In addition, he provided staff development about servant leadership and kept focusing on how educational leaders should serve students and the community.

In addition, the principal asked each department chair to develop a long-range plan of what their respective classrooms and labs should look like in the next 10 years. They were asked to include structural items as well as equipment. In other words, "What should our science labs look like? How should they be equipped? What should our writing labs look like? How should they be equipped? What should our math classrooms look like? How should they be equipped?" After each department submitted its plans, the principal shared them with all the department chairs. He then asked them how they expected to accomplish these plans. He further asked them to develop steps that would get them from here to there. It wasn't acceptable for them to say, "The district has to fund this." Instead, he asked them how the building budget could support their plans. He shared the entire building budget with them and worked with them with openness about all budgeting issues. He also showed them the unspent accounts that department chairs had requested but not used. Eventually, he won their trust, and they actually suggested a zero-based budgeting approach.

CHAPTER 4: ORGANIZATION AND DEVELOPMENT OF CURRICULUM

4-1. EVALUATING THE READING CURRICULUM REVISION (ISLLC STANDARD 1)

Here's What Happened

The principal brought the situation to the teachers in an honest and supportive manner. She did not criticize the board members or the superintendent, but rather explained the political realities of the situation. The superintendent has to show support of the board's needs. The board members have to show support of the needs of their constituents. Board members are steward of the district's finances, and when asked for an explanation regarding expenditures, they have to provide that explanation.

After engaging in some collective problem solving, the principal and the teachers came up with a plan to conduct a survey that would involve students, teachers, and parents. It would focus on key questions surrounding the new textbook. After compiling the results of this "customer satisfaction survey," the principal and a team of teachers would present their results to the board of education. They also planned to have some students bring the texts to the board meeting and demonstrate some of the well-liked features of the text. Typically board members enjoy seeing the enthusiasm of students and teachers, especially when they receive thanks for having purchased these new materials. As part of the presentation, the principal would explain the rationale for conducting a survey first, and then utilizing achievement test scores during the second year of implementation. This approach was a winner both with the superintendent and the board of education. As an added benefit, parents attended the board meeting to see their children make presentations to the board.

4-2. KINDERGARTEN CURRICULUM REVISION: PROMOTING AN EFFECTIVE LEARNING ENVIRONMENT AMID POLITICS (ISLLC STANDARD 3)

Here's What Happened

The principal and the assistant superintendent presented the kindergarten curriculum proposal to the other elementary principals as an information item. They liked the idea and asked if it could be done. The assistant superintendent reminded the principals that the proposal would compete with the superintendent's award acquisition plans for in-service time. The principals discussed the merits of the proposal and the disadvantages of waiting for another year. They reached consensus that they collectively would support the kindergarten curriculum proposal.

The assistant superintendent then asked the principals how they could address the superintendent's plan. The principals did some brainstorming, and then offered to make sure that the kindergarten teachers would receive the training about the awards acquisition program. Each principal would assume responsibility to train his or her kindergarten teachers. The assistant superintendent thought this would be acceptable by the superintendent and offered to present the proposal to him initially. He would ask the superintendent to include it on the next principals' meeting agenda.

At that meeting, the principals presented the kindergarten curriculum proposal, along with the promise to train their respective kindergarten teachers in the awards acquisition process. Because they recognized the value of the awards acquisition process but also wanted to take advantage of the kindergarten teachers' initiative, the superintendent accepted their proposal. Throughout the year, when the rest of the teachers were engaged in the awards acquisition process, the kindergarten teachers worked together on the development of a districtwide kindergarten curriculum. At mutually agreeable times, the principals trained their respective kindergarten teachers, as originally promised. The story had a good, positive ending!

4-3. THE LIFE SKILLS CURRICULUM: STUDENT LEARNING VS. BOARD POLITICS (ISLLC STANDARD 3)

Here's What Happened

The infighting between the two members of the board of education carried on, despite attempts on the part of the assistant superintendent to harness that energy into a productive direction. They seemed to enjoy their authority and their ability to lord it over the committee members. While the assistant superintendent and the principals who were members of the committee were able to keep the infighting in perspective, the teachers who were on the committee felt intimidated by it. They were afraid to offer suggestions that might appear to be contrary to either board member's opinion. The teachers also were becoming pessimistic in wondering if anything ever would happen to improve their curriculum. They began to believe that the initiative would go nowhere.

The assistant superintendent kept the superintendent informed, especially about the dynamics of the board members and the resulting negativity on the part of the teachers. He was reluctant to confront the board members about their actions and inability to get along. The superintendent opted to let their disagreement run itself out. Unfortunately, the teachers lost interest and stopped attending the committee meetings. Their lack of attendance convinced the two board members that a new curriculum wasn't really needed. Rather than commit to new sewing machines and kitchens, the board members on the committee convinced the other members of the board of education that the district would be best served by maintaining its current equipment and curriculum.

The assistant superintendent tried to convince them that this wouldn't be the best option, but the board insisted that because the teachers no longer were interested in renovating the labs and implementing new curriculum, it would be a waste of district money to buy them something that they didn't really believe in. While this was hard to argue with, the assistant superintendent knew that the teachers really wanted new equipment and curriculum, but they were afraid to cross either board member. When he mentioned this to the superintendent (in private), the assistant superintendent was told not to interfere with board politics.

There is a bright spot in this story, however. Two years later, one of the opposing board members moved out of the district. The assistant superintendent carefully worked with the other opposing board member (the retired home economics teacher) to gain her confidence. Whenever he could, the assistant superintendent would casually mention the need for a renovated home economics/life skills program. He also continued to work with the teachers to very clearly define exactly what they would like new labs to look like. Of course, the labs would be defined by the curriculum, so he also worked with them to rewrite the curriculum. They developed a hybrid. Instead of going with a module-based program in which each pair of students would be working on a different project, they developed a modified approach by which there would be more group work and individual projects going on simultaneously. In other words, instead of having 25 "workhorse" sewing machines, there were five well-optioned sewing machines. Instead of having four basic kitchens, there were two very well-equipped kitchens consisting of both gas and electric ranges, as well as microwave ovens and convection ovens.

Students would be working on different projects at the same time, but all those in the kitchen would be working on different aspects of the same meal. Some might be preparing the salad, others the main entree, the potatoes, the vegetables. While this group might be working on a meal, another group of students would be working on sewing projects. In other words, the teacher diversified the curriculum into various units that could be occurring simultaneously. She became the learning facilitator who "floated" from group to group, providing direction and assistance as needed.

4-4. THE MATH CURRICULUM COUNCIL: PROFESSIONAL ADVANCEMENT VS. WHAT'S BEST FOR KIDS (ISLLC STANDARD 2)

Here's What Happened

The assistant superintendent did investigate all the circumstances and concluded that the high school teacher was a hindrance to harmony on the council as well as any chance of progress on the part of the council. The teacher demonstrated an egotistical attitude and even referred to the other curriculum council members as being inferior to him in their knowledge of how to teach math. Needless to say, this attitude was counterproductive and injurious to the council's work. Also, the teacher admitted that he not only believed in the quality of his preferred math series, but also that he was a part-time sales representative and he would gain financially from a sale of the book to the district. Even after the assistant superintendent explained the conflict of interest and how that is contrary to the state ethic laws, which bind teachers as well as other public servants, the teacher refused to agree that it would be a conflict of interest. For these reasons, the assistant superintendent did not renew the math teacher's assignment to the curriculum council. Also, because of the potential legal issues related to a conflict of interest, the math teacher was removed from his leadership role as department chair of the high school math department. Through the department chair evaluation process, the principal had already expressed concern about the lack of leadership and the air of superiority demonstrated by the department chair.

The assistant superintendent met with the bilingual teacher prior to the end of the school year and reminded her of her summer duties as chair of the math curriculum council. The other curriculum council chairs had submitted their summary reports before the end of June, but the math curriculum council chair had not submitted hers. The assistant attempted to contact the bilingual teacher to remind her of the reports that were now overdue, but the teacher did not answer her phone nor did she respond to e-mails. The assistant superintendent then resorted to mailing a written request for the curriculum council reports. After two more weeks and still no response from the bilingual teacher, the assistant superintendent wrote a formal letter thanking the bilingual teacher for having served as chair of the math curriculum council, but because her duties as a bilingual teacher conflicted with those as a curriculum council chair, he was not going to re-appoint her as chair for the next year. Instead, he would consider her continued membership on the curriculum council, if she would like to serve in that capacity. He also asked that she contact him as to whether she would like to remain on the curriculum council.

The assistant superintendent then contacted the high school principal to learn who had been appointed as math department chair. The assistant principal met with that teacher and proposed that he consider assuming the role of chair of the math curriculum council chair. He explained the dynamics of the group as well as the interventions and decisions made by the assistant superintendent. The new department chair considered the scenario for a couple of days, and then notified the assistant superintendent that he would accept the role of chair, but only if the assistant superintendent would attend the first meeting of the year and formally introduce the new chair, as well as officially seek support from the council for the new chair. The assistant superintendent agreed to this.

It wasn't until new school year had already begun that the bilingual teacher and former math curriculum council chair finally contacted the assistant superintendent. She expressed anger and surprise at not being reappointed as chair. She also indicated that if she couldn't be chair, she didn't want to serve as a member on the council. When asked why she hadn't responded to his phone calls, e-mails, and written communication all summer, the bilingual teacher responded that she had recently gotten married, and she didn't have time to answer all the communications that she had received not only from the assistant superintendent, but also from her friends as well.

The assistant superintendent thought all had been concluded, and that the bilingual teacher's decision not to remain on the council brought an end to this year-old nightmare. Unfortunately, the bilingual education teacher filed a discrimination suit against the assistant superintendent. In the suit, she alleged that she had been discriminated against because of her ethnicity. She filed the suit with the superintendent, but did not go any further with it. The superintendent investigated, and while he agreed that the bilingual teacher had not fulfilled her duties, he did chastise the assistant superintendent for having removed her from the position of chair. Fortunately, the superintendent did not put anything in writing to the assistant superintendent.

4-5. MIDDLE SCHOOL PHILOSOPHY AND PERSONAL BELIEFS IMPACT STUDENT LEARNING OPPORTUNITIES (ISLLC STANDARD 3)

Here's What Happened

First of all, the principal agreed with the superintendent that the junior high schools needed to change in their instructional practices and in their curriculum. She then outlined a plan for leading the faculty through a process of recognizing the need for change, for investigating and determining what needed to be changed, and for implementing the identified changes through resources and staff development. The principal also included a timeline of three years for the process. Although the superintendent wasn't happy about the length of time it would take, he did recognize that he might have been trying to move things too quickly. He also agreed that ownership in the process is key to success.

Once the principal got the superintendent to this point, she casually mentioned that she had had a conversation with a board member who seemed to be against rapid change. Without directly quoting the board member, the principal indicated that she thought the board member might need some time to learn more about the change process and possible outcomes. The superintendent appreciated this insight and offered to work more closely with the board member about the need for initiating a change process. The principal felt comfortable knowing that she had addressed the challenge in a tactful and positive manner.

4-6. THE MOSQUITO UNIT: WHEN OWNERSHIP TAKES PRECEDENCE OVER STUDENT LEARNING (ISLLC STANDARD 2)

Here's What Happened

The principal met with the two teachers and heard their concerns. After letting them both express their feelings and to vent their frustrations, he was able to focus the discussion on the students and on the learning standards for each grade level. He asked if they would mind it if he were to involve the other sixth-grade and seventh-grade teachers in a discussion about the creative activities used in each grade level. They agreed to this idea.

Through a curriculum-mapping process, the teachers identified the creative activities, when they were currently used during the year, and in which grade level they were taught. The group then determined which creative units fit best in either of the two grade levels. They also agreed when the units should be used, by quarter (first quarter, second quarter, third quarter, or fourth quarter). Through this process the seventh-grade teacher, who originated the mosquito unit, recognized that it really belonged in the sixth-grade curriculum because it supported those learning standards. Interestingly, there was a unit currently used in the sixth grade that really belonged in the seventh grade. The net result was that no one lost a unit.

This process caused the faculty to realize that they need to involve the eighth-grade teachers as well. As a result, the principal was able to lead the faculty in a genuine curriculum mapping process for each grade level and content area. They not only identified creative units, but also types of assessment to be used. This information was made availabel to the teachers, students, and parents. It became a curriculum guide, which helped everyone to see the learning expectations for each grade level. Parents actually volunteered to assist with units of particular interest to them.

4-7. SELECTING A NEW READING SERIES: LET'S MAINTAIN A FOCUS! (ISLLC STANDARD 1)

Here's What Happened

The process was set up to involve teachers right up front in the development of characteristics that defined the needs regarding new texts. A reading philosophy also was developed because the current approach to teaching reading wasn't successful. Based on input from the teachers, a checklist was developed by which to judge the textbooks. The checklist was shared with the publishers, and they were asked to provide a presentation as to how their texts supported the characteristics and checklist.

After hearing the presentations, the teachers chose two texts to be piloted. Representative teachers volunteered to pilot both series. One teacher would pilot textbook A for nine weeks while another teacher would pilot textbook B for the same time. At the end of the nine weeks, they would swap classroom sets of texts and pilot the other series. Students and parents were asked to provide input as well as the piloting teachers. In addition, sample sets of texts were placed in the faculty lounge, and teachers were invited to review them as well as to talk with the teachers who were piloting them. At the end of 18 weeks, after both texts had been piloted by both teachers, a decision was made as to which text won. Please note that the piloting process was replicated in a number of schools. All the piloting teachers were asked to vote for their choice.

It also was stated that the same series would be used for grades kindergarten through 5. If one grade level preferred the opposite choice than another grade level, a consensus-building process was utilized until all grade levels agreed upon the same series. Then the textbook representatives were notified and the actual balloting results and comments were shared with each of them. The successful representative was asked what resources could be provided free, in light of the total cost of student textbooks. After the amount of free resources was determined, the teachers were called back together to determine which resources each grade level would want/need. Then the assistant superintendent for curriculum and instruction met with the textbook representative to negotiate a deal.

4-8. SELLING A NEW ASSESSMENT INITIATIVE TO YOUR DEPARTMENT (ISLLC STANDARD 2)

Here's What Happened

The department chair encouraged the teachers to put all their concerns on the proverbial table. He then utilized a plus-delta process of analyzing each of the concerns. Also, the department chair had done his homework by finding another district that already was utilizing the quarterly assessments. He and some of the teachers visited this district. The teachers included both the supporters and the dissenters.

After their visit, the teachers were asked to present their impressions and opinions at the next department meeting. Interestingly, the contract required teachers to attend one department meeting per month, but the teachers were quite willing to attend additional department meetings as the proposal was being analyzed. Over a period of three months, as the teachers discussed and shared, enthusiasm grew, and even the dissenters came on board. As a result of suggestions from the department, the department chair asked the assistant superintendent if the teachers could begin working on the project earlier than the summer. Some of them wanted to work on weekends and during spring break. The request was approved, and the project moved ahead nicely. Its implementation experienced some growing pains, but it was successful, and it continues to be utilized today.

4-9. THE SPEECH TEACHER'S PERSONAL AGENDA VS. THE INSTRUCTIONAL PROGRAM GOALS (ISLLC STANDARD 3)

Here's What Happened

The department chair continued to build on the teachers' enthusiasm for developing a new program. He asked the assistant superintendent for resources that would pay for the teachers' visiting other schools as well as to pay for after-school and summer curriculum writing. He involved as many of the teachers as he could in the development of the new program. The speech teacher began to feel left out, and the peer pressure to be part of this enthusiastic project caused her to ask if she could join the others in the curriculum development as well as the visits to other schools. Of course, the department chair welcomed her request.

While the speech teacher continued to express her concern about how she would be able to teach English, the department chair reminded her that she had been certified to do so and that the new program would include lessons for the teachers to use. Although she proposed that she should be the one to teach the speech component for each lesson, that wouldn't be practical. Furthermore, the teachers all wanted to teach the speaking component of their lessons. When she heard her colleagues say that they wanted to teach the speaking component themselves, she offered to help them. They, in turn, offered to help her with the reading and writing components of her lessons. The result was a more cohesive department, as well as a better curriculum. Also, some curriculum mapping occurred and sharing of resources.

CHAPTER 5: SUPERVISION OF PERSONNEL

5-1. ASSIGNMENT OF CLASSROOMS TO BENEFIT A NEW TEACHER (ISLLC STANDARD 5)

Here's What Happened

The department chair spoke with both the new teacher and the complaining teacher separately to do some fact-finding and to determine the extent of the dislike between the two. The new teacher didn't harbor any ill feelings against the complaining teacher, other than those of not feeling accepted. The complaining teacher admitted that she didn't like the new teacher and that she resented having to share her classroom with anyone else. The department chair pursued this further with the complaining teacher, asking her if she'd at least give it a try without complaining so much. Eventually, she agreed to cut back on the complaining.

The department chair also made it a point to be especially supportive of both teachers. When observing the complaining teacher as part of the evaluation process, he noticed that she was uncomfortable at his presence in the classroom. He made every attempt possible to assure her that she was doing a good job of teaching. He raised his hand to answer questions and joined in classroom discussions. This seemed to help her to feel more relaxed. During the postconference, the department chair was complimentary of her lessons. She clearly appreciated this. Little by little he won her over.

Unrelated to her teaching, the complaining teacher developed some health problems. The department chair phoned her regularly to check on her health. Again, she appreciated his concern and began to see him as a caring supervisor. When she returned to school, she definitely had changed her attitude and became more cordial and helpful to the new teacher. Interestingly, the shared classroom schedule became "institutionalized" without any more questions by any of the teachers.

5-2. THE DYNAMIC READING PROGRAM EQUALS A RECIPE FOR SUCCESS? (ISLLC STANDARD 2)

Here's What Happened

Unfortunately, the principals couldn't get beyond their own negative feelings. Their presentations to their respective faculty members were obviously full of resentment, and the faculty members quickly picked up on the resentful feelings. Without faculty buy-in, the program became a mandate that was supported only superficially. The state test results did not improve, and the superintendent was most discouraged that his other schools did not realize the same results as the piloting school did. He could not understand why, but it was obvious to everyone else that the lack of success of the reading program was directly due to the way by which it was delivered to the schools. No one wants to support a mandate in which they don't believe.

5-3. THE FIRST-YEAR TEACHER AND THE SUPERVISION PROCESS (ISLLC STANDARD 2)

Here's What Happened

The division chair was negligent in his duties to mentor the new teacher. He did not provide her the guidance and assistance that he should have. He also did not provide her opportunities to visit and observe other classrooms. He did not keep the principal apprised of Laura's progress or lack thereof. In addition to his negligence of duties, the division chair was on a personal mission to undermine the principal. He did not agree with the superintendent's choice when the principal was hired. While the division chair made some public overtures of acceptance and even took the principal to lunch immediately after the superintendent named the new principal, the division chair never gave full support to the principal. The division chair actually tried to use his own mismanagement of the new teacher as a way to turn his division staff against the principal.

Despite many attempts on the part of the principal to help the new teacher, the proverbial well had been poisoned by the division chair, resulting in the new teacher's rejecting the principal's comments and suggestions. Ultimately, the principal chose to not renew the new teacher's contract. Because this had to be determined in March, as per state law, there was a risk that the new teacher would "shut down" and merely put in her time during the last few months of the school year. To try to control the potential damage, the principal became very directive toward the division chair to make sure that the new teacher would be closely monitored by the division chair until the end of the school year. In addition, the principal and the assistant principal also made frequent visits to the new teacher's classroom during the last months of the school year.

The principal also had a serious conversation with the division chair about the situation. The division chair indicated that he was retiring in another year and that he wasn't interested in professional growth as a division chair during his last year. The principal assumed more of the supervisory duties of the new teacher and decided to let the division chair have a peaceful and uneventful last year of teaching.

5-4. FOUR INTERNAL CANDIDATES DON'T GET THE ADMINISTRATIVE JOB (ISLLC STANDARD 6)

Here's What Happened

The internal candidates did what they promised. One withdrew from any future consideration. Another complained to the superintendent and even told him that there would be no future extra duties for this person. One of them complained to the board and was politely thanked for sharing his opinion. Ten years later, he still did not have an administrative position. The department chair went to the superintendent and said, "I don't agree with your decision, but I am a team player. I will continue to do my best as a department chair, and I will help the new assistant principal in any way that I can."

The department chair then approached the new assistant principal and said, "I don't know if you were told, but I also applied for your position. I don't blame you for accepting the job, and I want you to know that I have no hard feelings against you. If I can be of any help, I'll gladly do so." The assistant principal thanked him and promised to help the department chair in his administrative pursuit. They became good friends.

Later that school year, an assistant principalship opened in a neighboring district. The assistant principal helped the department chair with his application process. The superintendent also put in a good word for the department chair. When he got an interview, the department chair sought the assistant principal's help in preparing for the interview. Interestingly, one of the other internal candidates also applied for this position. The department chair got it, and his colleague (the one who refused to do any extra duties) didn't.

5-5. JAKE'S CLASSROOM MANAGEMENT (ISLLC STANDARD 2)

Here's What Happened

The superintendent assembled the disciplinary referral data and shared it both with the board of education as well as with the teachers' union president. They discussed many options, but because of the safety issues, the board member whose son was in that class was able to convince the other board members that they should seek dismissal of the teacher. The union president reminded them that a remediation plan had to be created first to at least give the teacher a reasonable amount of time to address the concerns in the plan.

Such a plan was developed both with the district lawyer and the union lawyer. The teacher reviewed the plan and realized that he either was unable or unwilling to meet the conditions of the plan. He agreed to a buy-out. The union negotiated a three-year buy-out for the teacher. He was dismissed at the end of the school year and received his salary for the next three years. Unfortunately, the teacher displaced the blame and his anger onto the assistant principal. Jake assumed no responsibility for his lack of classroom management and blamed the assistant principal for not being able to control the students for him. He believed that his job was to teach, and the administrators' job was to make sure that the students behaved themselves.

The assistant principal was a caring individual and felt bad about this. He tried to reason with Jake in a private meeting later and even offered to help him find a new job. But Jake was rude and visibly angry toward the assistant principal. A few months later, the assistant principal heard of a vocational teaching position in a neighboring district. They were having a difficult time finding a certified person to hire. The assistant principal notified Jake about the job and suggested that Jake might have a good chance of starting all over if he'd admit his mistakes and make appropriate changes to his classroom management strategies. Who wouldn't want to hire someone who has reflected on his mistakes, learned from them, and has made changes to prevent their recurrence? Unfortunately, Jake was not interested in this position and still continued to harbor his ill feelings toward the assistant principal.

5-6. THE OUTDOOR EDUCATION PROGRAM THAT GOES BAD (ISLLC STANDARD 6)

Here's What Happened

After thinking through this situation and consulting with her assistant principal, the principal called a meeting with the sixth-grade teachers and the teachers' aides prior to their leaving for the outdoor education program. She thanked them for their dedication to service and for all the good that they would be doing through this event. The principal also indicated that she didn't want them to think that once they were gone on the field trip, they were forgotten about. She told them that in order to show her support of their efforts, she and her assistant principal would be helping them to supervise the students in their cabins at night. She further indicated that it was only right that she and her assistant principal share in the supervisory duties. The principal would be there for the first night, and the assistant principal would be there for the second night, in a spirit of teamwork between the administrators and the sixth-grade teachers and aides. She went on to emphasize the importance of being good role models for the sixth-grade students and that it was everyone's responsibility to share in that role. In short, she put somewhat of a "guilt trip" on the teachers.

Needless to say, this not only squelched any plans to go to the bar, but it also set expectations to be strong role models for the students. Also, this showed a spirit of support on the part of the administration. The result was a good one in that the teachers respected their administrators for "rolling up their sleeves" and joining them in the nighttime supervision of the cabins. There was no more talk of going to a bar during any of the subsequent outdoor education program field trips.

5-7. THE MOVE FROM ASSOCIATE CHAIR TO DEPARTMENT CHAIR: HOW TO EVALUATE MY PREDECESSOR (ISLLC STANDARD 3)

Here's What Happened

The new department chair addressed the multifaceted situation in a comprehensive way. First of all, he recognized that the former department chair had a group of personal supporters in the department members at that campus. The new department chair had to dissemble this power base and infuse some fresh insights into the culture. He believed that if he could get some new teachers into the department, perhaps the present department members would become competitive and resume their effective teaching practices rather than appear lazy to the new teachers.

The new department chair knew he couldn't simply hire new teachers, especially during the semester. Instead, he approached his teachers at the other campus and asked if any of them would like to trade assignments with their counterparts at the other campus. So as not to disrupt the educational process, the change would occur at a natural break such as the beginning of the second semester. Fortunately, two of the department members volunteered to teach at the other campus for the second semester. The new department chair then asked the teachers at the other campus if any of them would like to try a new adventure of teaching at another campus. None volunteered, but the new department chair devised a lottery system to select who would teach at the opposite campus. He didn't have to utilize the lottery system because eventually two teachers agreed to the switch.

To address the former department chair's teaching, the new department chair observed his classes several times, but instead of forming his own conclusions, he asked the former department chair to analyze his own lessons.

"What were you trying to accomplish in today's lesson? What did you expect the students to do by the end of the class period? Did they meet your expectations?"

These questions forced the former department chair to reflect on his lessons, although he seemed to want the new department chair simply to pass a judgment on him and write up an evaluation. The new department chair persisted with his approach of reflective questioning and forcing the former department chair to create effective lessons through this approach.

He did not regain the former department chair's respect, but he did get him to improve his lessons and to stop showing the movies instead of teaching lessons. Unfortunately, the former department chair's personal issues did not improve, and the new department chair suspected that the former department chair was still using alcohol to escape the reality of his problems. He did not come to school under the influence of alcohol, and he did prepare at least satisfactory lessons. That was an accomplishment in itself.

5-8. A NEW ASSISTANT SUPERINTENDENT IS CHOSEN OVER AN INTERNAL CANDIDATE (ISLLC STANDARD 3)

Here's What Happened

The assistant superintendent used a combination of a collegial and a directive approach with the language arts coordinator. He affirmed her desire to set high expectations, but he also explained to her that he could not live with those expectations because they were unreasonable for many of the students. They compromised on a lower percentage. Instead of saying that 100% of the students would gain at least a year's growth, they agreed to state that 75% of the students would gain at least a year's growth. While the assistant superintendent still wasn't sure if this percentage would be too high, he felt better knowing that it could be within reach.

Although the assistant superintendent hoped that this compromise would quell any possible end-runs to the superintendent on the part of the language arts coordinator, he nevertheless decided to quickly notify the superintendent of the entire situation. He believed that good communication was imperative not only to show his own credibility, but also to prevent the superintendent from being blindsided by unexpected information. It was difficult to read the superintendent, and the assistant superintendent did not know if he was being fully supported by the superintendent, but at least he was able to prevent the language arts coordinator from getting to the superintendent first and thereby putting the assistant superintendent on the defensive.

At the end of the school year, only 60% of the student showed a year's growth, but the vast majority of the students did score above their own grade levels. They just didn't show a full year's worth of growth. The assistant superintendent phoned the state department of education and explained that they might have set their expectations too high, but that the grant money had resulted in the vast majority of the students' being above grade level. The state department of education accepted this explanation and allowed the assistant superintendent to amend the grant. Unfortunately, the language arts coordinator would not admit that she had set her expectations too high. Instead she blamed the teachers for not pushing the students more. Even though the majority of students were above grade level, she still would not consider this acceptable.

5-9. THE SCIENCE TEACHER'S SENIORITY VS. THE INSTRUCTIONAL PROGRAM (ISLLC STANDARD 5)

Here's What Happened

The assistant principal tried to reason with the department chair, but was unable to convince him to change the schedule. The department chair stuck tightly to the union position. The assistant principal had no choice but to exert his administrative authority and to redo the schedule to keep the teacher employed. He did stipulate to the teacher that it would be in her best interests to take coursework to acquire the additional science certification endorsement. The department chair was not happy about this decision, but deep in his heart he seemed to know that this was the right thing to do. He accepted the decision and was equally supportive of both of the teachers. He realized that he had to work hard to regain the confidence of both of the teachers.

CHAPTER 6: SCHOOL COMMUNITY RELATIONS AND STRATEGIC PLANNING

6-1. THE BAND BOOSTERS AND A TRAILER: A SCHOOL COMMUNITY RELATIONS DILEMMA (ISLLC STANDARD 4)

Here's What Happened

With the superintendent's permission, the principal investigated the actual costs of licensing and insuring the trailer. He found that the license in his state was a one-time fee for a municipal vehicle license. His budget could cover that cost. The cost of insuring the trailer and the towing vehicle was negligible, but the insurance company did require that any drivers be approved by the school district. The maintenance staff actually was relieved to learn that they would not have to share their pickup truck with the band parents. They agreed to store the towing vehicle in the district garage and to maintain it.

The principal met with the band director to make sure that no more surprises were on the horizon. The band director agreed to keep the principal apprised of the projects undertaken by the band parents, and he invited the principal to attend periodic band parents' meetings. The principal and the band director created a little ceremony at which the band parents' president presented the principal with the keys to the trailer. The local news media was invited and covered the event with a front-page photo and story in the newspaper. It was a great public relations opportunity!

6-2. THE CENTRAL OFFICE SNITCH (ISLLC STANDARD 3)

Here's What Happened

The assistant for curriculum and instruction did meet with the director of bilingual education to ask about the comment made by the superintendent, and she admitted having reported her information to him. She went on to explain that the superintendent was the number one supervisor, and everyone else in the organization owed him a great deal of respect. She did not think that laughing at his behavior was respectful. She further explained that the superintendent was her number one role model for educational leadership. The assistant superintendent for curriculum and instruction quietly processed this revelation.

The superintendent's practice of finding a victim to criticize at each cabinet meeting wasn't his idea of good educational leadership, but he couldn't say that to her, because she was so obviously enamored by the superintendent's power. The director of bilingual education went on to explain that she someday hoped to become superintendent and that she had told the superintendent about her goals. According to her, he had offered her his support for her plans. The assistant superintendent wondered where his plans stood in this scheme.

Regardless of his own aspirations, the assistant superintendent realized that he had to address the situation at hand. He attempted to assure her that he and the others weren't showing any disrespect by laughing at the situation. They all still recognized the superintendent's authority, but they were laughing at the way his veins stood out when the grants administrator was challenging him. There is a difference between laughing at a situation and laughing at an individual. She didn't see the difference. The assistant superintendent again attempted to convince her that no one was trying to show disrespect, but when the superintendent engaged in his shouting match, he really wasn't acting with a lot of respect toward the grants administrator. Maybe they shouldn't get hung up on the respect and disrespect displayed at the cabinet meeting, but rather they should move ahead with this as a learning experience.

Again the director of bilingual education was unwilling to move beyond this situation. She was convinced in her own mind that the group was being disrespectful to the superintendent, and she no longer would go out to lunch with any of them. The assistant superintendent tried to calm her and asked her to take some time to think this over before disassociating herself from the rest of the cabinet.

The assistant superintendent then met individually with each of the other cabinet members who had been present at the recent lunch. He asked them to be careful of what they might say or how they might act regarding the superintendent's outbursts. He explained that the director of bilingual education had expressed feeling uncomfortable about the recent lunch conversation. They all agreed and in the future were careful about what they said regarding the superintendent. Unfortunately, the director of bilingual education made a point of not even sitting near any of the cabinet members at future meetings. Instead, she sat directly next to the superintendent at each meeting. Whenever there was any discussion, she always would side with the superintendent. He became very protective of her and her opinions, and it became clear that she was the "heir-apparent" to the superintendency in his eyes.

6-3. CRISIS MANAGEMENT: A STUDENT FATALITY (ISLLC STANDARD 5)

Here's What Happened

The principal enjoyed a good relationship with the local ministerial society. He often called upon the ministers to serve as role models to the students. They had a standing invitation to come in during the lunch periods to visit with students. Now was the time to tap into that resource. The principal quickly found out to which church the deceased student's family belonged. He contacted the pastor and sought his assistance. Fortunately, the pastor spoke Spanish and was able to assist the parents as they went to the morgue and then to a funeral home to make arrangements.

The principal put the crisis plan into effect, which included calling social workers across the district as well as from the local mental health agencies. They provided direct assistance to classrooms. In addition, central office administrators were asked to be visible in the hallways and in the library, which was designated as a drop-in grief center. The goal was to provide a safe and comfortable environment that allowed faculty and students to process their grief. In some cases, counseling was required; in other cases, a quiet place for reflection was all that was needed.

Later that day the pastor and the parents returned to the school and asked to speak with the students in the grief center. This was reassuring to the students to see that the parents were handling the situation as best they could. The pastor and the parents then met privately with the principal and expressed concern about holding the funeral church services on a school day. The principal agreed with them that to do so would present the school with attendance issues, but he assured them that the students' absence would be considered as excused absences pending parental permission. The deceased student's parents then offered to hold the funeral church services on Saturday so as not to interfere with the school day.

6-4. THE DUMPSTER INCIDENT: INTERNAL AND EXTERNAL PUBLIC RELATIONS (ISLLC STANDARD 6)

Here's What Happened

The principal phoned the neighbor/board president and explained the situation. He made sure that it was clearly understood that that school could file charges with the police, but that was not his intent. Rather, the principal wanted to protect the high school's costs. He appealed to the neighbor/board president's sense of fiscal responsibility for schools and likened it to the president's own responsibility to the elementary school district that he served. The neighbor/board president became angry and tried to bully the principal, but the principal stuck to the facts and the issue at hand. He remained calm and asked that the neighbor/board president work with him on this.

He gave the neighbor/board president two options: either to remove the deck material from the dumpster or to write a check for half the cost of the dumpster, because the deck material had taken up half of the dumpster's load capacity. The neighbor/board president hung up the phone in anger, and the principal went to his superintendent to report the situation. The superintendent suggested that the principal contact the elementary school district superintendent and ask him to talk with his board president. The principal did this, and the elementary school district superintendent agreed to try to mediate the situation. Later that day, the neighbor/board president left an envelope with the principal's secretary. When the principal opened it, he found a check made out to the high school for half the cost of the dumpster.

6-5. GRADUATING STUDENTS' FAMILIES GET INTO A FIGHT IN THE SCHOOL PARKING LOT (ISLLC STANDARD 4)

Here's What Happened

The principal tried to resolve the situation and when it became obvious that he was not being successful, he phoned the police. Because there was a police officer assisting with traffic at the exit of the school parking lot, response was very quick. The principal asked the police officer to help him to calm things down. No arrests were made and the conflicting parties got into their respective cars and drove away. No comments appeared in the letters to the editor section of the local newspaper either.

6-6. LET MY SON GRADUATE EVEN THOUGH HE FAILED TWO COURSES (ISLLC STANDARD 5)

Here's What Happened

Although the principal felt bad for the parent, he felt an obligation to uphold the school district policy. He personally had tried to change the policy by doing comparison studies and presenting them to the board of education. He believed that the correct way to handle this situation was to try to change the policy. Because the board was not willing to do so, all members of the high school (students, faculty, administration) had to abide by the policies set forth by the board of education.

From a public relations perspective, the principal worked with the parent to try to get her to understand this. He also met with the student's teachers to find out just what the student had to complete in order to graduate. The principal directed the guidance counselor to meet weekly with the student and his teachers to check on the student's progress. The parent was kept apprised of the student's progress. Unfortunately, the student chose not to complete all the missing assignments and was not allowed to participate in the graduation ceremony. While the parent was upset and threatened to bad-mouth the school to the newspaper, she never did. Most likely she was too embarrassed to put her family's name in the newspaper.

6-7. LOCAL FLORIST COMPLAINS ABOUT THE DATE OF THE PROM (ISLLC STANDARD 4)

Here's What Happened

The principal listened carefully to the florist and asked questions that showed her interest in solving the problem. She explained the process for determining the prom date and further explained that avoiding Mother's Day wasn't always a possibility. But she also promised to take that into consideration when next year's date was chosen. The principal also offered to notify the florist as soon as the prom date was chosen, thereby giving the florist ample time to prepare, should additional resources be needed to complete the flower orders. While this wasn't exactly what the florist was hoping for, he was relieved to know that his concerns had been heard and that some attempt to resolve the problem was being attempted.

6-8. MEDIA SCOOPS AND THE SCHOOL'S PUBLIC IMAGE (ISLLC STANDARD 4)

Here's What Happened

The principal met with the editor of the local newspaper and let her vent and fume away at him. She acted very unprofessionally and angrily. The principal's suspicions that she really didn't support the high school were proven by her comments and her demeanor. However, to attempt to build good school community relations, the principal agreed to follow her schedule for submitting press releases, but he also indicated that in a case like this, he would not hold back a story. He did offer to phone her to give her a "heads-up" about stories of special interest. The principal also expressed his concern that the high school had not been receiving very good coverage in her newspaper, to which the editor replied that she didn't have the staff to cover all the things going on at the high school, but she would try to do a better job.

6-9. A PARENT'S CONCERNS ABOUT THE TECHNOLOGY CURRICULUM (ISLLC STANDARD 4)

Here's What Happened

The principal did not agree with the teacher that the parent was an annoyance and should be told to back off. Instead, the principal thanked the parent both for bringing this to her attention and for his desire to support his son's learning at home. She explained that the exploratory program had preceded her, but now that she knew about its shortcoming, she would address that need immediately. The parent was pleased with this response.

The next day, the teacher contacted the assistant superintendent for curriculum and instruction to explain the situation. Because the same program was in use in all three junior high schools, the assistant superintendent agreed to provide a stipend for all three teachers to develop a curriculum guide for parents. To meet the immediate concern of the parent, the assistant superintendent asked the principal to find out which module the student in question was working on. The assistant superintendent then created a prototype for this unit. Not only did this serve as a model for the teachers to follow when creating the other units, but it also met the immediate need of the parent. Like the principal, the assistant superintendent was relatively new to the district and had been working on other curriculum areas, but had not gotten to this one yet. He personally contacted the parent and thanked him for alerting the school district to this need. This actually was a positive public relations situation. Now that the parent felt valued, he volunteered for various school and district committees and later ran for a seat on the board of education.

6-10. THE PRINCIPAL BANS THE LOCAL NEWSPAPER EDITOR FROM THE SCHOOL (ISLLC STANDARD 4)

Here's What Happened

The principal spoke privately with the department chair and asked if he thought it wise to be using school time to meet with the new editor. The principal explained that while he understood the arrangement, he was concerned that it might set a precedent for other department chairs and teachers to use their planning periods for personal business. The principal went on to admit that he appreciated the department chair's willingness to come to school early and to stay late, but his use of planning periods was not setting the tone that the rest of the faculty should embrace.

The department chair didn't argue and said that he understood the principal's perspective. He assured the principal that he would change the meeting arrangement with the new editor, but that they had already planned to meet today. The principal agreed that today's meeting would not have to be cancelled. Later, the principal was in the hall when the new editor was leaving her meeting with the department chair. She approached the principal and said sarcastically, "Thanks a lot! I have children in the elementary school, and I like to be home with them in the evening. That's why I was meeting here during the day. Thanks to you, I have to deprive my family of my presence." She quickly stormed out of the building. The principal ran after her, but she jumped into her car and drove away. He later tried to phone her, but she didn't answer. He left several messages for her to contact him, but she didn't.

6-11. STUDENTS AGAINST DRINKING AND DRIVING:
A GOOD IDEA GOES BAD (ISLLC STANDARD 3)

Here's What Happened

The principal contacted the club sponsor and explained the situation. He thanked her for getting the car and for doing all that she did to send a powerful message to the students about the risks of drinking and driving. He told her that he believed in good communication and wanted her to be aware of the situation. The principal asked if the car could be promptly removed the day after the prom. The club sponsor explained that usually the towing company would pick it up at their convenience, but considering the situation she would ask them to expedite its removal.

The principal then contacted the family and assured them that he understood their concerns, but that it was not so easy to have the car removed right away. He told them that it would be promptly removed the day after the prom. The principal also explained that the likelihood of anyone's recognizing the car as belonging to their family was quite slim. Also, he had not heard any of the students trying to identify the owner of the car. The principal also thanked the family because of the good that had come from the wrecked car. It had become a teaching tool that would have an impact on many students. While the family wasn't happy with the outcome because they wanted the car to be removed immediately, they did understand the school's position.

6-12. STUDENTS DRINKING IN FRONT OF THE SCHOOL AND
THE POLITICAL IMPLICATIONS (ISLLC STANDARD 6)

Here's What Happened

The principal chose to place the call to the police department. He opted to directly phone the police chief and reported the situation. The police chief thanked him for the call and personally responded in a marked police car. Both students were taken away in the squad car. Arrangements were made to remove the students' car, but only after the chief had dispatched his evidence technicians to photograph the evidence (beer bottles in the car). From all appearances, the situation had been handled appropriately by the police chief.

Later the local newspaper reported that the two students had been arrested for underage drinking in a car. No names were given due to laws protecting minors, but the student body recognized the situation.

While the teacher who reported the incident didn't directly tell the principal, a guidance counselor confided that the faculty had not only heard about the situation but that they supported his decision.

6-13. A STUDENT VISA: A NEIGHBORING DISTRICT CHARGES
TUITION (ISLLC STANDARD 4)

Here's What Happened

The assistant superintendent made the presentation based on a factual accounting of what had transpired. He downplayed the role of the neighboring school district and commended his board of education for authorizing him to seek a legal appeal. He also commended the legal counsel to the state department of education for being open-minded enough to look at individual circumstances and to overturn its own decision in favor of the individual. In other words, he tried to make all parties look good and to cast blame on the circumstances, not on any agencies.

CHAPTER 7: DIVERSITY ISSUES IN EDUCATIONAL LEADERSHIP

7-1. BILINGUAL ISSUES (ISLLC STANDARD 4)

Here's What Happened

The principal invited the board member to visit a number of the bilingual classrooms. She also sought the help of her faculty to not only allow the board member to visit their classes, but also to have their students show her their projects that were written in English. She also assembled recent test score data along with transition rates of the students in the bilingual program and presented these to the board of education. Because this was a presentation at a public forum, the principal distributed copies of her presentation to all in attendance at the meeting, including the news media. Although the board member still wasn't entirely convinced, she was willing to listen to the educators' and parents' views about bilingual education. The board member asked to see long-term data so she could study the trends of bilingual students as they transitioned and eventually mainstreamed into the regular education program.

7-2. THE BLIND ELL STUDENT: WHO'S RESPONSIBLE? (ISLLC STANDARD 2)

Here's What Happened

The principal explored this issue from many different angles as outlined in the *ethical considerations* for this case study. He worked diligently with the faculty of both departments together and separately to help each of them determine a tentative primary and support plan. They also explored possible interventions both from the internal and external sources. He asked each department to present their primary plan from a positive, "we want to do this" perspective. Then he asked the two departments to critique each other's plan. Finally, he asked, "Who can provide the best services to the student?" Both departments agreed that the special education department should be responsible for the primary plan, and the bilingual department should be responsible for the supporting plan. The strongest rationale for this decision was that the student actually had two handicaps related to special education: blindness and an educational deficit.

7-3. COMMUNICATION WITH A STUBBORN SUPERINTENDENT (ISLLC STANDARD 6)

Here's What Happened

The principal attempted to get the superintendent into his office in order to allow the teachers to do their work with the student. He also wanted to have an opportunity to give the principal the bigger picture of what had transpired so far in this student's behavior plan. After getting the student into class with the assurance that the student would receive appropriate consequences for his behavior, the principal was finally able to get the superintendent in his office.

While the superintendent was still reeling from a blow to his ego based on the student's disrespectful behavior, he was able to understand the bigger picture. The principal eventually got the superintendent to a point where he could laugh about the situation, but that took a lot of time and assurance that the behavior disorders program was working in this school.

7-4. FACULTY ISSUES RELATED TO GENDER (ISLLC STANDARD 5)

Here's What Happened

The principal began the next faculty meeting with some general questions about faculty beliefs regarding boys' and girls' abilities and behaviors. He followed up with a gender attitude survey, which was used to stimulate small-group discussion among the faculty. After a sufficient period of time, the principal then called the small groups back to engage in a debriefing session with the whole faculty. From this process, the faculty began to realize that they didn't all hold the same beliefs about gender.

The principal suggested that they form some research groups who would explore this topic further. This continued throughout the school year, resulting in good discussions at each of the faculty meetings. The principal also arranged for some gender-sensitivity training as the focus of an institute day. By the end of the school year, the faculty was very aware of and sensitive to gender biases. They were able to examine their curriculum and teaching materials, including texts and library books to make sure that boys and girls were portrayed as successful in all fields of study. The following year, the state test scores showed a more equal distribution of achievement between both genders in all areas tested. This assured the principal that his plan had worked.

7-5. HOMOSEXUALITY ISSUES AND A BOARD MEETING (ISLLC STANDARD 5)

Here's What Happened

The superintendent did not intervene, but rather left the principal to handle this situation. As suggested in the *ethical considerations* section, the principal tactfully thanked the parent for sharing her concerns. The principal went on to assure the parent that all teachers were hired on the basis of their teaching credentials and retained on the basis of their demonstrated performance in the classroom. The principal went on to say, "Teachers' personal lives are just that—personal. There should be no reason to inquire about any teacher's personal life, and this comment should not be taken to affirm or to dispute any allegations. I want to further discuss this matter with you because I sense that this is very important to you. The board meeting is not the appropriate forum to continue this discussion, but I am grateful that you brought it to my attention. Please phone my office tomorrow morning. Here is my business card with my phone number."

The parent did make the appointment, during which the principal was told that one of the books the students were asked to read made reference to two male penguins that had adopted an egg in the Central Park Zoo in New York. The true story emphasized that families take many different formats, but the bottom line is that the children are loved by their parents. The parent was upset by the story because of its reference to same-gender parents. Furthermore, the parent alleged that the teacher had been promoting homosexual relationships through the book discussion. The principal promised to investigate further and found that the teacher's use of the book was within district guidelines and that no inappropriate promotion of particular lifestyles had been made by the teacher.

During the follow-up conversation with the parent, the principal tried to help the parent to understand the importance of tolerance and acceptance of diversity. She assured the parent that in the future, teachers would notify parents if any potentially controversial books would be used in class. The principal also explained that the book used by the teacher had been approved by a parent advisory council, but nevertheless because of its controversial nature, advance notice would be given to parents via the grade-level newsletter.

7-6. PLACEMENT IN THE GIFTED PROGRAM? (ISLLC STANDARD 3)

Here's What Happened

The principal personally met with Bob Murphy, the board member, to discuss his son's placement criteria. He explained that the boy didn't meet all the criteria and that the criteria were there to make sure that students would be successful in the program, not to create an elite group of students. The board member admitted that he hadn't thought about it from that perspective and that he was looking for ways to challenge his son and to stretch his critical thinking. The principal assured the board member that he would share this with the student's teacher, and he would ask the teacher to address those needs through activities that would benefit not only the board member's son but also all the students in her class.

The principal also decided to head off another question. He told the board member that he couldn't have the son retested because standardized tests have a window during which they can be administered. Any tests given outside that window can't be scored on the same scale as tests taken earlier. This is due to the norming group as well as the fact that as the school year progresses, the students should have learned more. It would be an unfair comparison. The board member understood this and thanked the principal for his time. The principal assured the board member that his son would be retested next year along with other students wanting to qualify for the program.

Regardless of the principal's concerns about the parking situation, the issue never arose between him and the board member. However, to address that issue with the board of education because it had been brought up at a board meeting, the principal invited Arlene McDougal to join the school safety committee, which included members of the police and fire departments as well as faculty and parents. This committee had been investigating the traffic problem and was ready to unveil its plan to solve the problems. Arlene was grateful to be part of the committee and took much credit for the plan as it was explained at a board of education meeting.

7-7. PRIDE AND SNOBBERY BETWEEN SCHOOL DISTRICTS (ISLLC STANDARD 5)

Here's What Happened

The principal from the less fortunate school district decided to win over the educational leaders from the affluent school district, little by little. He began by contacting the principals of similar schools from the affluent district and inviting them to visit his school. He asked them to brainstorm about activities and programs that they could share. He explained that he felt it would provide a rich opportunity for students to work together with students from other districts.

One of the first activities they tried was Operation Snowball. The principal from the less fortunate school offered to sponsor a local chapter and to invite students from the other district to join it. Not only would the students from different districts be engaged in problem-solving activities, but also they would learn how to work with team members from different backgrounds. This program was so successful that others followed, and within two years both districts were sponsoring various student activities to which the students from the other district were invited.